# BLADE RUNNER 2019

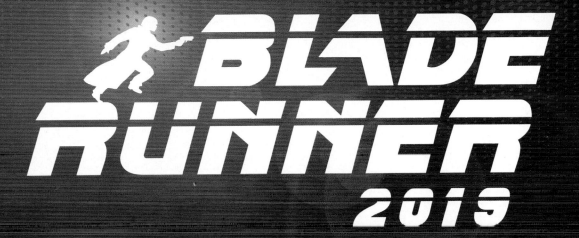

## DEDICATED TO:

The Memory of Rutger Hauer who played Roy Batty in the original *Blade Runner* movie and who died on July 19, 2019. It's true to say he saw things that we people wouldn't believe.

Thank you to: Syd Mead for your exceptional work on *Blade Runner* and for allowing us the honor of using your artwork for our covers. Your extraordinary vision remains an inspiration even after 27 years.

Special thanks to: Roger Servick for your invaluable assistance. Thank you Philip K. Dick, Ridley Scott, Hampton Fancher, David Peoples and Michael Deeley for creating such an incredible world.

## BLADE RUNNER 2019: LOS ANGELES

Senior Creative Editor | DAVID LEACH
Senior Designer | ANDREW LEUNG

### TITAN COMICS

Managing Editor | MARTIN EDEN
Art Director | OZ BROWNE
Production Controller | PETER JAMES
Senior Production Controller | JACKIE FLOOK
Sales & Circulation Manager | STEVE TOTHILL
Publicist | IMOGEN HARRIS
Ad & Marketing Assistant | BELLA HOY

Marketing Assistant | GEORGE WICKENDEN
Commercial Manager | MICHELLE FAIRLAMB
Head of Rights | JENNY BOYCE
Publishing Director | DARRYL TOTHILL
Operations Director | LEIGH BAULCH
Executive Director | VIVIAN CHEUNG
Publisher | NICK LANDAU

### ALCON PUBLISHING

Director/Editor | JEFF CONNER
Associate Editor | AL CUENCA
COO/CEO | SCOTT PARISH
Legal/Business Affairs | JEANNETTE HILL
Publishers | ANDREW KOSOVE & BRODERICK JOHNSON

STANDARD EDITION ISBN 9781787731615
FORBIDDEN PLANET EXCLUSIVE ISBN 9781787734159
BARNES AND NOBLE EXCLUSIVE ISBN 9781787734494

A CIP catalogue for this title is available from the British Library.

First Edition November 2019
10 9 8 7 6 5 4 3 2 1
Printed in Canada

www.titan-comics.com
Follow us on twitter@ComicsTitan | Visit us at facebook.com/comicstitan
For rights information contact: jenny.boyce@titanemail.com

# BLADE RUNNER 2019

WRITTEN BY
MICHAEL GREEN
& MIKE JOHNSON

ART BY
ANDRES GUINALDO

COLORS BY
MARCO LESKO

LETTERING BY
JIM CAMPBELL

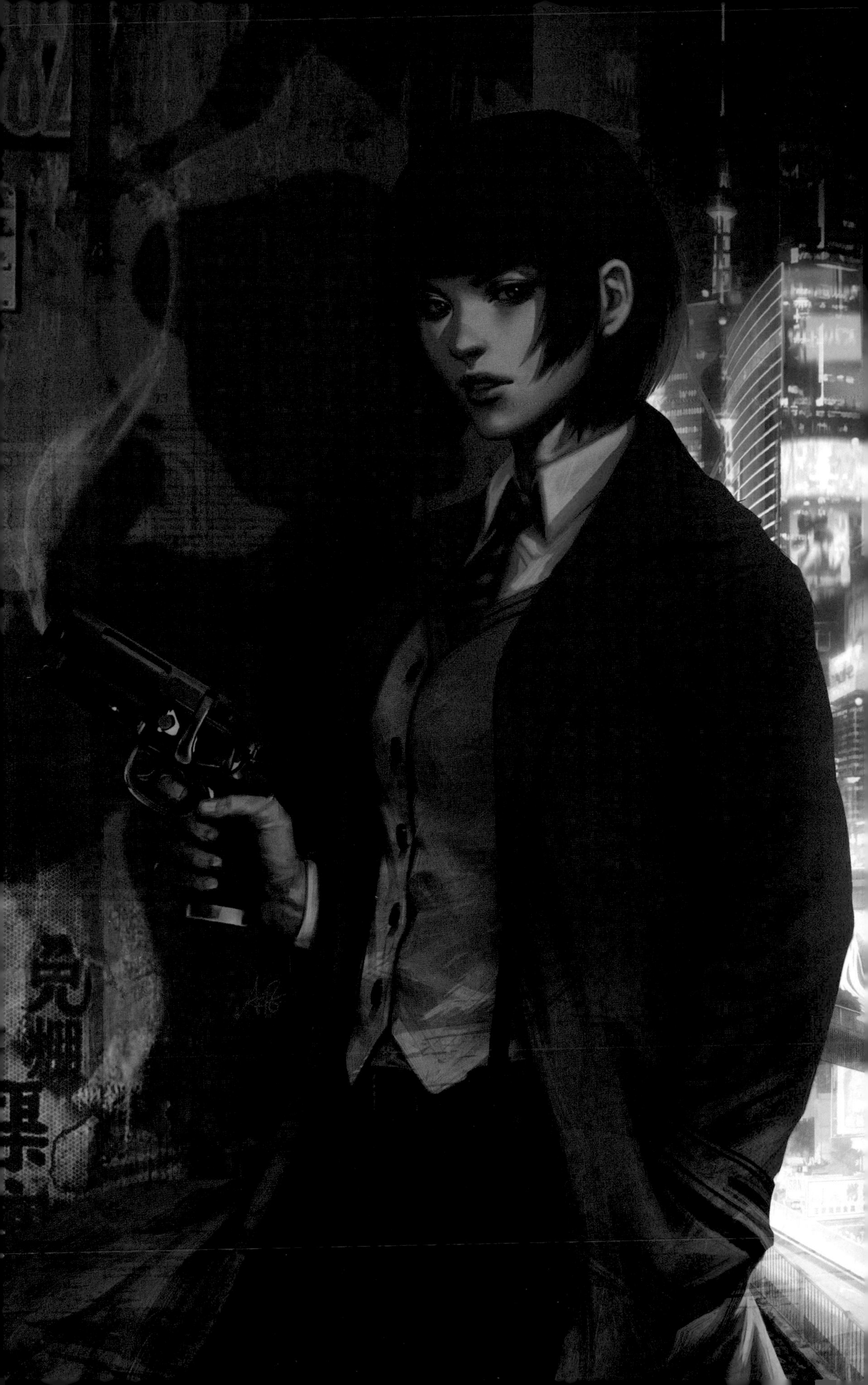

EARLY IN THE 21ST CENTURY, THE TYRELL CORPORATION ADVANCED ROBOT EVOLUTION TO THE NEXUS PHASE – CREATING ARTIFICIAL BEINGS VIRTUALLY IDENTICAL TO HUMANS – KNOWN AS REPLICANTS.

SUPERIOR IN STRENGTH AND AGILITY, THE REPLICANTS FUNCTIONED PRIMARILY AS OFF-WORLD SLAVE LABOR OR IN HAZARDOUS, HIGH-COLLATERAL COMBAT SITUATIONS.

AFTER REPLICANTS WERE DECLARED ILLEGAL ON EARTH, SPECIAL POLICE OPERATIVES – CALLED BLADE RUNNERS – HAD ORDERS TO KILL OR 'RETIRE' ANY TRESPASSERS UPON DETECTION.

DETECTIVE AAHNA ASHINA OF THE LOS ANGELES POLICE DEPARTMENT WAS ONE OF THE FIRST TO QUALIFY FOR THE ASSIGNMENT.

HER COLLEAGUES CALLED HER ASH.

SHE WAS THE BEST OF THEM.

LOS ANGELES
2019

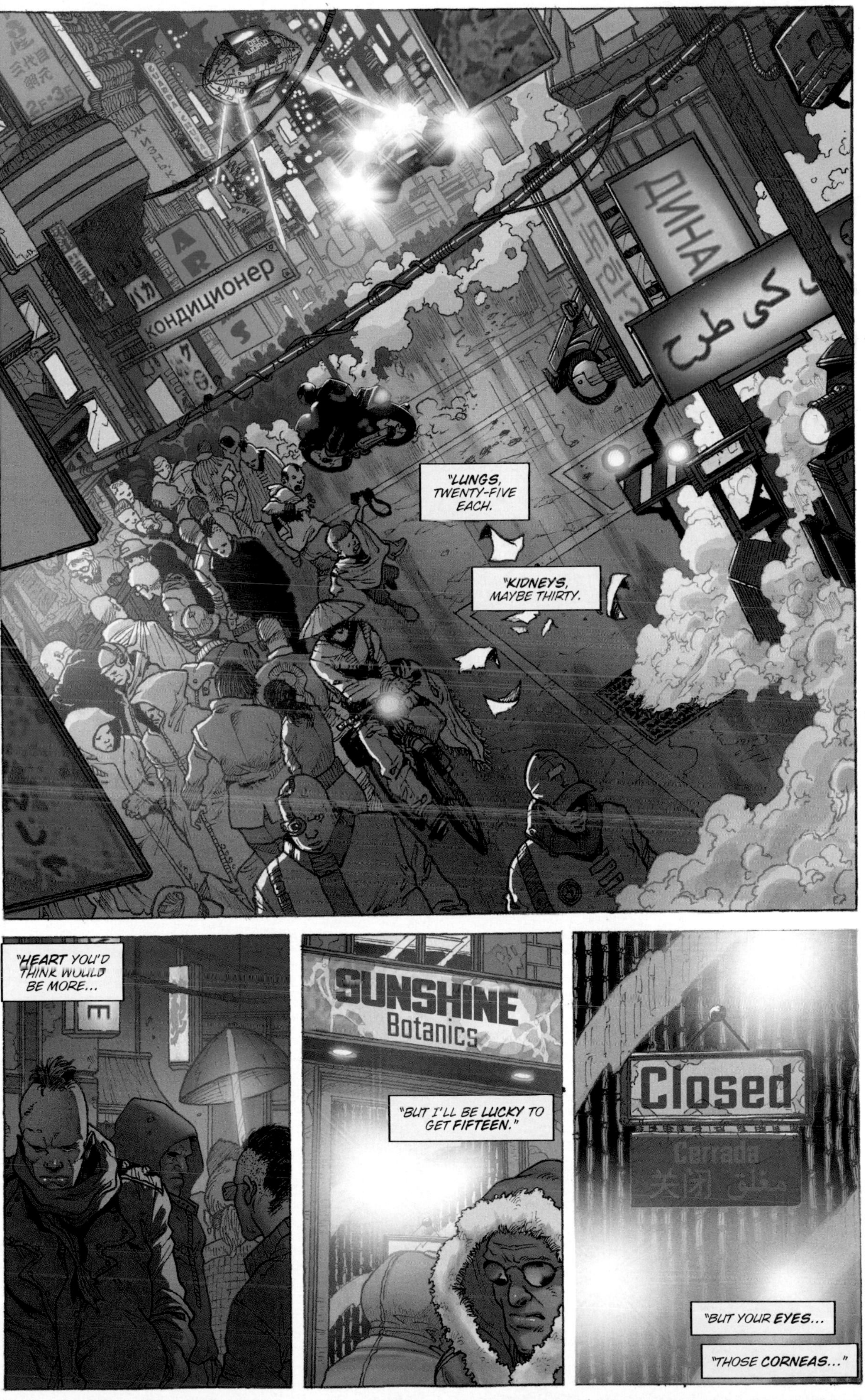
Кондиционер
"LUNGS, TWENTY-FIVE EACH.
"KIDNEYS, MAYBE THIRTY.
"HEART YOU'D THINK WOULD BE MORE...
SUNSHINE
Botanics
"BUT I'LL BE LUCKY TO GET FIFTEEN."
Closed
Cerrada
关闭 مغلق
"BUT YOUR EYES...
"THOSE CORNEAS..."

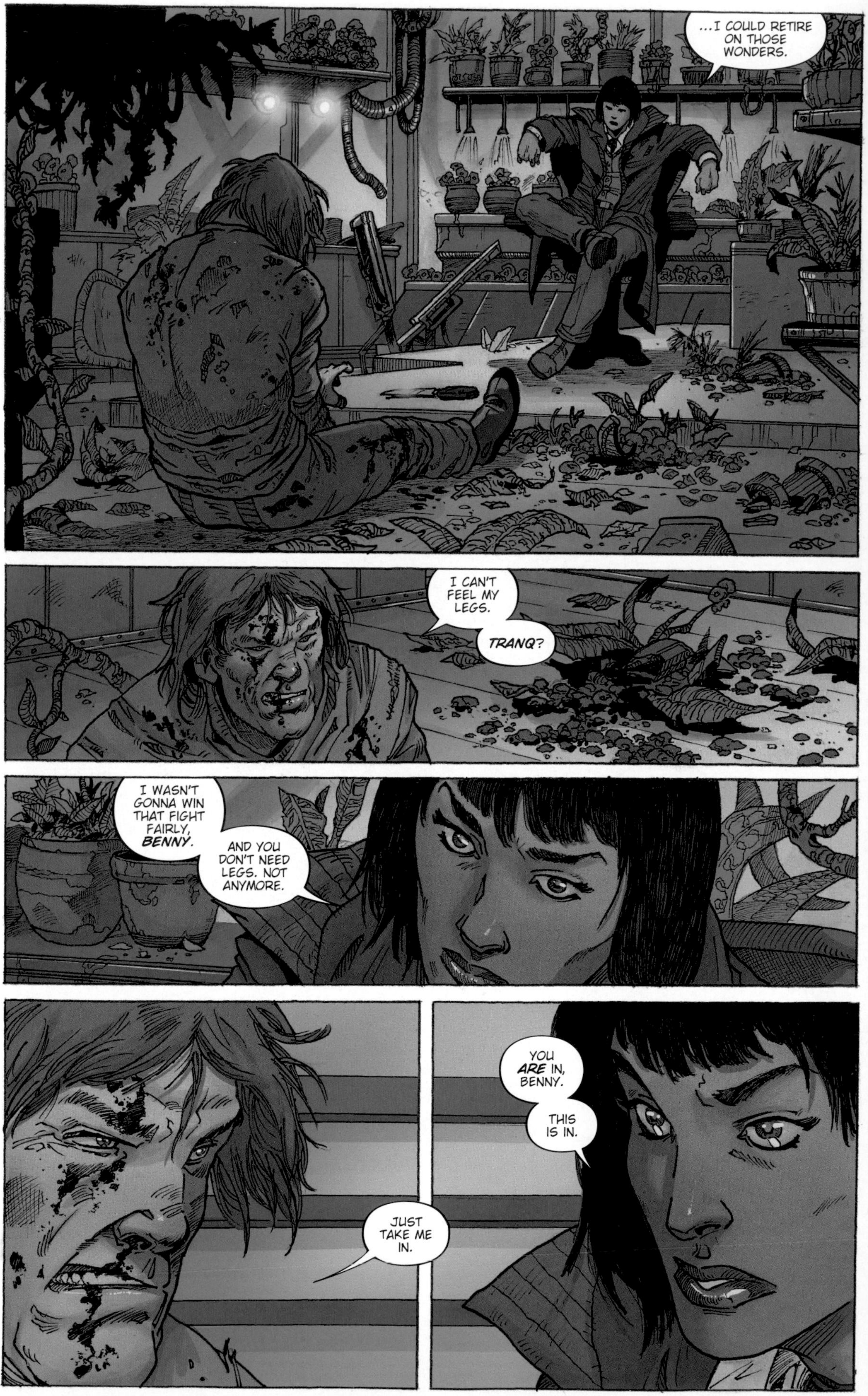
...I COULD RETIRE ON THOSE WONDERS.
I CAN'T FEEL MY LEGS.
TRANQ?
I WASN'T GONNA WIN THAT FIGHT FAIRLY, BENNY.
AND YOU DON'T NEED LEGS. NOT ANYMORE.
JUST TAKE ME IN.
YOU ARE IN, BENNY.
THIS IS IN.

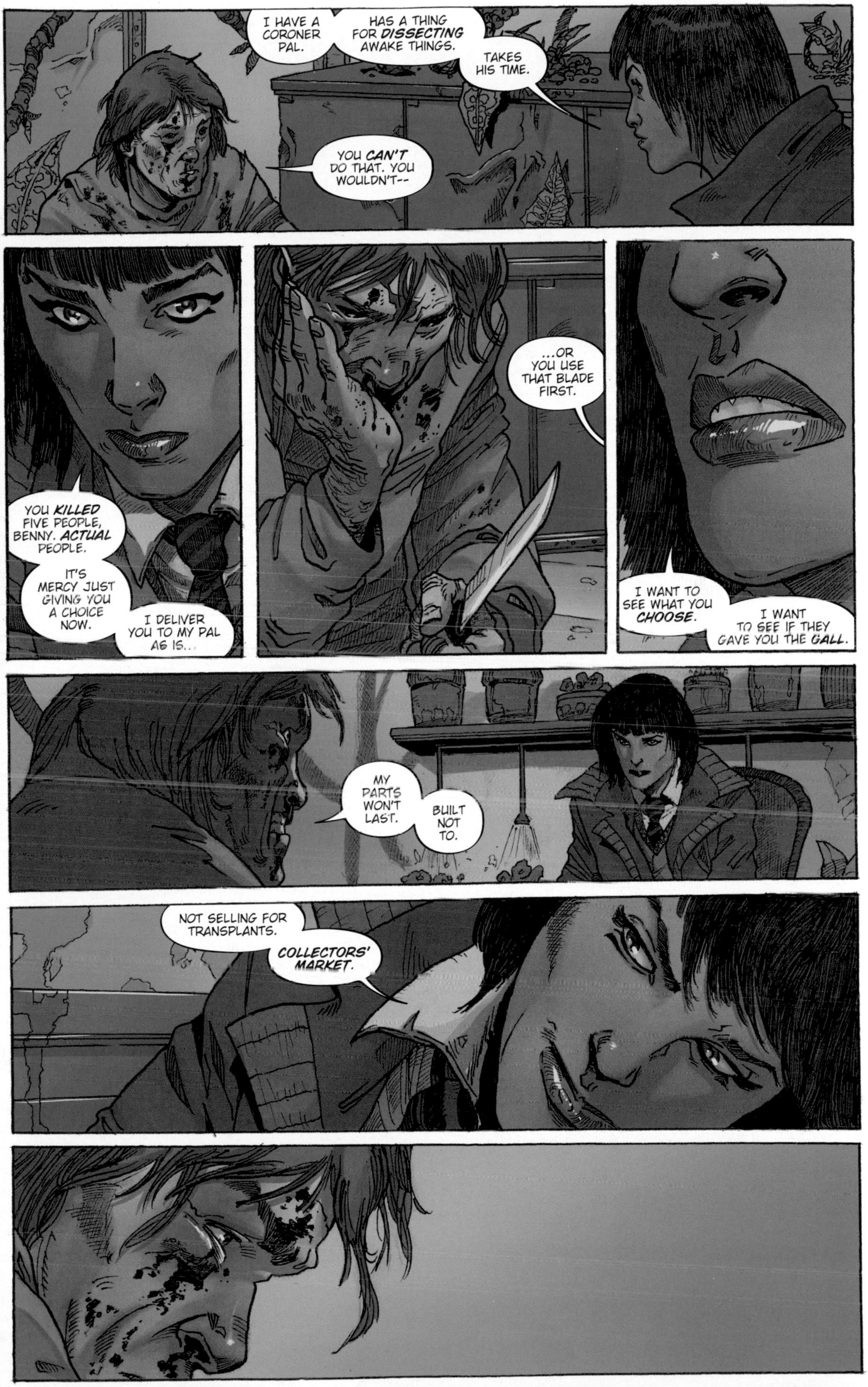
I HAVE A CORONER PAL.
HAS A THING FOR DISSECTING AWAKE THINGS.
TAKES HIS TIME.
YOU CAN'T DO THAT. YOU WOULDN'T--
YOU KILLED FIVE PEOPLE, BENNY. ACTUAL PEOPLE.
IT'S MERCY JUST GIVING YOU A CHOICE NOW.
I DELIVER YOU TO MY PAL AS IS...
...OR YOU USE THAT BLADE FIRST.
I WANT TO SEE WHAT YOU CHOOSE.
I WANT TO SEE IF THEY GAVE YOU THE GALL.
MY PARTS WON'T LAST.
BUILT NOT TO.
NOT SELLING FOR TRANSPLANTS.
COLLECTORS' MARKET.

MY NAME IS
BENJAMIN.

I GOT
GALL.

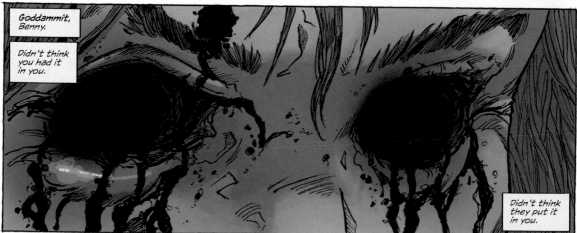

Goddammit,
Benny.

Didn't think
you had it
in you.

Didn't think
they put it
in you.

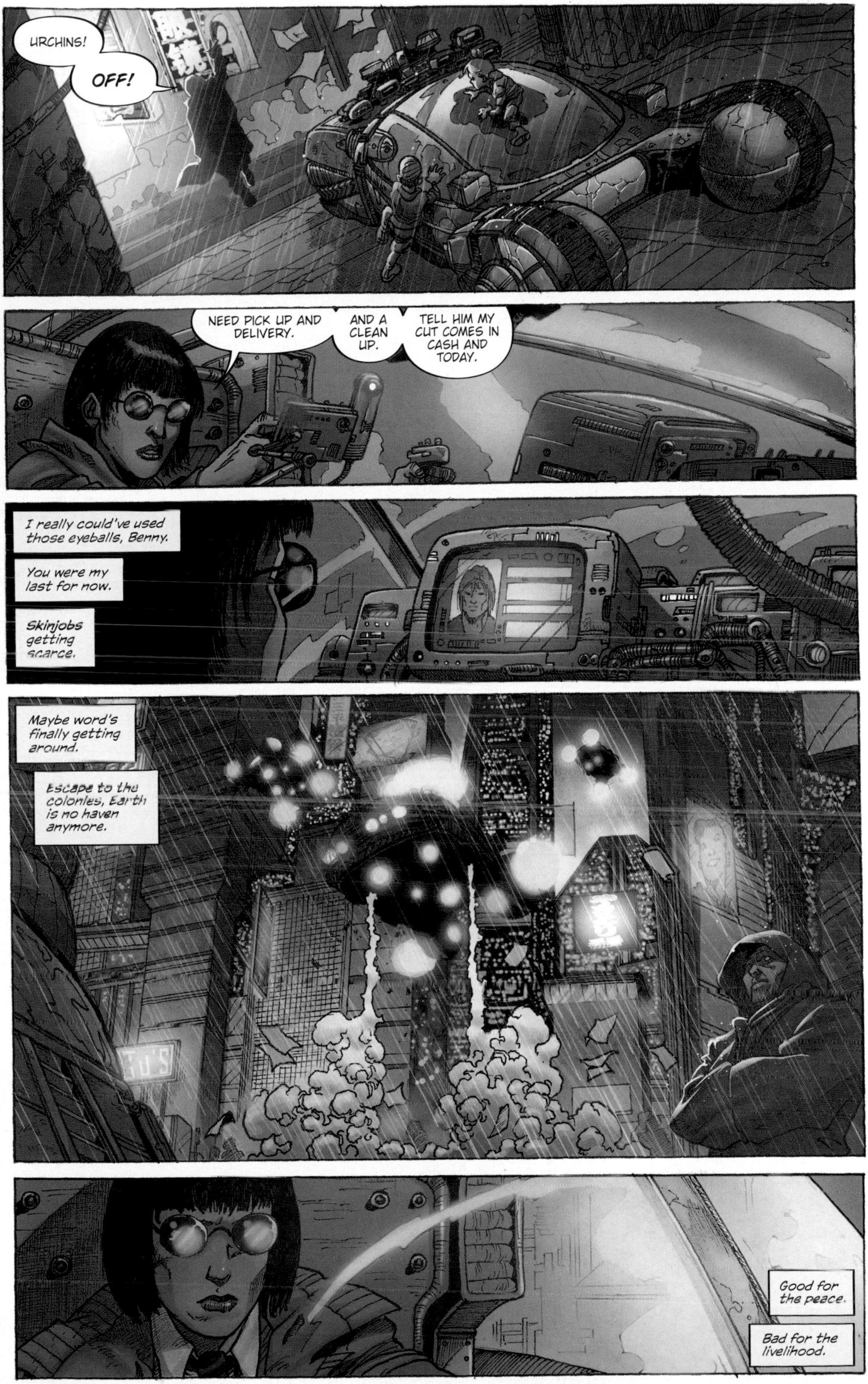
URCHINS!
OFF!
NEED PICK UP AND DELIVERY.
AND A CLEAN UP.
TELL HIM MY CUT COMES IN CASH AND TODAY.
I really could've used those eyeballs, Benny.
You were my last for now.
Skinjobs getting scarce.
Maybe word's finally getting around.
Escape to the colonies, Earth is no haven anymore.
Good for the peace.
Bad for the livelihood.

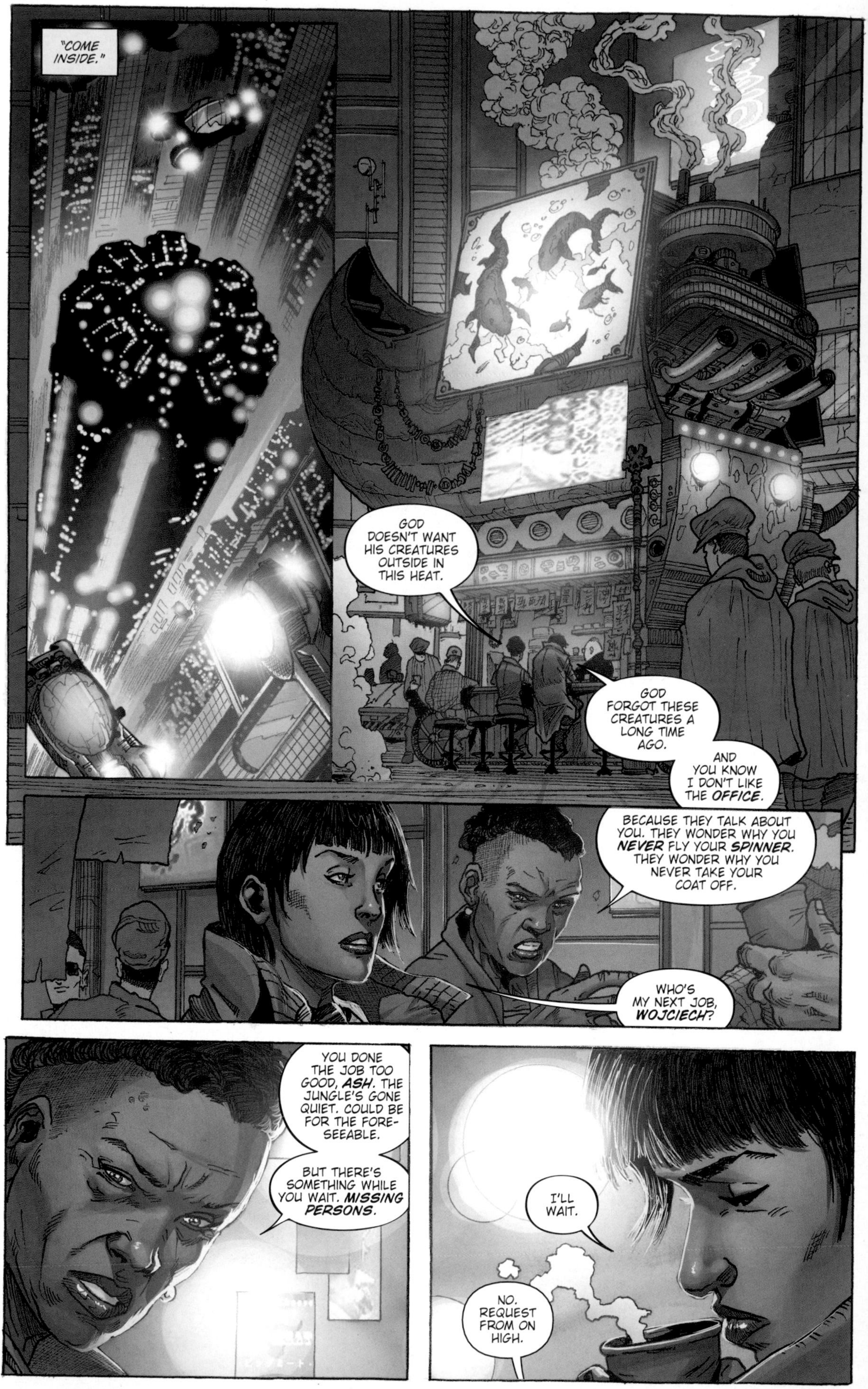
"COME INSIDE."
GOD DOESN'T WANT HIS CREATURES OUTSIDE IN THIS HEAT.
GOD FORGOT THESE CREATURES A LONG TIME AGO.
AND YOU KNOW I DON'T LIKE THE OFFICE.
BECAUSE THEY TALK ABOUT YOU. THEY WONDER WHY YOU NEVER FLY YOUR SPINNER. THEY WONDER WHY YOU NEVER TAKE YOUR COAT OFF.
WHO'S MY NEXT JOB, WOJCIECH?
YOU DONE THE JOB TOO GOOD, ASH. THE JUNGLE'S GONE QUIET. COULD BE FOR THE FORE-SEEABLE.
BUT THERE'S SOMETHING WHILE YOU WAIT. MISSING PERSONS.
I'LL WAIT.
NO. REQUEST FROM ON HIGH.

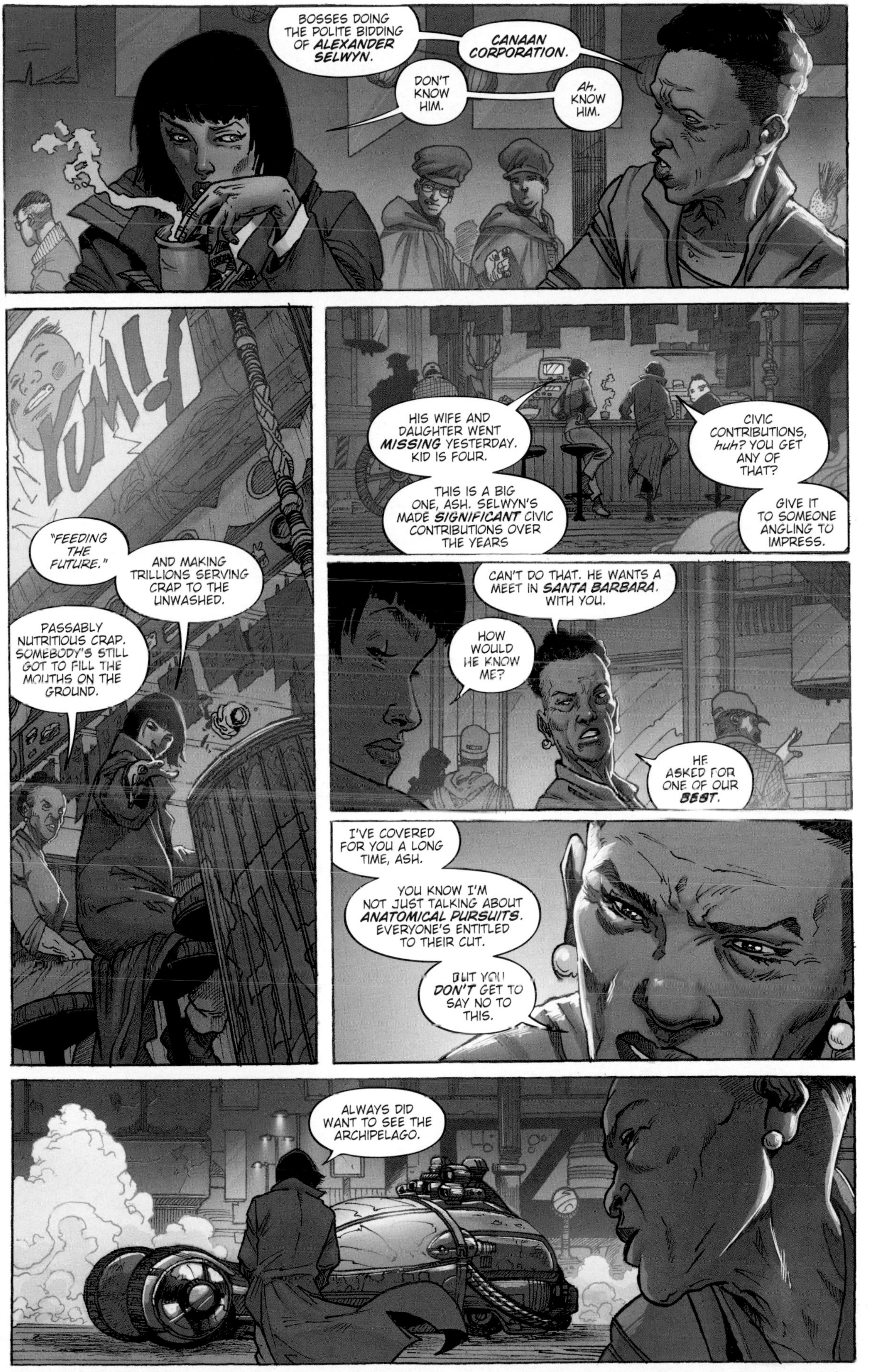
BOSSES DOING THE POLITE BIDDING OF ALEXANDER SELWYN.
CANAAN CORPORATION.
DON'T KNOW HIM.
AH. KNOW HIM.
"FEEDING THE FUTURE."
AND MAKING TRILLIONS SERVING CRAP TO THE UNWASHED.
PASSABLY NUTRITIOUS CRAP. SOMEBODY'S STILL GOT TO FILL THE MOUTHS ON THE GROUND.
YUM!
HIS WIFE AND DAUGHTER WENT MISSING YESTERDAY. KID IS FOUR.
THIS IS A BIG ONE, ASH. SELWYN'S MADE SIGNIFICANT CIVIC CONTRIBUTIONS OVER THE YEARS
CIVIC CONTRIBUTIONS, HUH? YOU GET ANY OF THAT?
GIVE IT TO SOMEONE ANGLING TO IMPRESS.
CAN'T DO THAT. HE WANTS A MEET IN SANTA BARBARA. WITH YOU.
HOW WOULD HE KNOW ME?
HE ASKED FOR ONE OF OUR BEST.
I'VE COVERED FOR YOU A LONG TIME, ASH.
YOU KNOW I'M NOT JUST TALKING ABOUT ANATOMICAL PURSUITS. EVERYONE'S ENTITLED TO THEIR CUT.
BUT YOU DON'T GET TO SAY NO TO THIS.
ALWAYS DID WANT TO SEE THE ARCHIPELAGO.

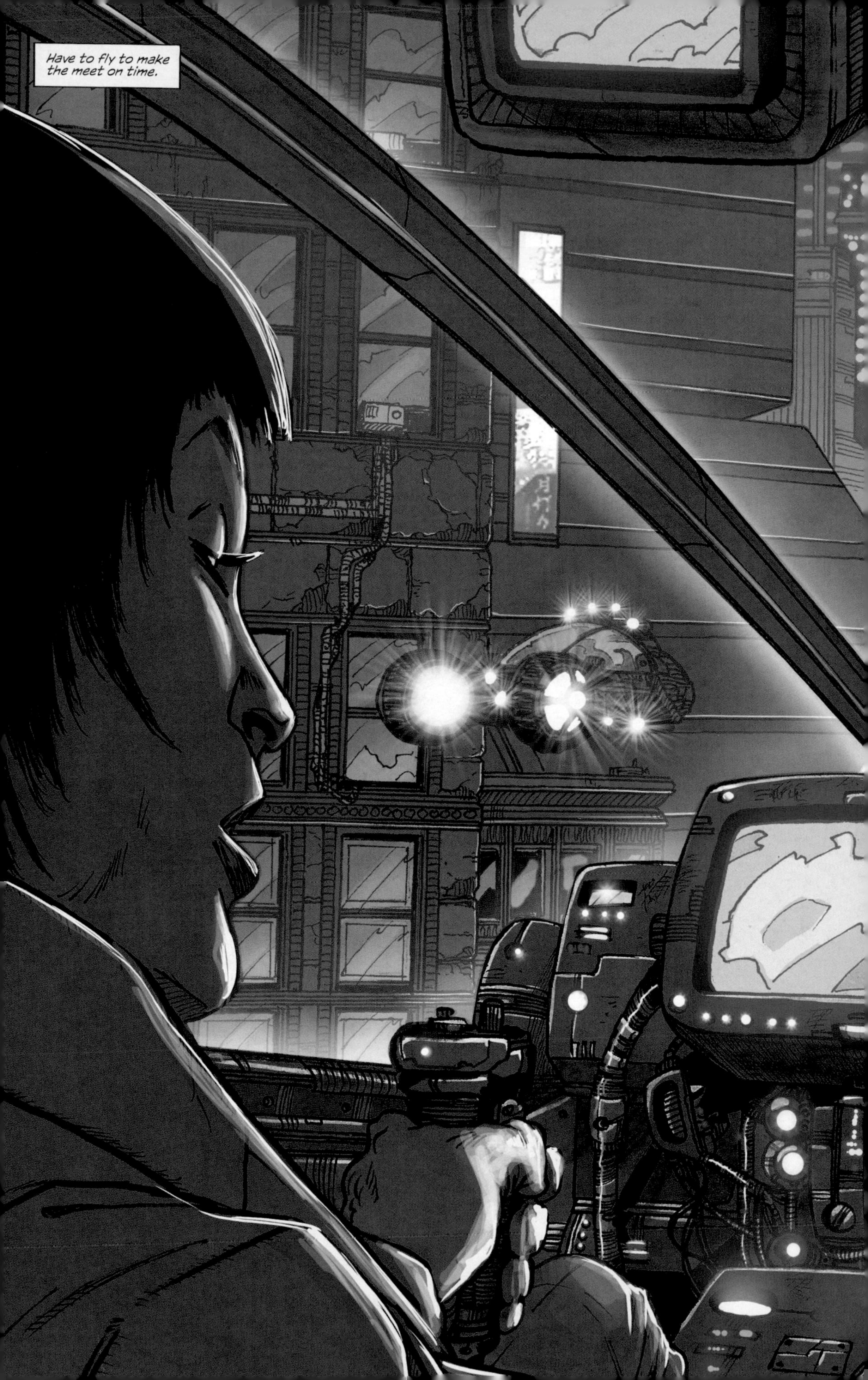
Have to fly to make the meet on time.

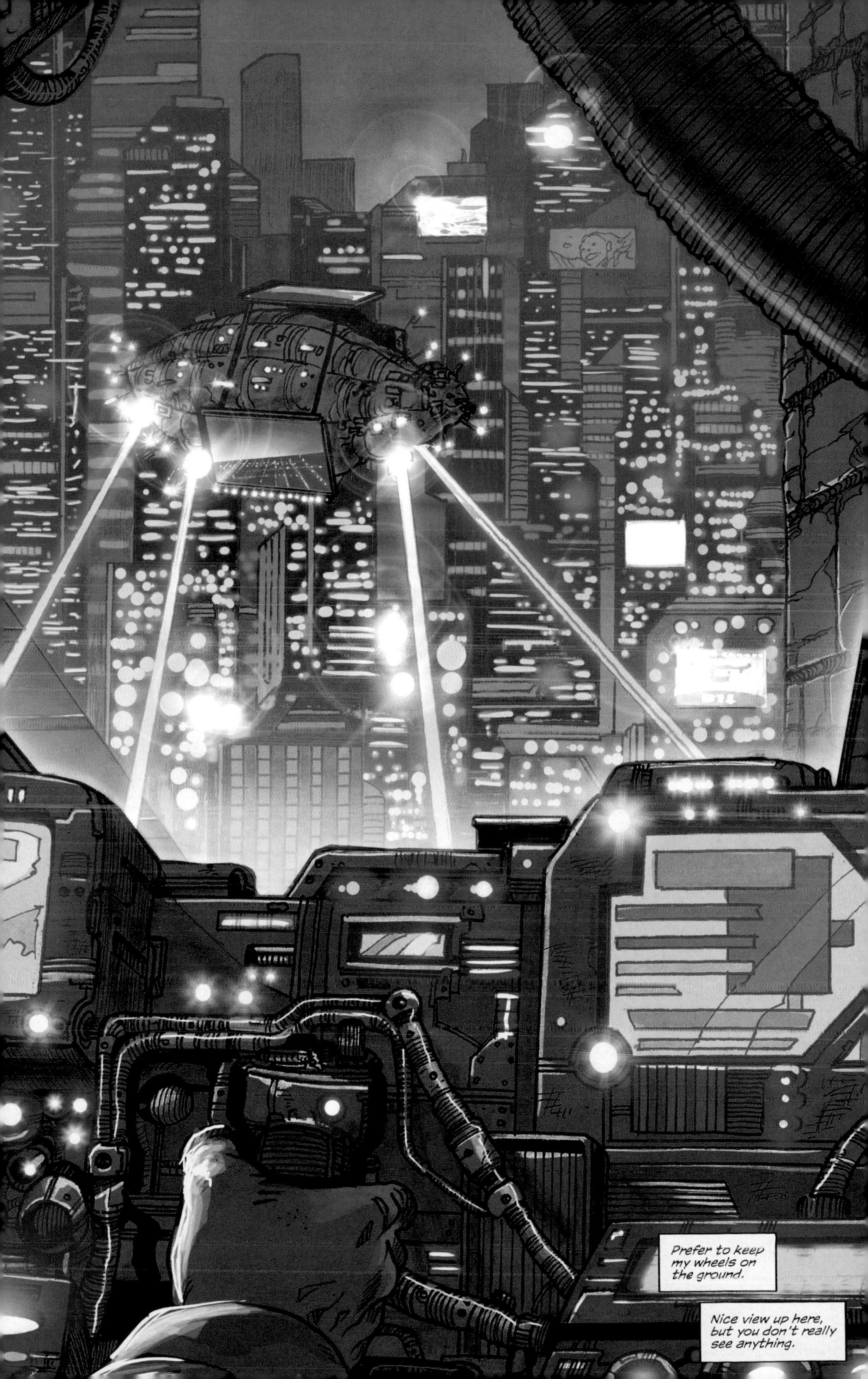
Prefer to keep my wheels on the ground.
Nice view up here, but you don't really see anything.

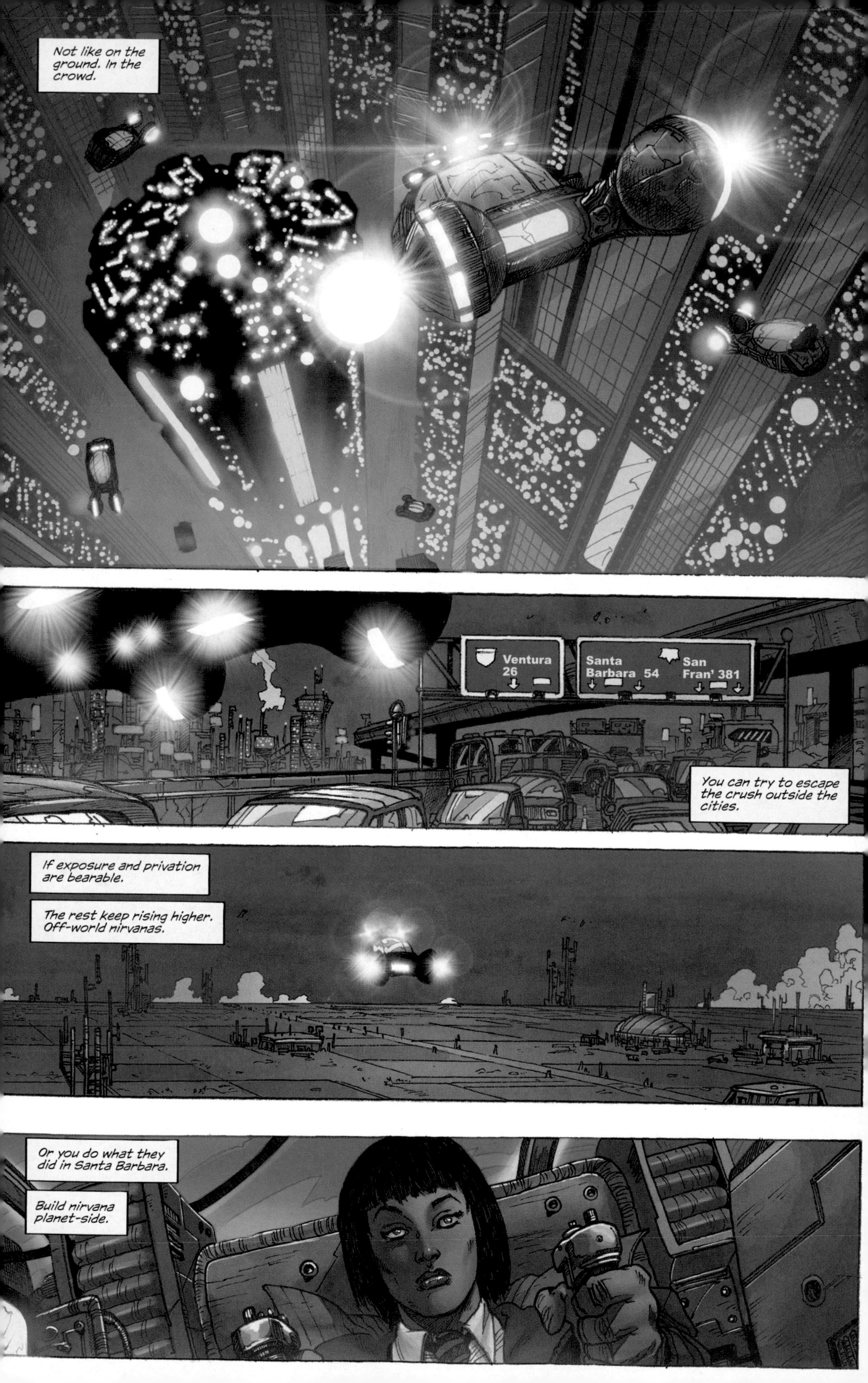
Not like on the ground. In the crowd.
Ventura 26
Santa Barbara 54
San Fran' 381
You can try to escape the crush outside the cities.
If exposure and privation are bearable.
The rest keep rising higher. Off-world nirvanas.
Or you do what they did in Santa Barbara.
Build nirvana planet-side.

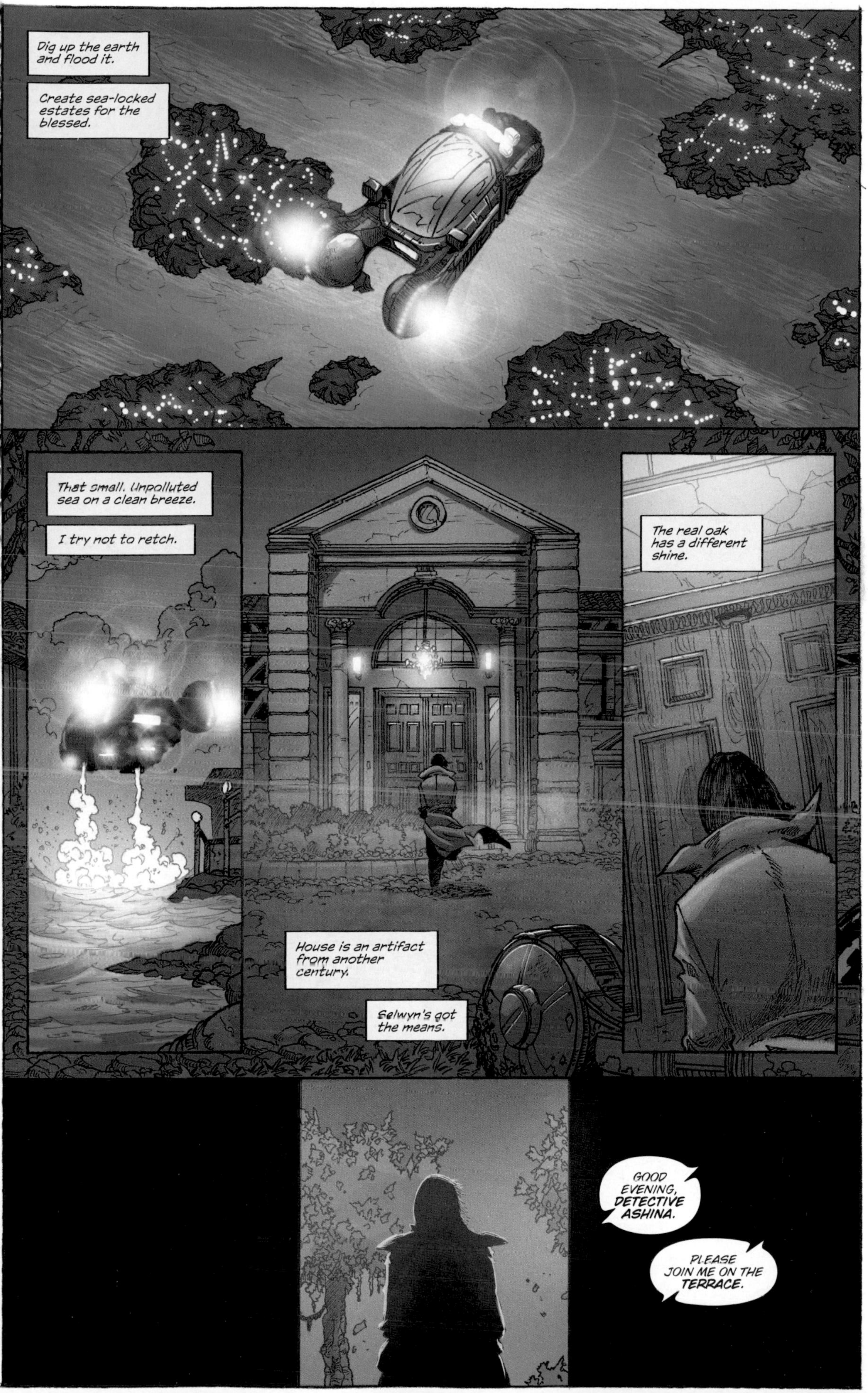

Dig up the earth and flood it.
Create sea-locked estates for the blessed.
That small. Unpolluted sea on a clean breeze.
I try not to retch.
House is an artifact from another century.
Selwyn's got the means.
The real oak has a different shine.
GOOD EVENING, DETECTIVE ASHINA.
PLEASE JOIN ME ON THE TERRACE.

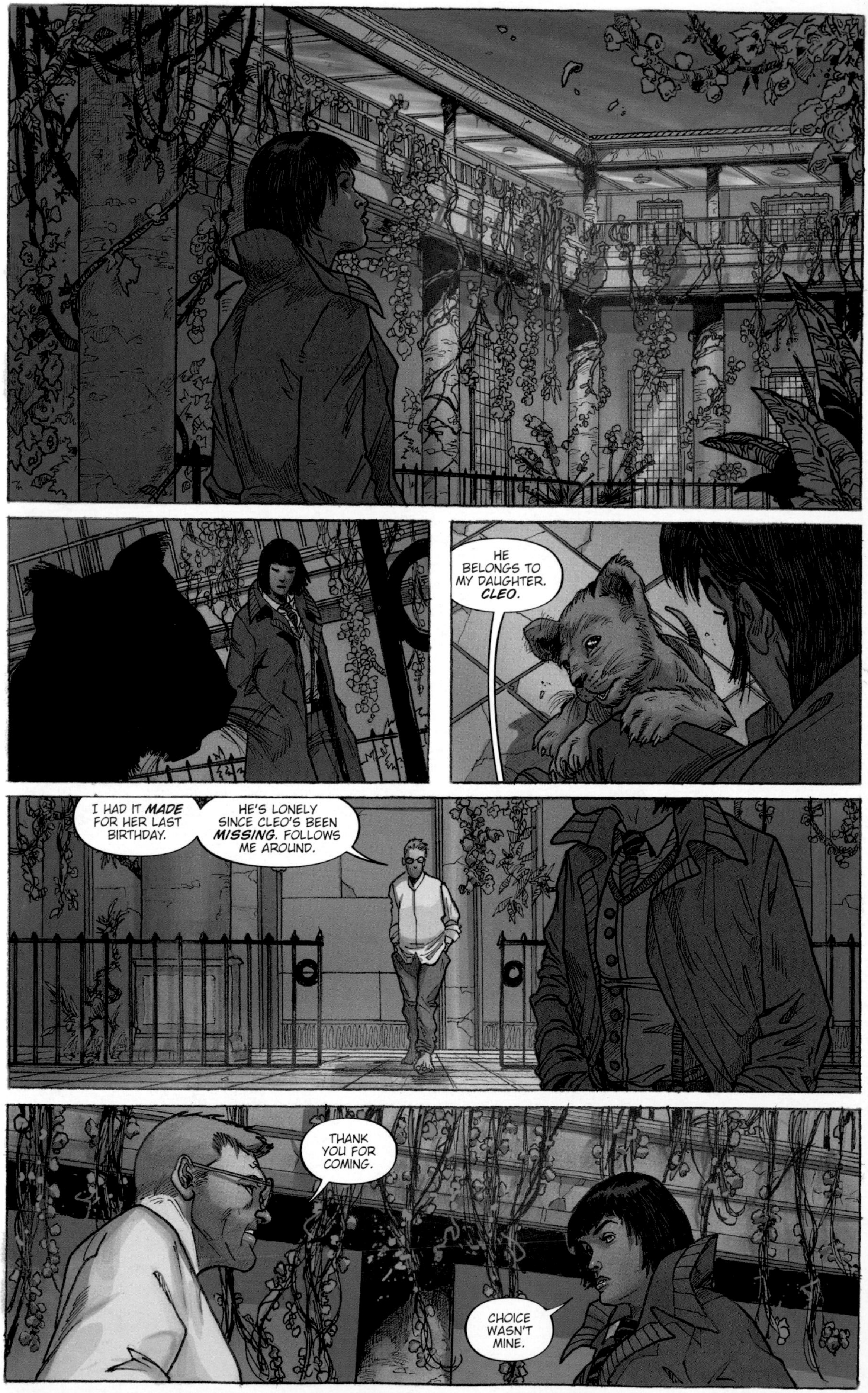
HE BELONGS TO MY DAUGHTER. CLEO.
I HAD IT MADE FOR HER LAST BIRTHDAY.
HE'S LONELY SINCE CLEO'S BEEN MISSING. FOLLOWS ME AROUND.
THANK YOU FOR COMING.
CHOICE WASN'T MINE.

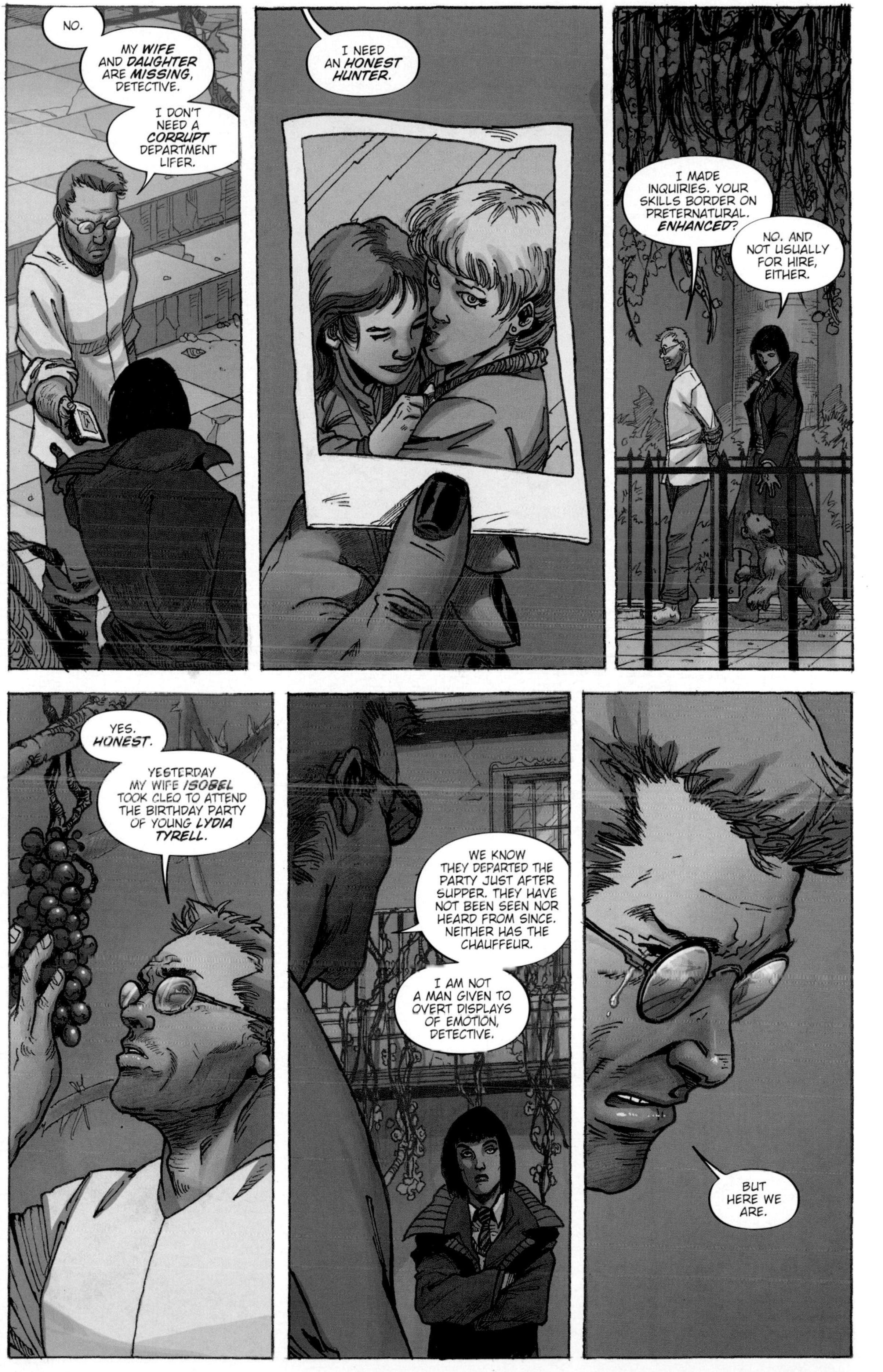
NO.
MY WIFE AND DAUGHTER ARE MISSING, DETECTIVE.
I DON'T NEED A CORRUPT DEPARTMENT LIFER.
I NEED AN HONEST HUNTER.
I MADE INQUIRIES. YOUR SKILLS BORDER ON PRETERNATURAL. ENHANCED?
NO. AND NOT USUALLY FOR HIRE, EITHER.
YES. HONEST.
YESTERDAY MY WIFE ISOBEL TOOK CLEO TO ATTEND THE BIRTHDAY PARTY OF YOUNG LYDIA TYRELL.
WE KNOW THEY DEPARTED THE PARTY JUST AFTER SUPPER. THEY HAVE NOT BEEN SEEN NOR HEARD FROM SINCE. NEITHER HAS THE CHAUFFEUR.
I AM NOT A MAN GIVEN TO OVERT DISPLAYS OF EMOTION, DETECTIVE.
BUT HERE WE ARE.

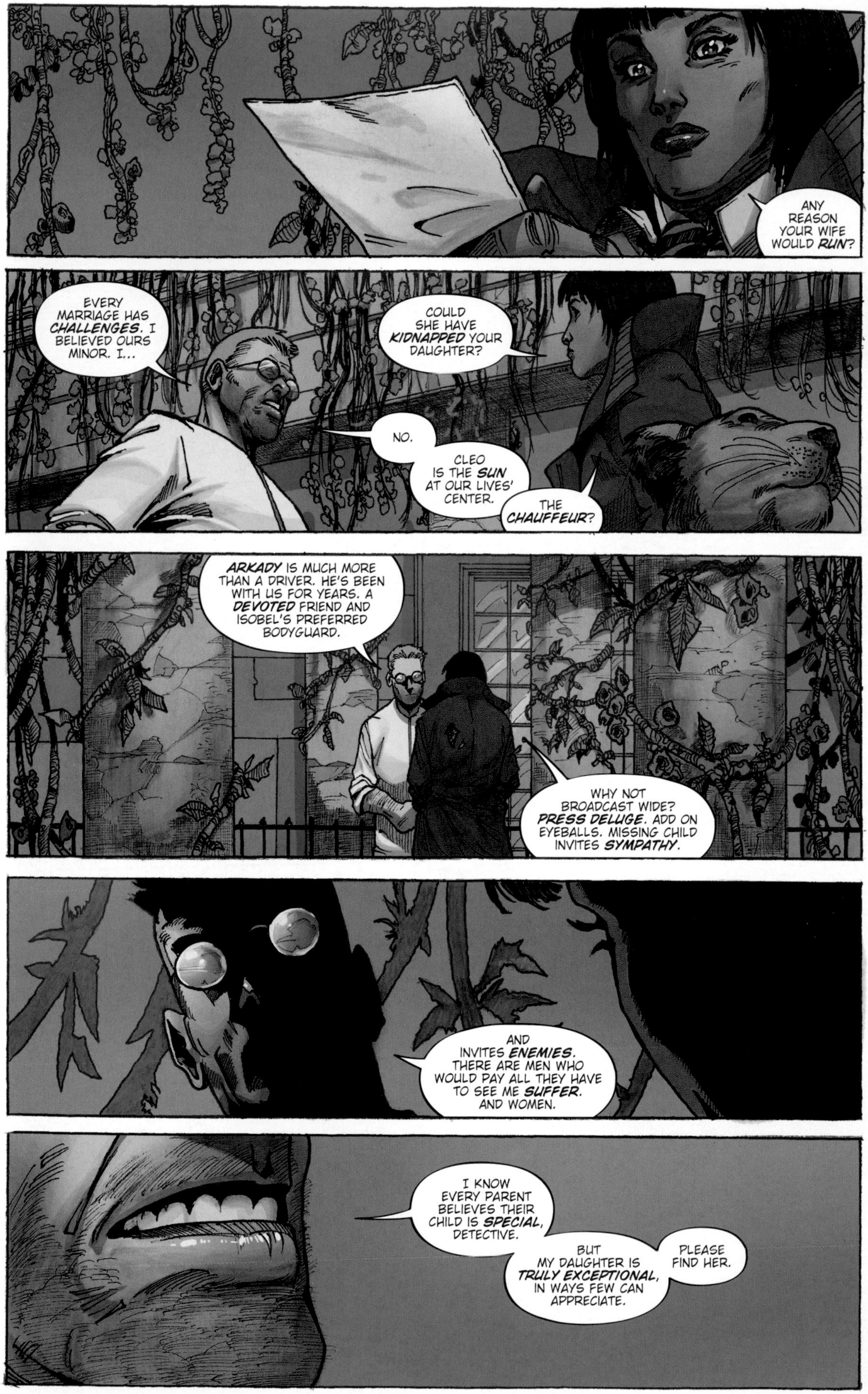
ANY REASON YOUR WIFE WOULD RUN?
EVERY MARRIAGE HAS CHALLENGES. I BELIEVED OURS MINOR. I...
COULD SHE HAVE KIDNAPPED YOUR DAUGHTER?
NO.
CLEO IS THE SUN AT OUR LIVES' CENTER.
THE CHAUFFEUR?
ARKADY IS MUCH MORE THAN A DRIVER. HE'S BEEN WITH US FOR YEARS. A DEVOTED FRIEND AND ISOBEL'S PREFERRED BODYGUARD.
WHY NOT BROADCAST WIDE? PRESS DELUGE. ADD ON EYEBALLS. MISSING CHILD INVITES SYMPATHY.
AND INVITES ENEMIES. THERE ARE MEN WHO WOULD PAY ALL THEY HAVE TO SEE ME SUFFER. AND WOMEN.
I KNOW EVERY PARENT BELIEVES THEIR CHILD IS SPECIAL, DETECTIVE.
BUT MY DAUGHTER IS TRULY EXCEPTIONAL, IN WAYS FEW CAN APPRECIATE.
PLEASE FIND HER.

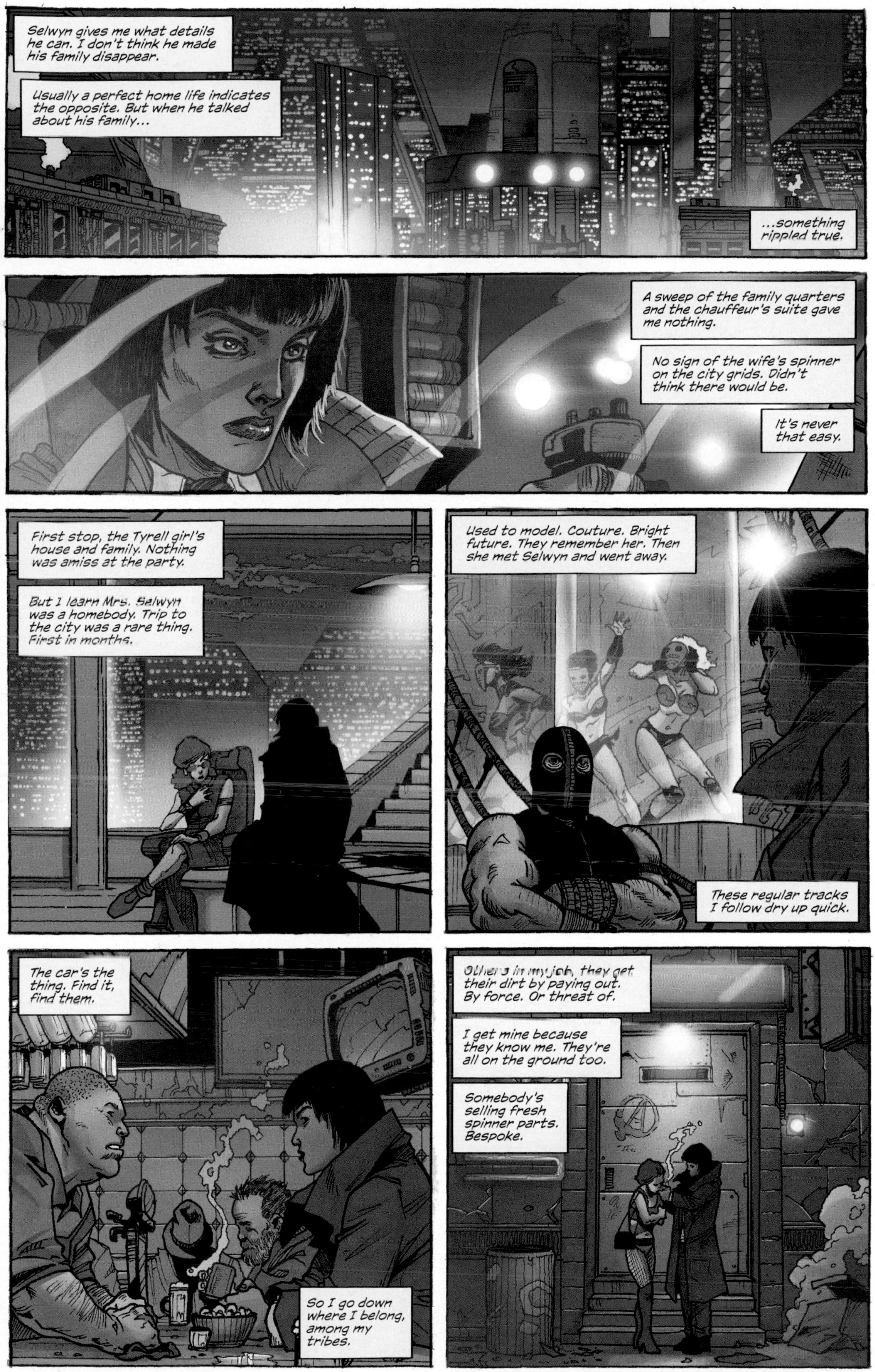
Selwyn gives me what details he can. I don't think he made his family disappear.
Usually a perfect home life indicates the opposite. But when he talked about his family...
...something rippled true.
A sweep of the family quarters and the chauffeur's suite gave me nothing.
No sign of the wife's spinner on the city grids. Didn't think there would be.
It's never that easy.
First stop, the Tyrell girl's house and family. Nothing was amiss at the party.
But I learn Mrs. Selwyn was a homebody. Trip to the city was a rare thing. First in months.
Used to model. Couture. Bright future. They remember her. Then she met Selwyn and went away.
These regular tracks I follow dry up quick.
The car's the thing. Find it, find them.
So I go down where I belong, among my tribes.
Others in my job, they get their dirt by paying out. By force. Or threat of.
I get mine because they know me. They're all on the ground too.
Somebody's selling fresh spinner parts. Bespoke.

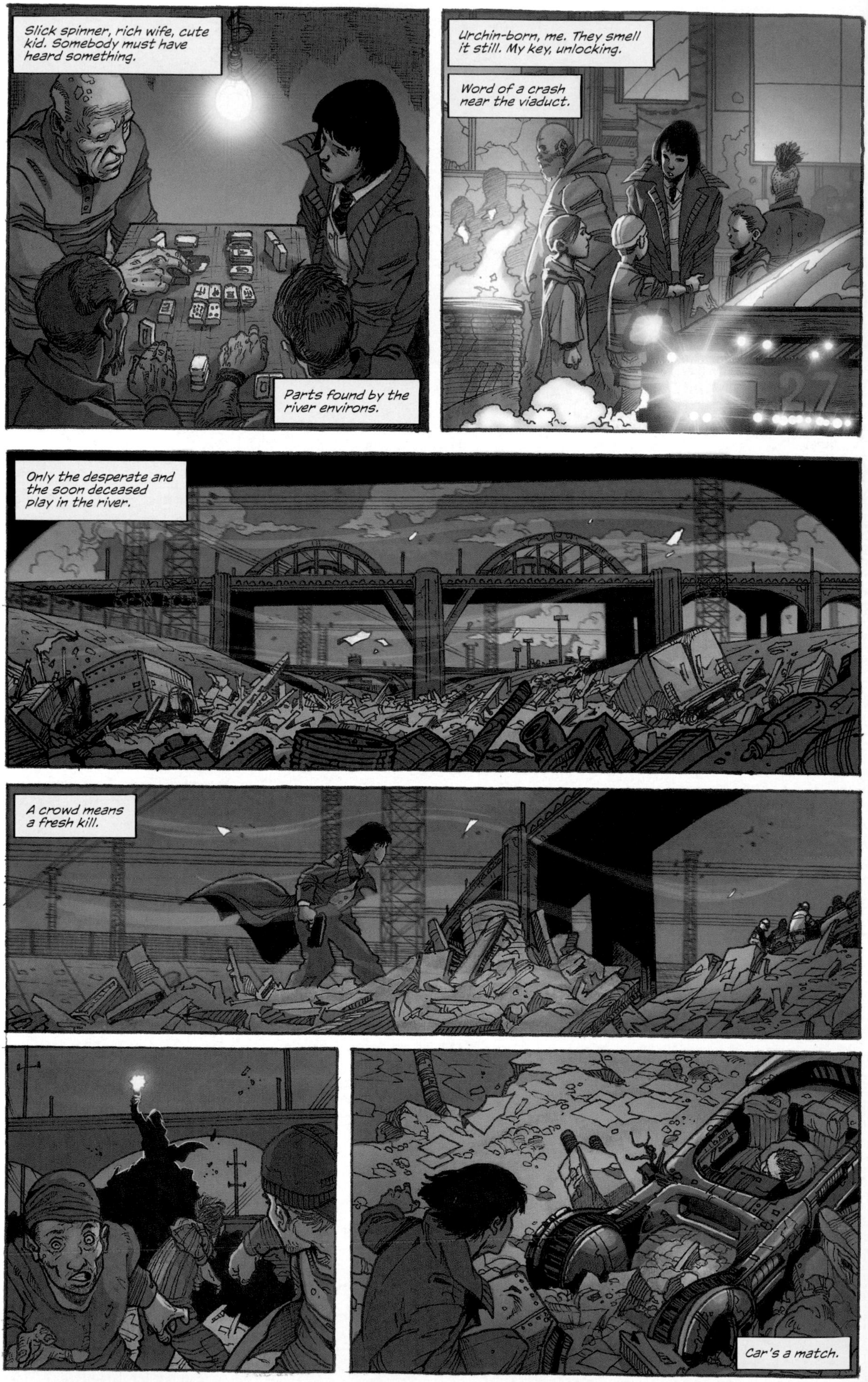
Slick spinner, rich wife, cute kid. Somebody must have heard something.
Parts found by the river environs.
Urchin-born, me. They smell it still. My key, unlocking.
Word of a crash near the viaduct.
Only the desperate and the soon deceased play in the river.
A crowd means a fresh kill.
Car's a match.

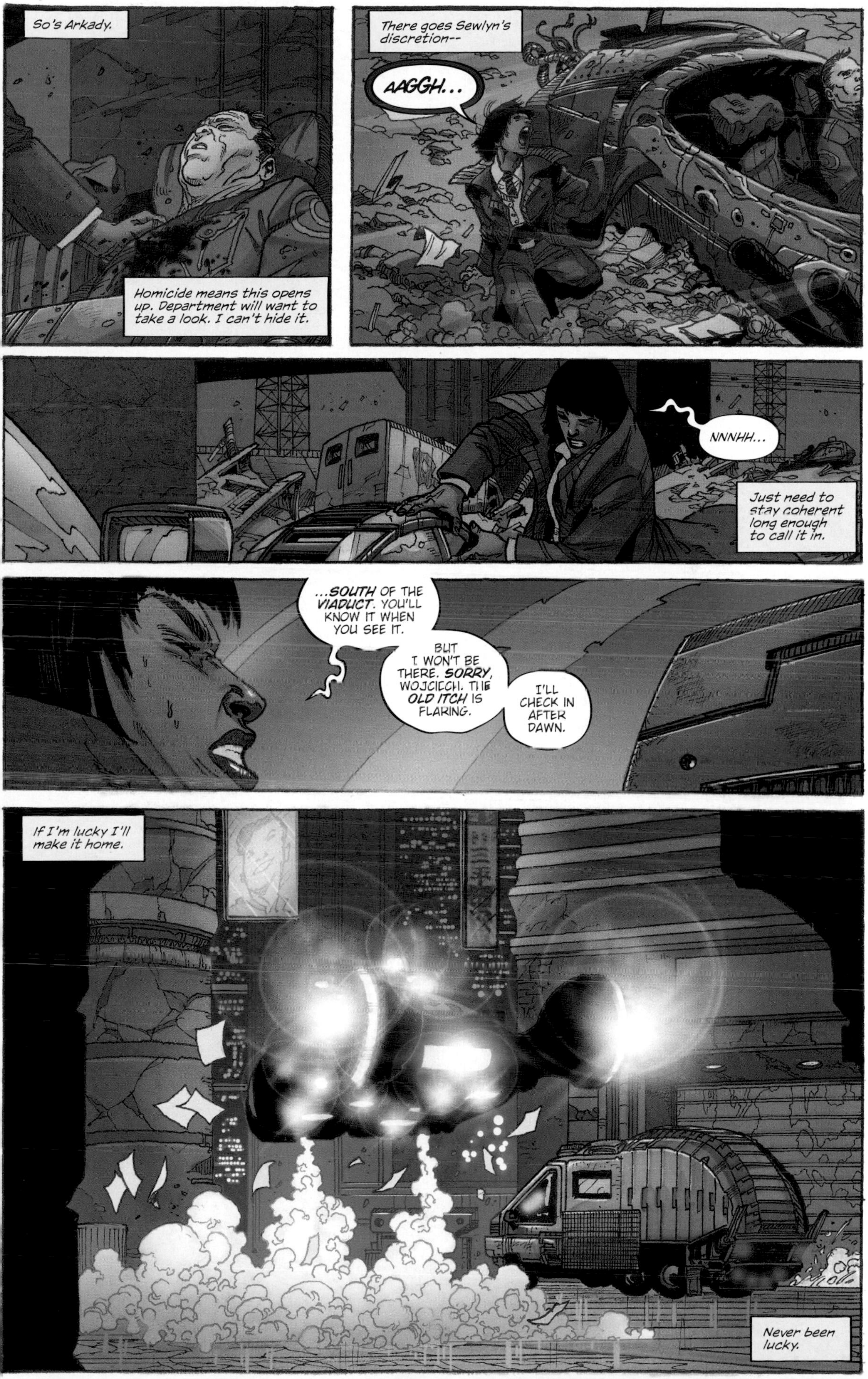
So's Arkady.
Homicide means this opens up. Department will want to take a look. I can't hide it.
There goes Sewlyn's discretion--
AAGGH...
NNNHH...
Just need to stay coherent long enough to call it in.
...SOUTH OF THE VIADUCT. YOU'LL KNOW IT WHEN YOU SEE IT.
BUT I WON'T BE THERE. SORRY, WOJCIECH. THE OLD ITCH IS FLARING.
I'LL CHECK IN AFTER DAWN.
If I'm lucky I'll make it home.
Never been lucky.

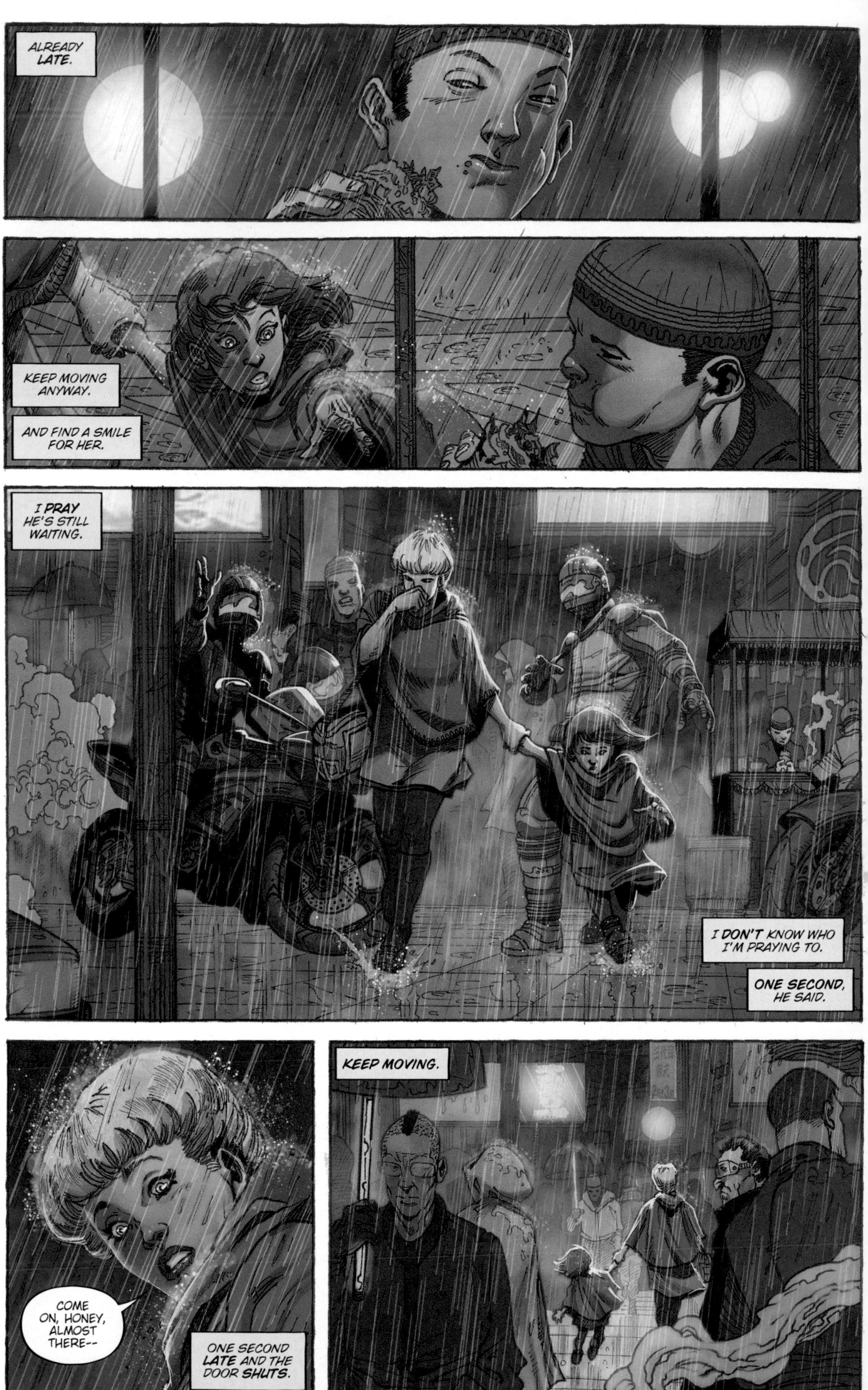
ALREADY LATE.
KEEP MOVING ANYWAY.
AND FIND A SMILE FOR HER.
I PRAY HE'S STILL WAITING.
I DON'T KNOW WHO I'M PRAYING TO.
ONE SECOND, HE SAID.
COME ON, HONEY, ALMOST THERE--
ONE SECOND LATE AND THE DOOR SHUTS.
KEEP MOVING.

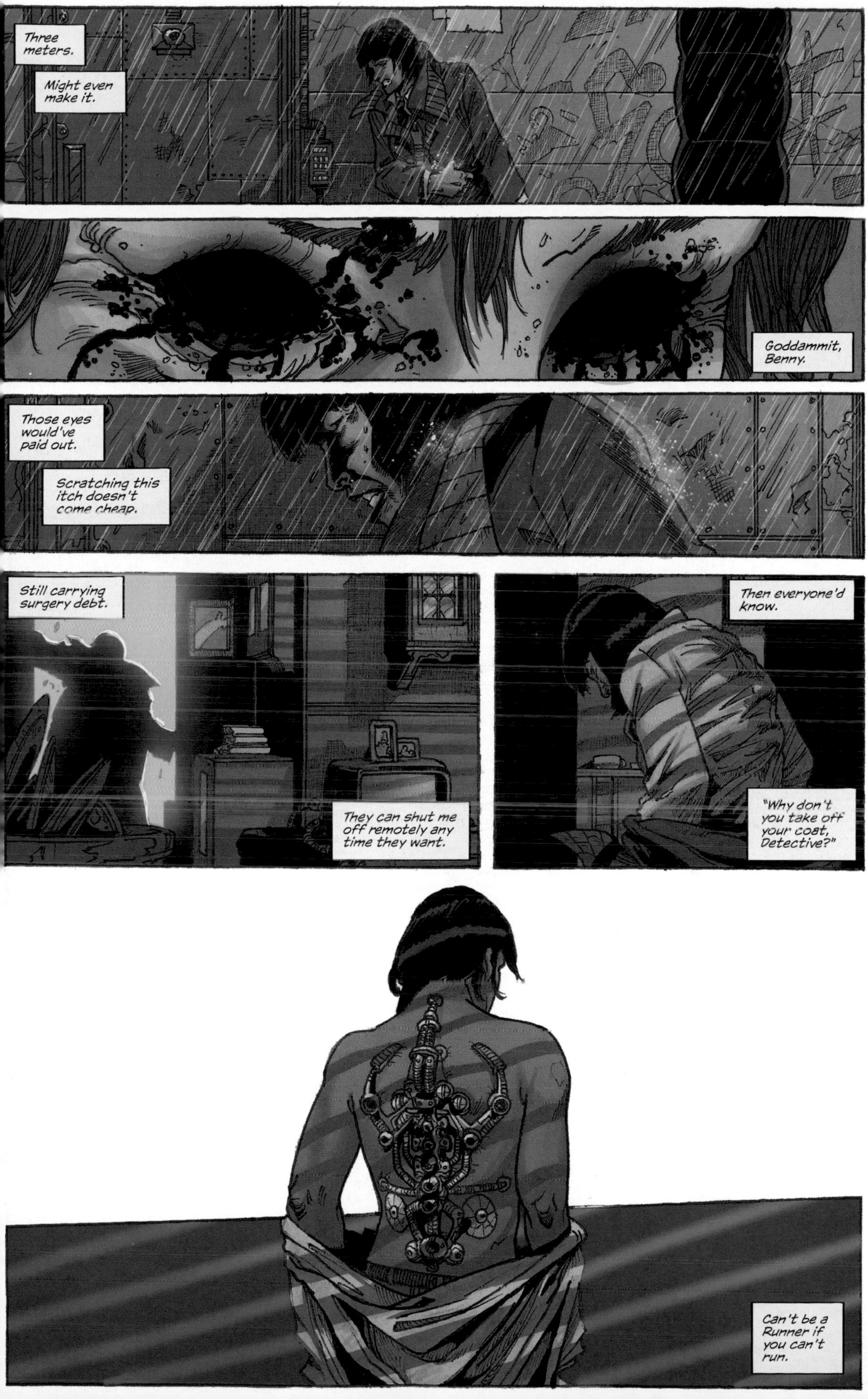
Three meters.
Might even make it.
Goddammit, Benny.
Those eyes would've paid out.
Scratching this itch doesn't come cheap.
Still carrying surgery debt.
They can shut me off remotely any time they want.
Then everyone'd know.
"Why don't you take off your coat, Detective?"
Can't be a Runner if you can't run.

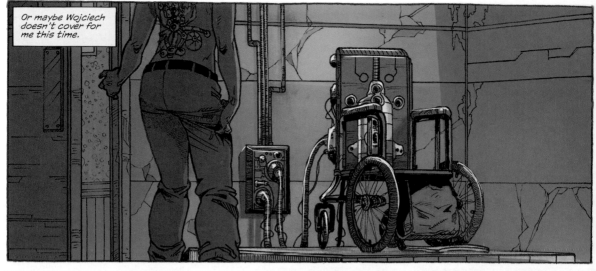

Or maybe Wojciech doesn't cover for me this time.

Maybe this time she tells the bosses her best bet won't pass the physical.

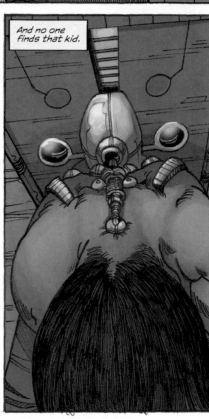

And no one finds that kid.

Four years old.

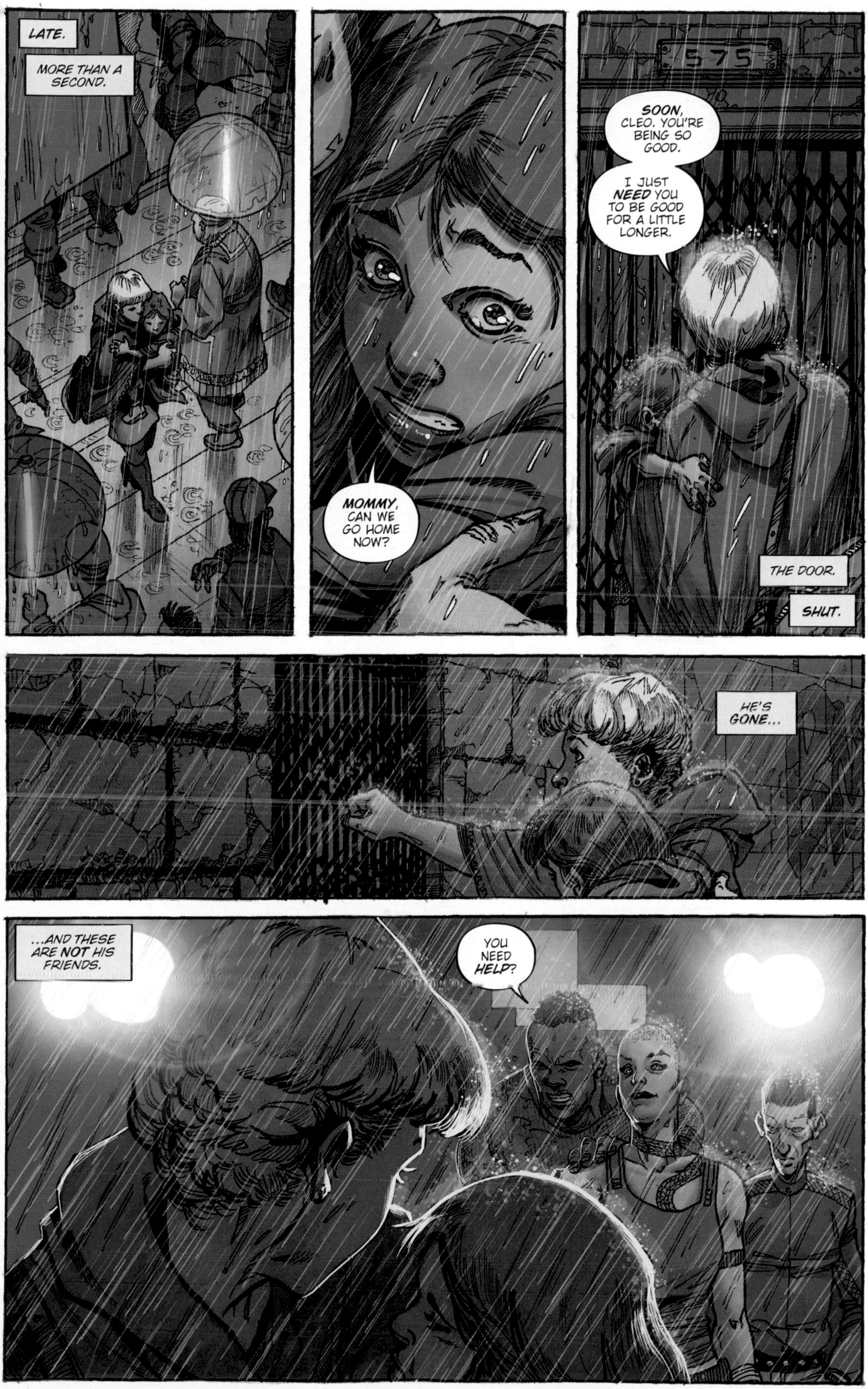
LATE.
MORE THAN A SECOND.
MOMMY, CAN WE GO HOME NOW?
SOON, CLEO. YOU'RE BEING SO GOOD.
I JUST NEED YOU TO BE GOOD FOR A LITTLE LONGER.
575
THE DOOR.
SHUT.
HE'S GONE...
...AND THESE ARE NOT HIS FRIENDS.
YOU NEED HELP?

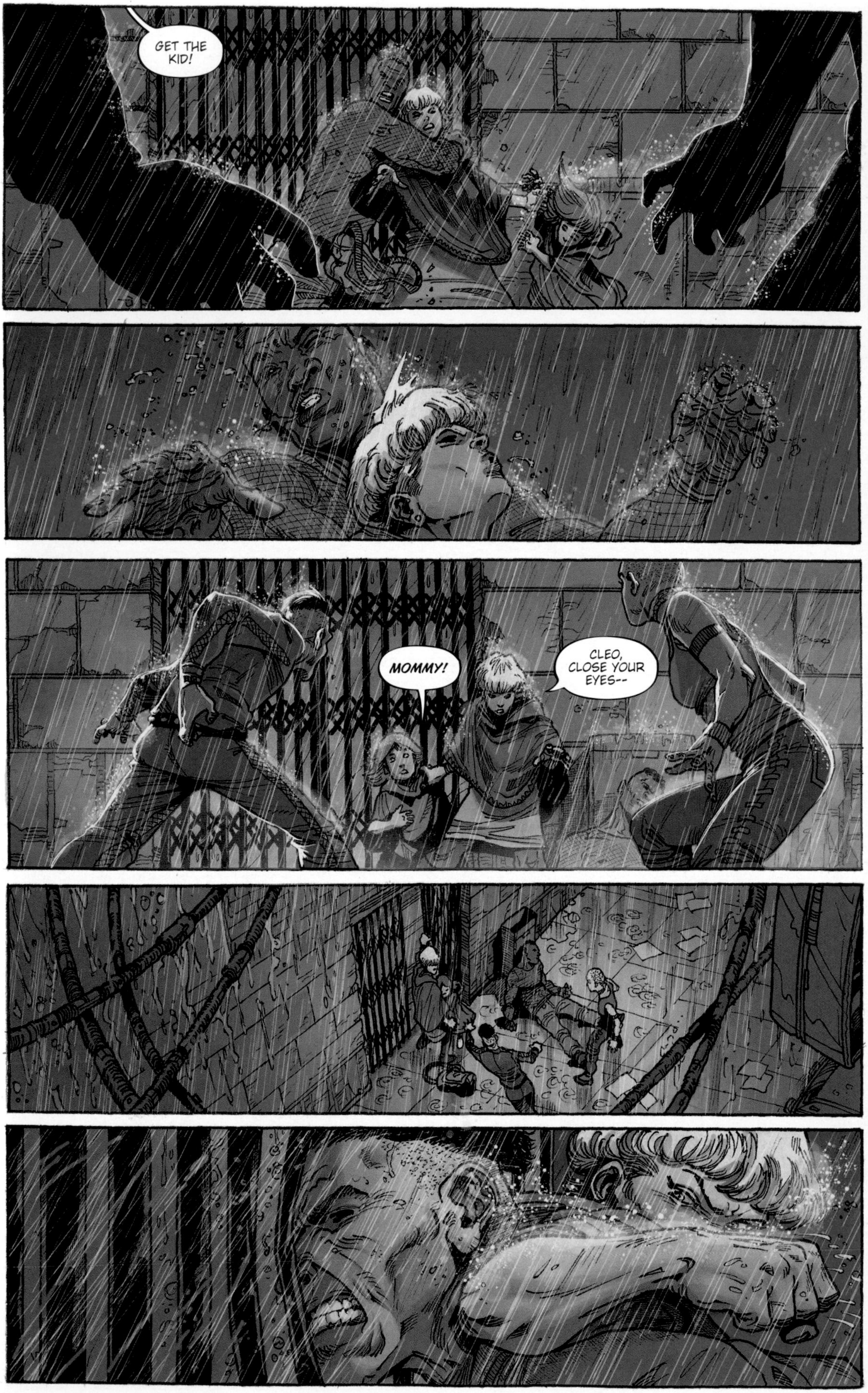
GET THE KID!
MOMMY!
CLEO, CLOSE YOUR EYES--

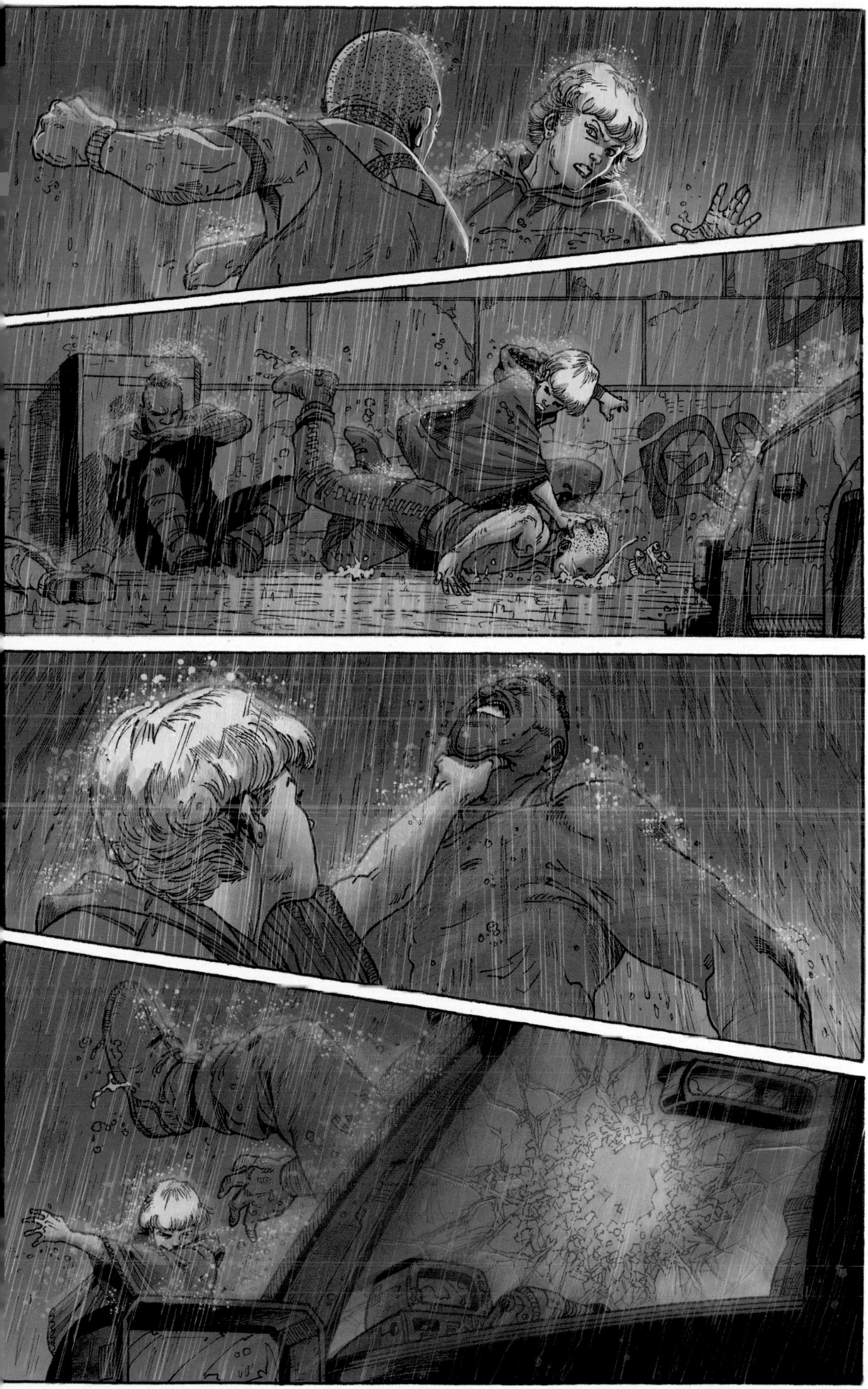

MOMMY...

I'M *SORRY*, BABY, I'M SORRY--

YOU WERE *LATE*...

...SO I CAME LOOKING.

M-*MALAK*?

YES.

THE DOOR...

TIME IS NOT OUR ALLY.

COME.

...CRACKS OPEN.

JUST ENOUGH.

WE SLIP THROUGH.

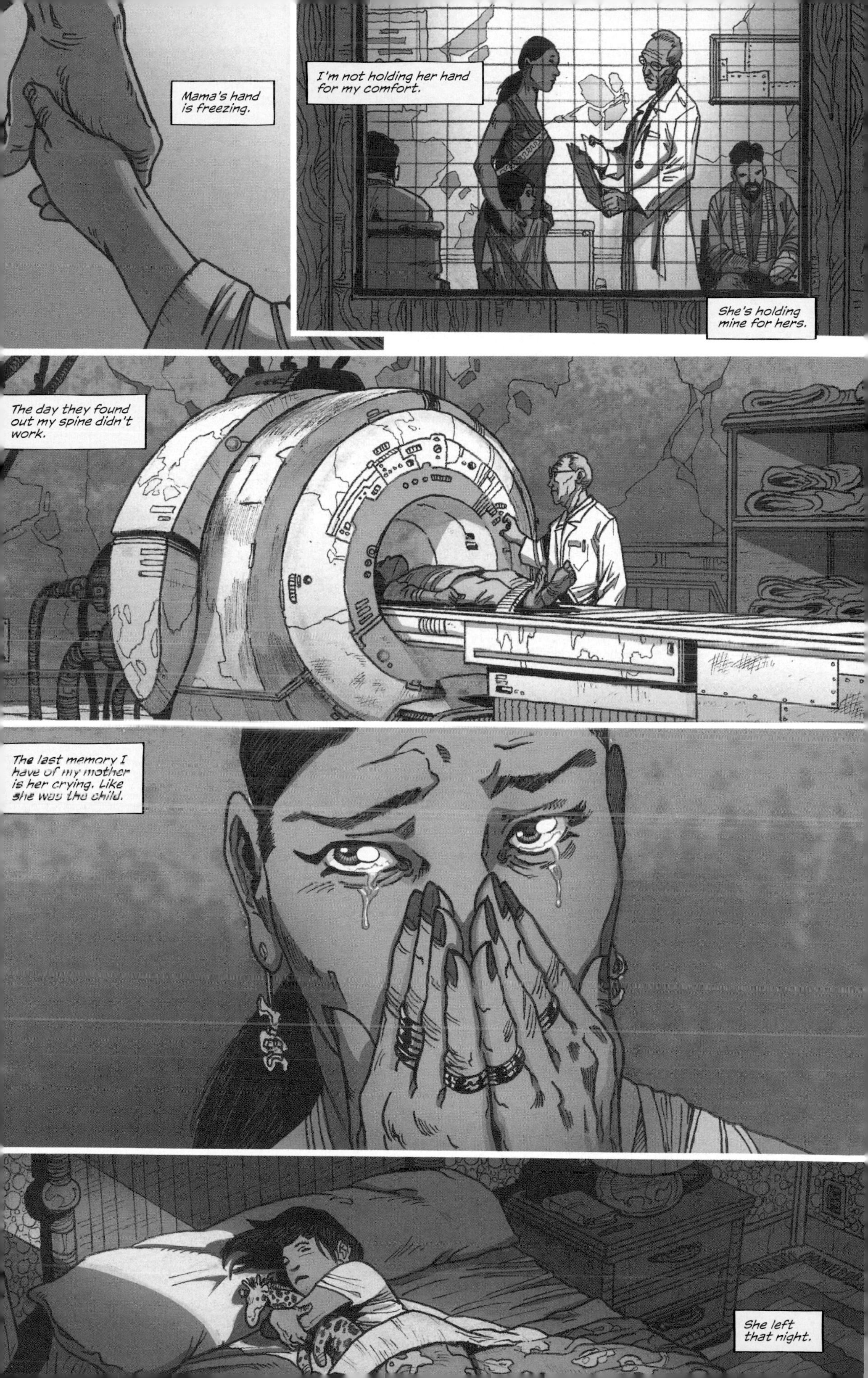
Mama's hand is freezing.
I'm not holding her hand for my comfort.
She's holding mine for hers.
The day they found out my spine didn't work.
The last memory I have of my mother is her crying. Like she was the child.
She left that night.

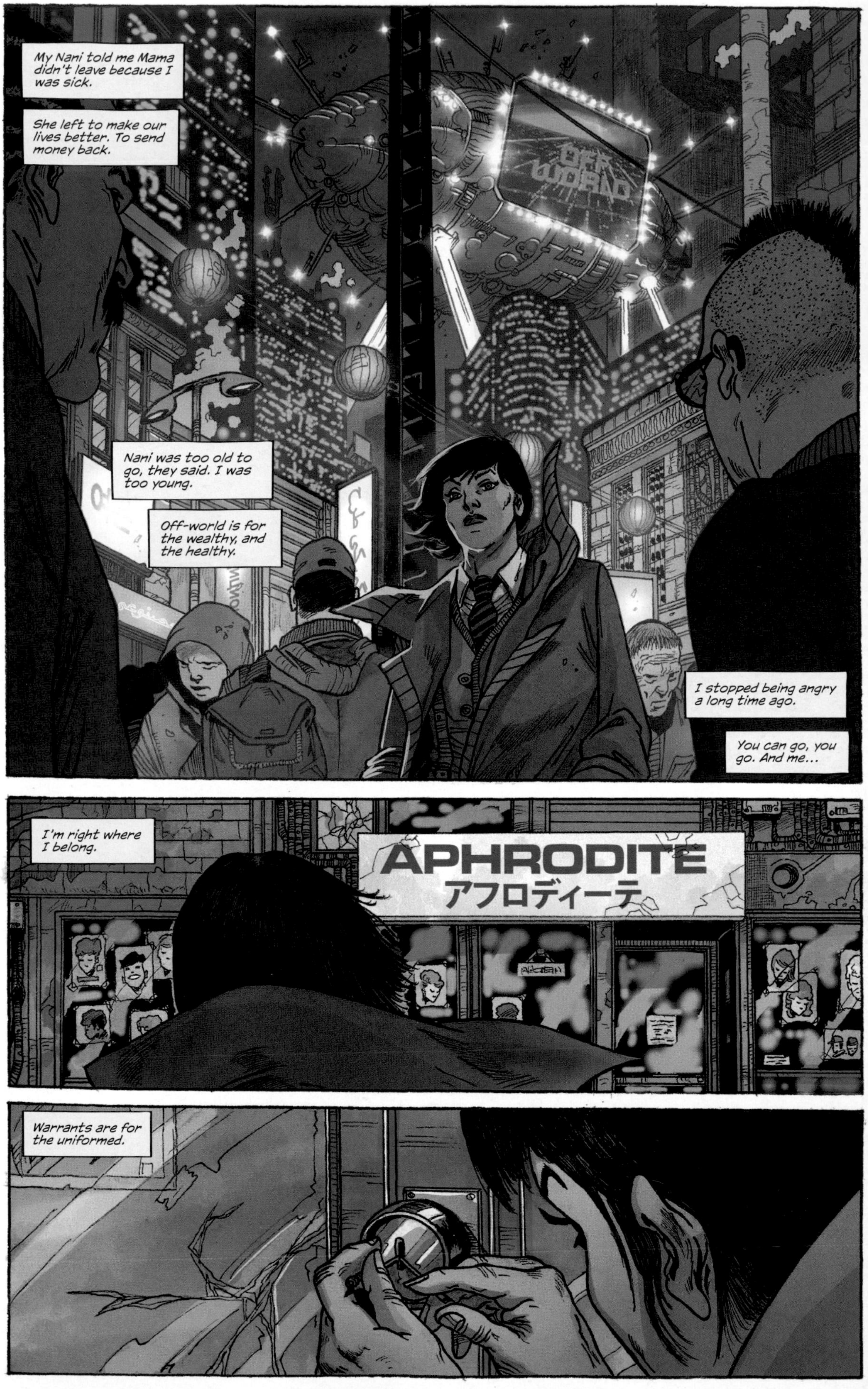
My Nani told me Mama didn't leave because I was sick.
She left to make our lives better. To send money back.
OFF WORLD
Nani was too old to go, they said. I was too young.
Off-world is for the wealthy, and the healthy.
I stopped being angry a long time ago.
You can go, you go. And me...
I'm right where I belong.
APHRODITE
アフロディーテ
Warrants are for the uniformed.

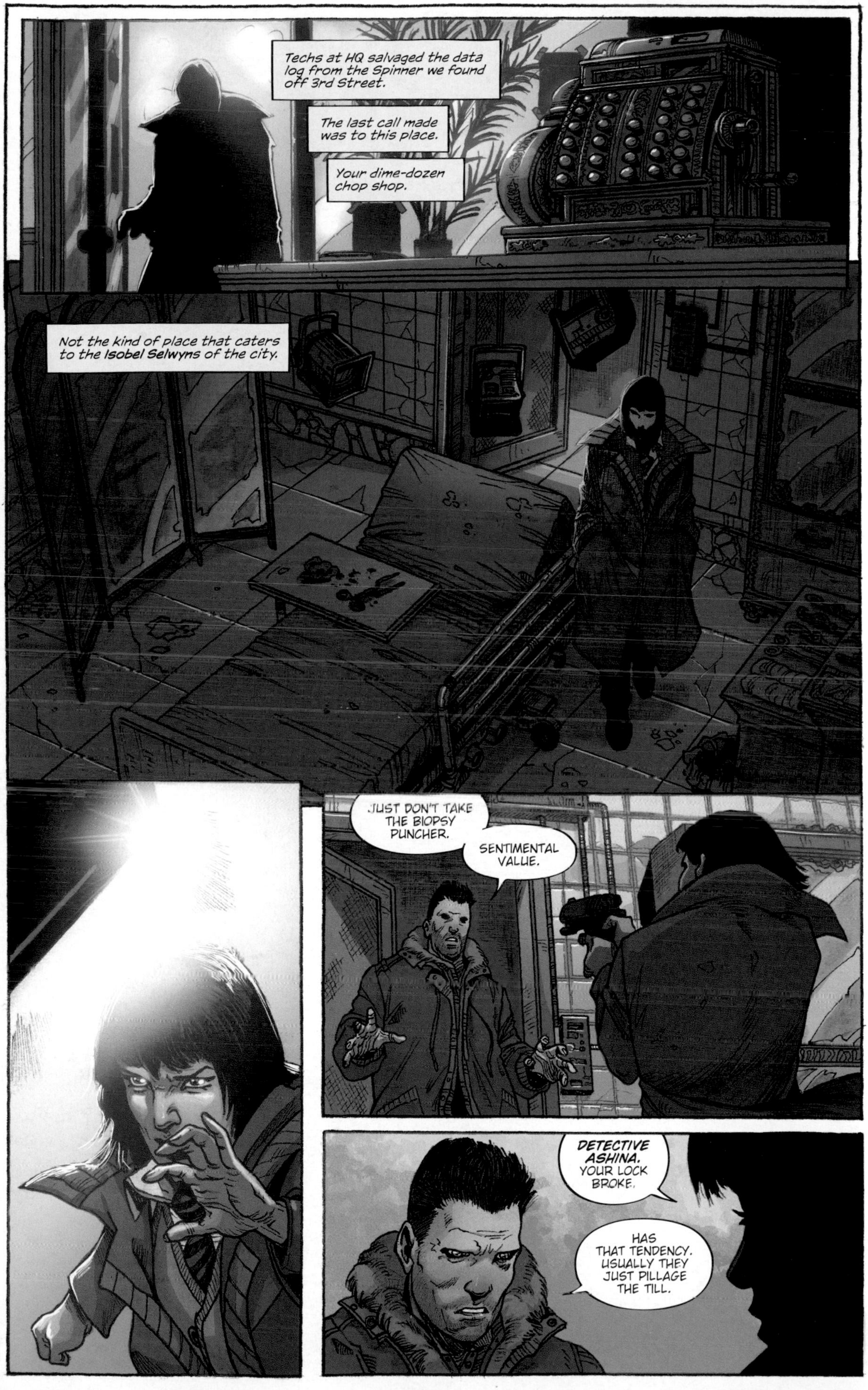

Techs at HQ salvaged the data log from the Spinner we found off 3rd Street.
The last call made was to this place.
Your dime-dozen chop shop.
Not the kind of place that caters to the Isobel Selwyns of the city.
JUST DON'T TAKE THE BIOPSY PUNCHER.
SENTIMENTAL VALUE.
DETECTIVE ASHINA. YOUR LOCK BROKE.
HAS THAT TENDENCY. USUALLY THEY JUST PILLAGE THE TILL.

WORKING LATE?

OFFICE IS HOME.

YOU GOT A CALL LAST NIGHT.

I'M LOOKING FOR THE CALLER.

LADY NAMED *ISOBEL*.

*Cops right to it.*

*Innocent. Or clever, this one.*

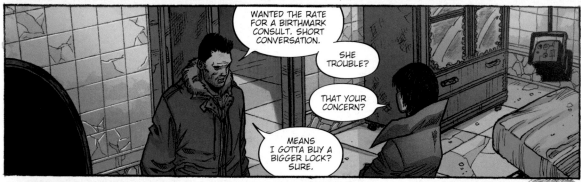

WANTED THE RATE FOR A BIRTHMARK CONSULT. SHORT CONVERSATION.

SHE TROUBLE?

THAT YOUR CONCERN?

MEANS I GOTTA BUY A BIGGER LOCK? SURE.

SHE CALLS BACK, YOU CALL ME NEXT.

HOW LONG YOU BEEN WEARING A *BRACE*, DETECTIVE?

SHE SAID SHE WAS ON HER WAY HOME. FOR WHAT IT'S WORTH.

GOOD LUCK WITH YOUR TILL.

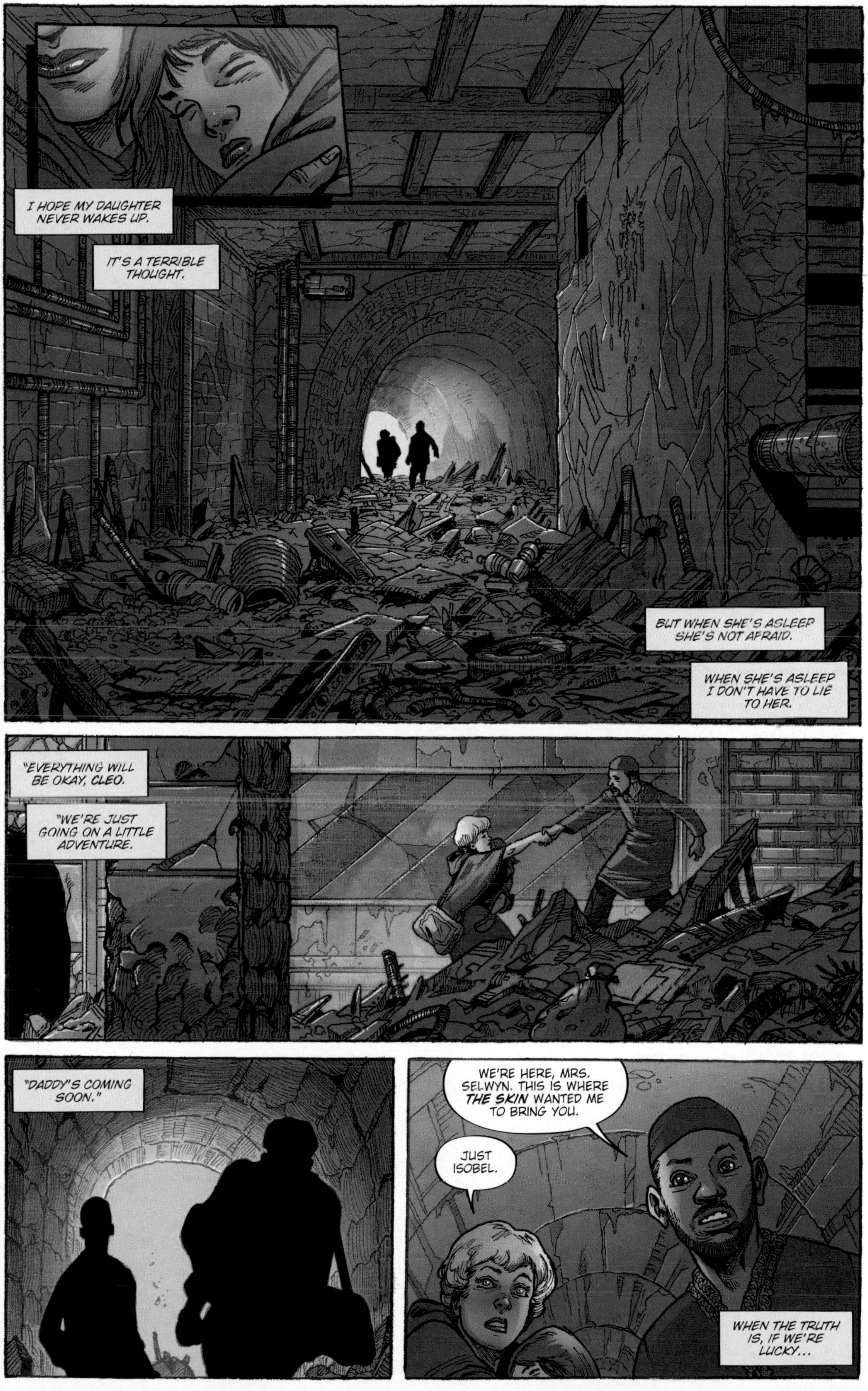
I HOPE MY DAUGHTER NEVER WAKES UP.
IT'S A TERRIBLE THOUGHT.
BUT WHEN SHE'S ASLEEP SHE'S NOT AFRAID.
WHEN SHE'S ASLEEP I DON'T HAVE TO LIE TO HER.
"EVERYTHING WILL BE OKAY, CLEO.
"WE'RE JUST GOING ON A LITTLE ADVENTURE.
"DADDY'S COMING SOON."
WE'RE HERE, MRS. SELWYN. THIS IS WHERE THE SKIN WANTED ME TO BRING YOU.
JUST ISOBEL.
WHEN THE TRUTH IS, IF WE'RE LUCKY...

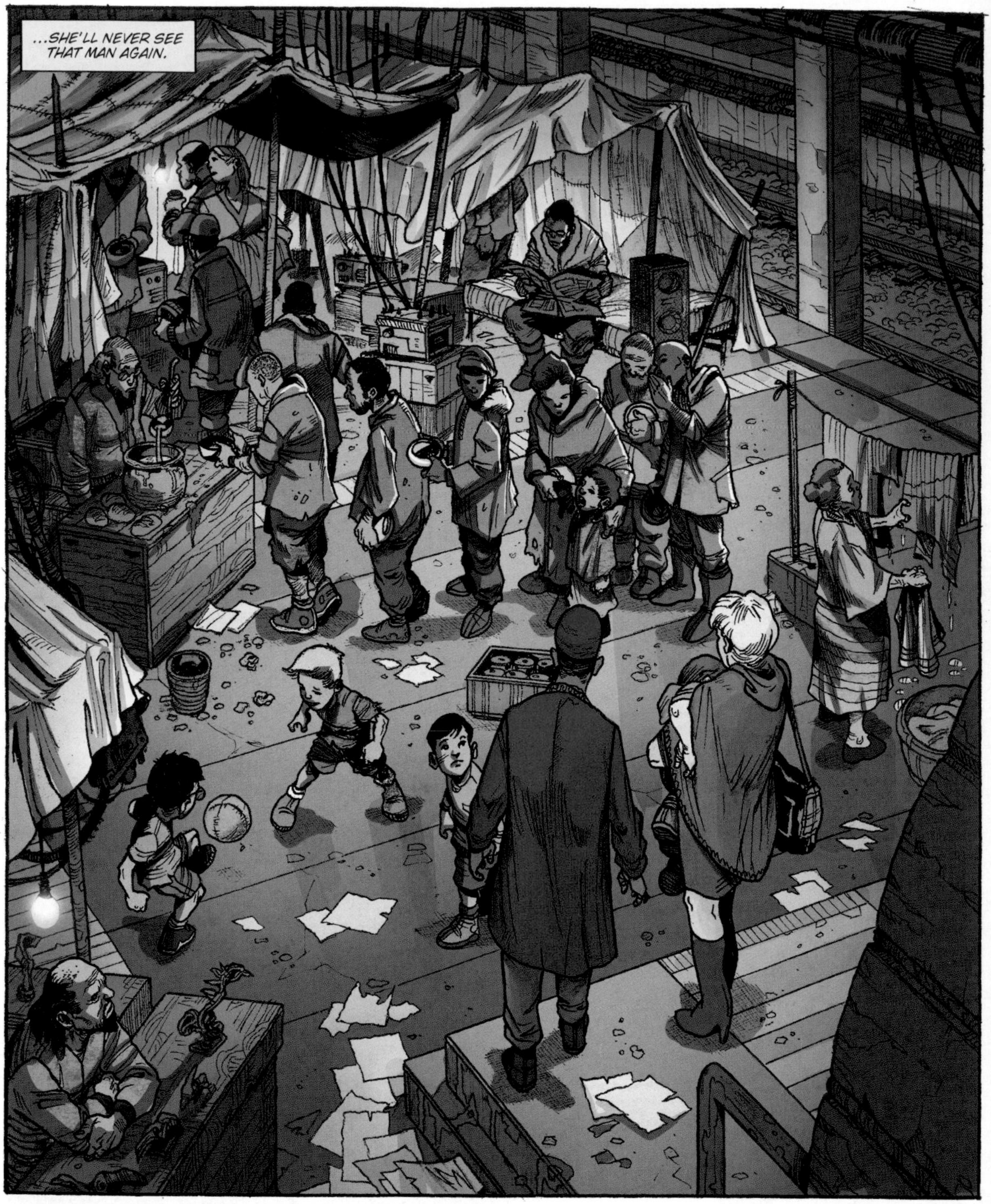
...SHE'LL NEVER SEE THAT MAN AGAIN.

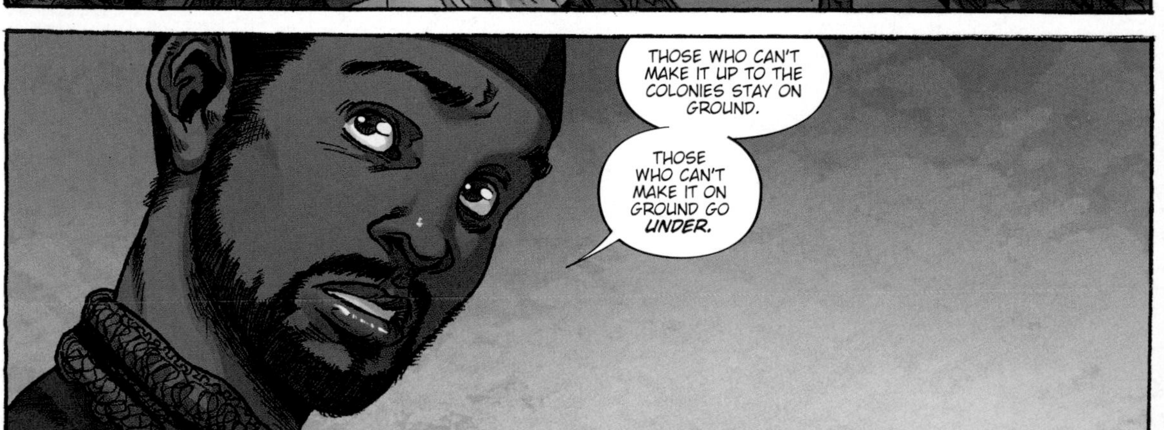
THOSE WHO CAN'T MAKE IT UP TO THE COLONIES STAY ON GROUND.
THOSE WHO CAN'T MAKE IT ON GROUND GO **UNDER.**

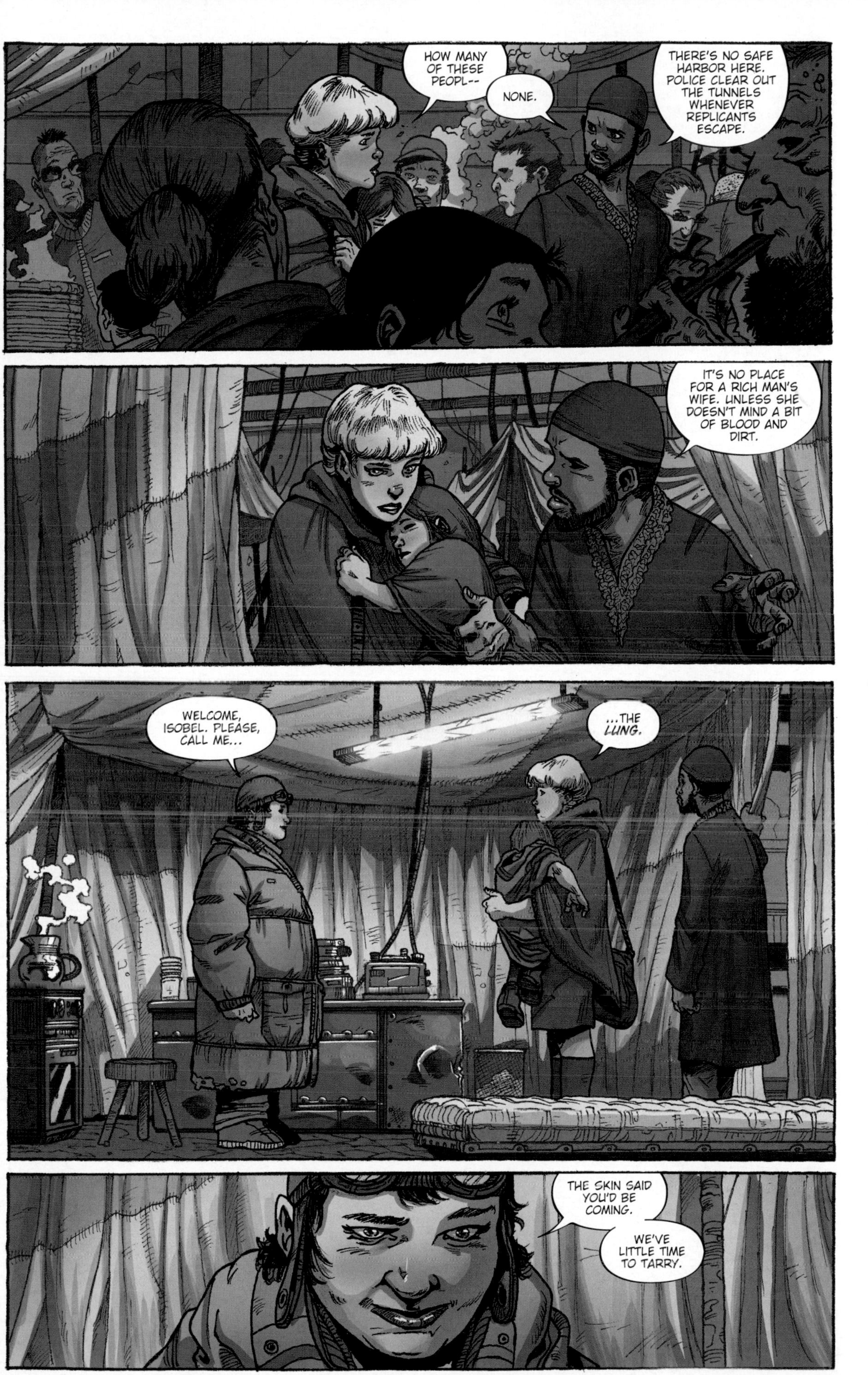
HOW MANY OF THESE PEOPL--
NONE.
THERE'S NO SAFE HARBOR HERE. POLICE CLEAR OUT THE TUNNELS WHENEVER REPLICANTS ESCAPE.
IT'S NO PLACE FOR A RICH MAN'S WIFE. UNLESS SHE DOESN'T MIND A BIT OF BLOOD AND DIRT.
WELCOME, ISOBEL. PLEASE, CALL ME...
...THE *LUNG.*
THE SKIN SAID YOU'D BE COMING.
WE'VE LITTLE TIME TO TARRY.

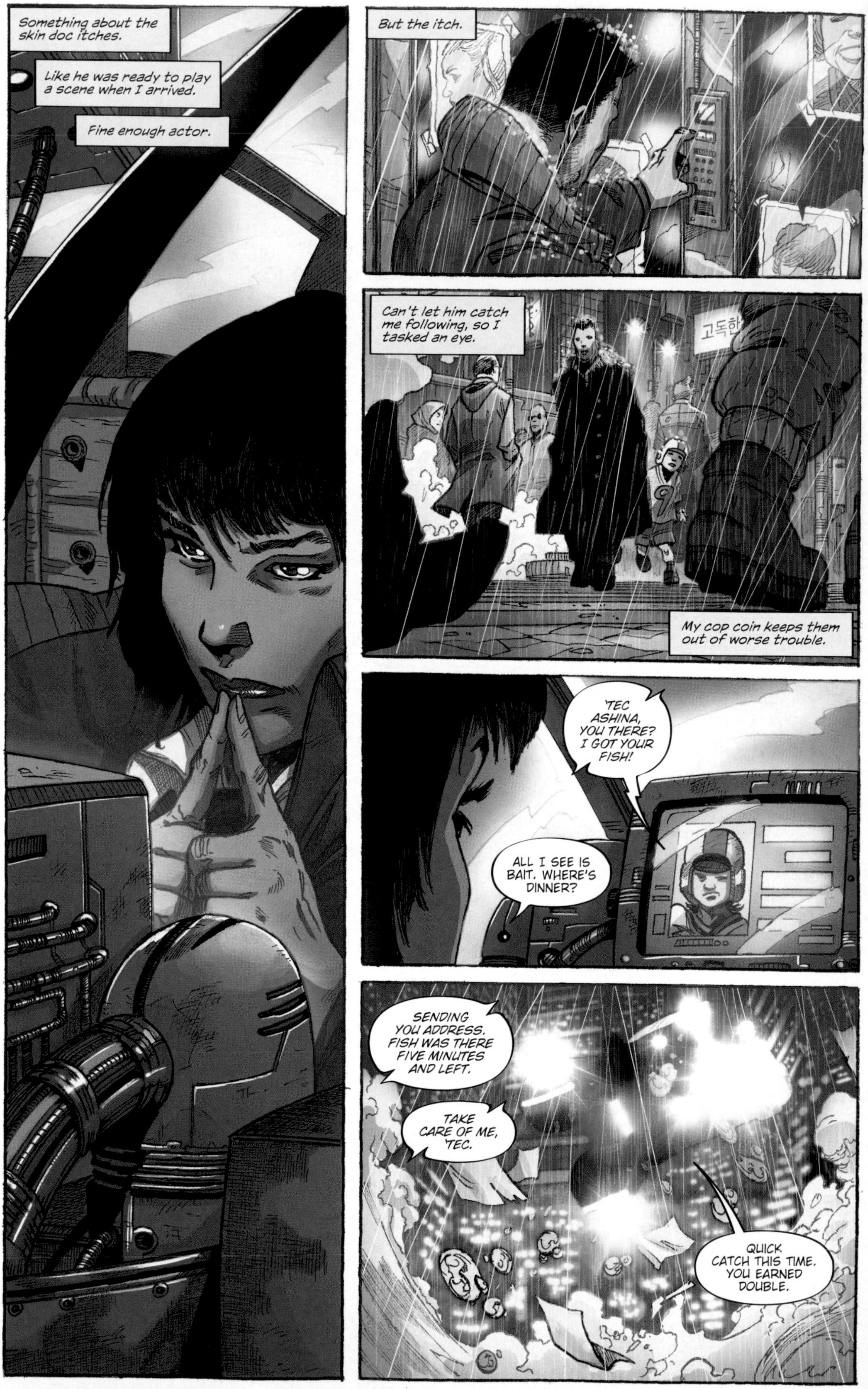
Something about the skin doc itches.
Like he was ready to play a scene when I arrived.
Fine enough actor.
But the itch.
Can't let him catch me following, so I tasked an eye.
고독한
My cop coin keeps them out of worse trouble.
'TEC ASHINA, YOU THERE? I GOT YOUR FISH!
ALL I SEE IS BAIT. WHERE'S DINNER?
SENDING YOU ADDRESS. FISH WAS THERE FIVE MINUTES AND LEFT.
TAKE CARE OF ME, 'TEC.
QUICK CATCH THIS TIME. YOU EARNED DOUBLE.

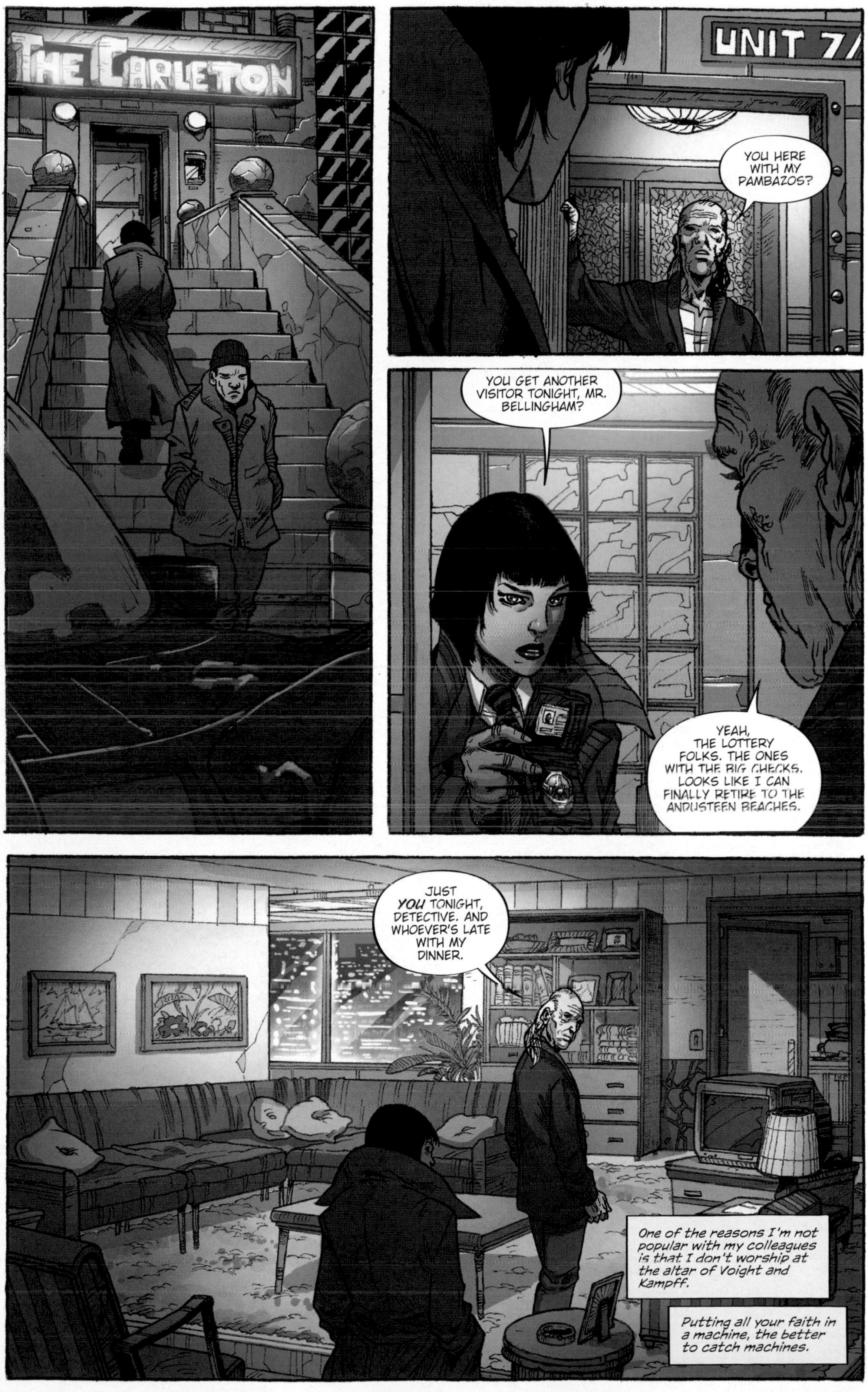
THE CARLETON
UNIT 7
YOU HERE WITH MY PAMBAZOS?
YOU GET ANOTHER VISITOR TONIGHT, MR. BELLINGHAM?
YEAH, THE LOTTERY FOLKS. THE ONES WITH THE BIG CHECKS. LOOKS LIKE I CAN FINALLY RETIRE TO THE ANDUSTEEN BEACHES.
JUST *YOU* TONIGHT, DETECTIVE. AND WHOEVER'S LATE WITH MY DINNER.
One of the reasons I'm not popular with my colleagues is that I don't worship at the altar of Voight and Kampff.
Putting all your faith in a machine, the better to catch machines.

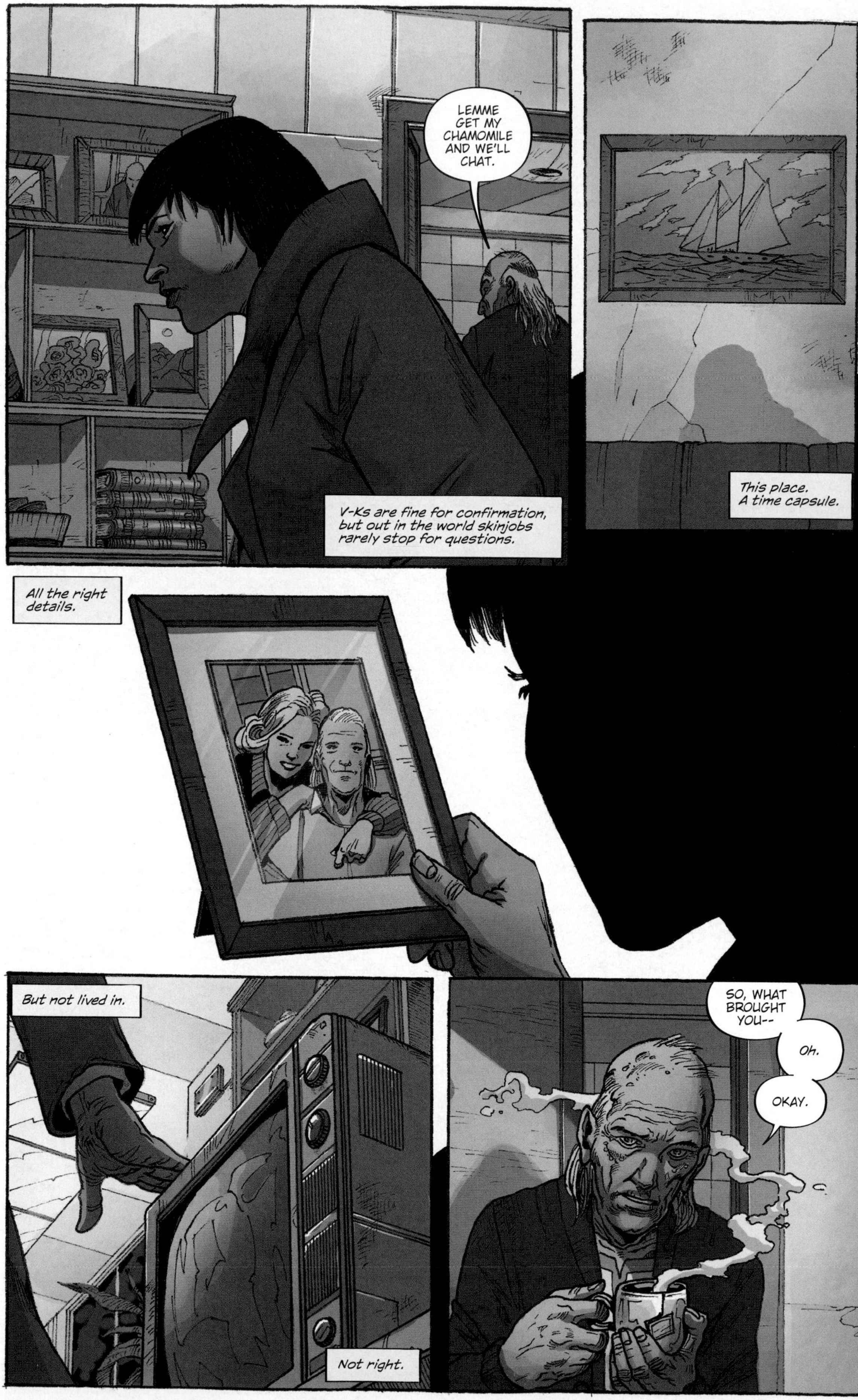
LEMME GET MY CHAMOMILE AND WE'LL CHAT.
V-Ks are fine for confirmation, but out in the world skinjobs rarely stop for questions.
This place. A time capsule.
All the right details.
But not lived in.
Not right.
SO, WHAT BROUGHT YOU--
Oh.
OKAY.

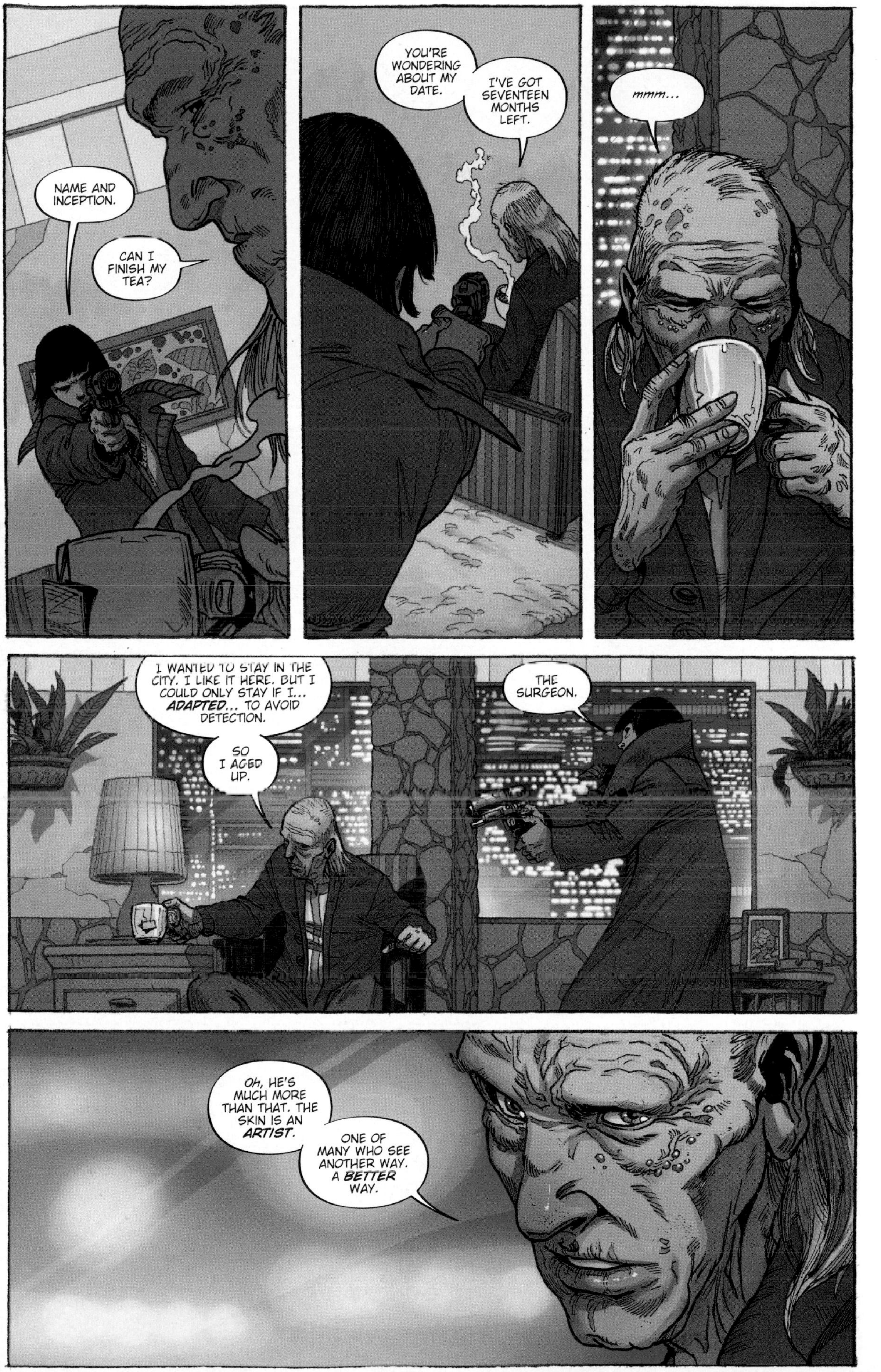
NAME AND INCEPTION.
CAN I FINISH MY TEA?
YOU'RE WONDERING ABOUT MY DATE.
I'VE GOT SEVENTEEN MONTHS LEFT.
mmm...
I WANTED TO STAY IN THE CITY. I LIKE IT HERE. BUT I COULD ONLY STAY IF I... ADAPTED... TO AVOID DETECTION.
SO I AGED UP.
THE SURGEON.
OH, HE'S MUCH MORE THAN THAT. THE SKIN IS AN ARTIST.
ONE OF MANY WHO SEE ANOTHER WAY. A BETTER WAY.

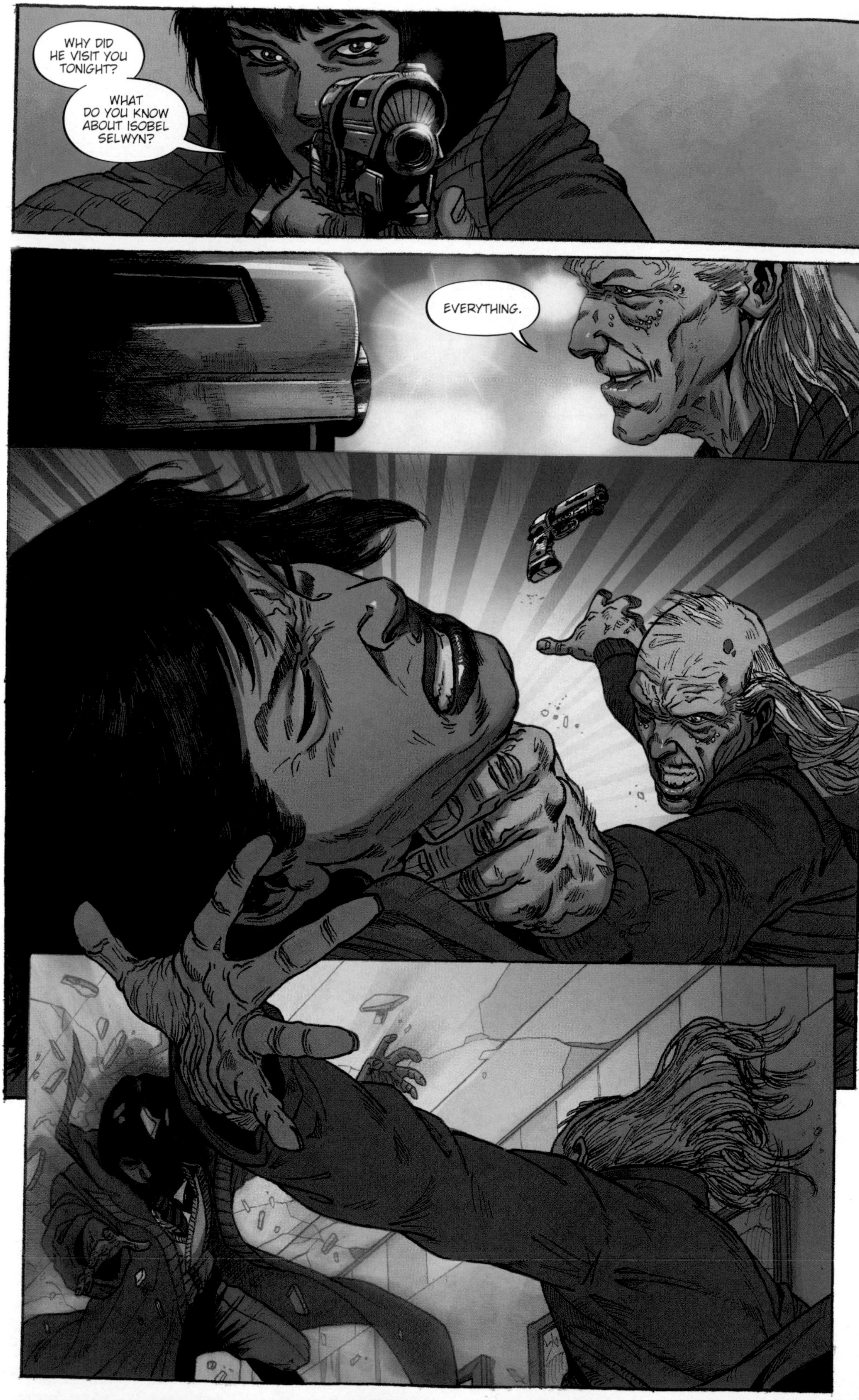
WHY DID HE VISIT YOU TONIGHT?
WHAT DO YOU KNOW ABOUT ISOBEL SELWYN?
EVERYTHING.

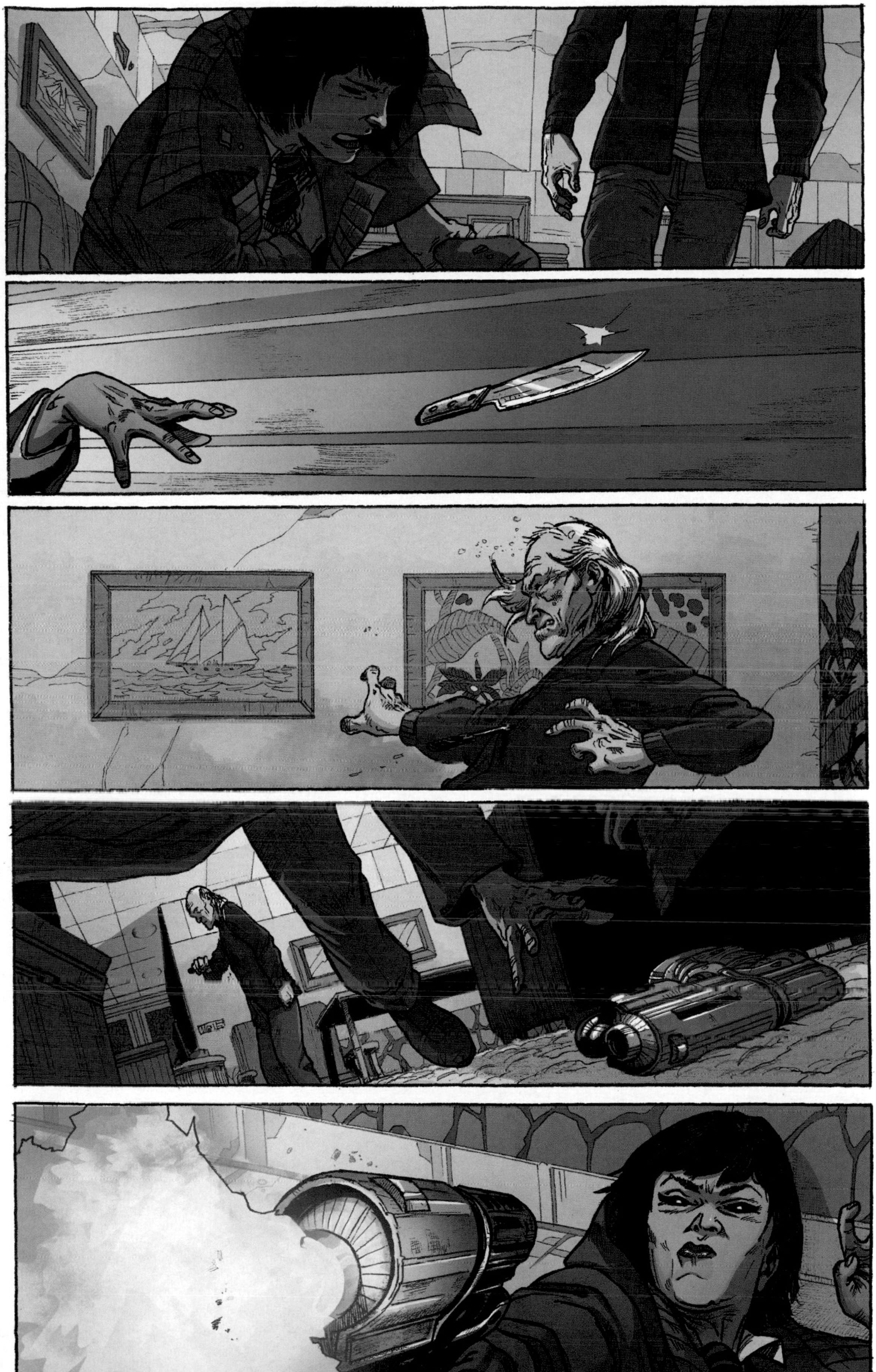

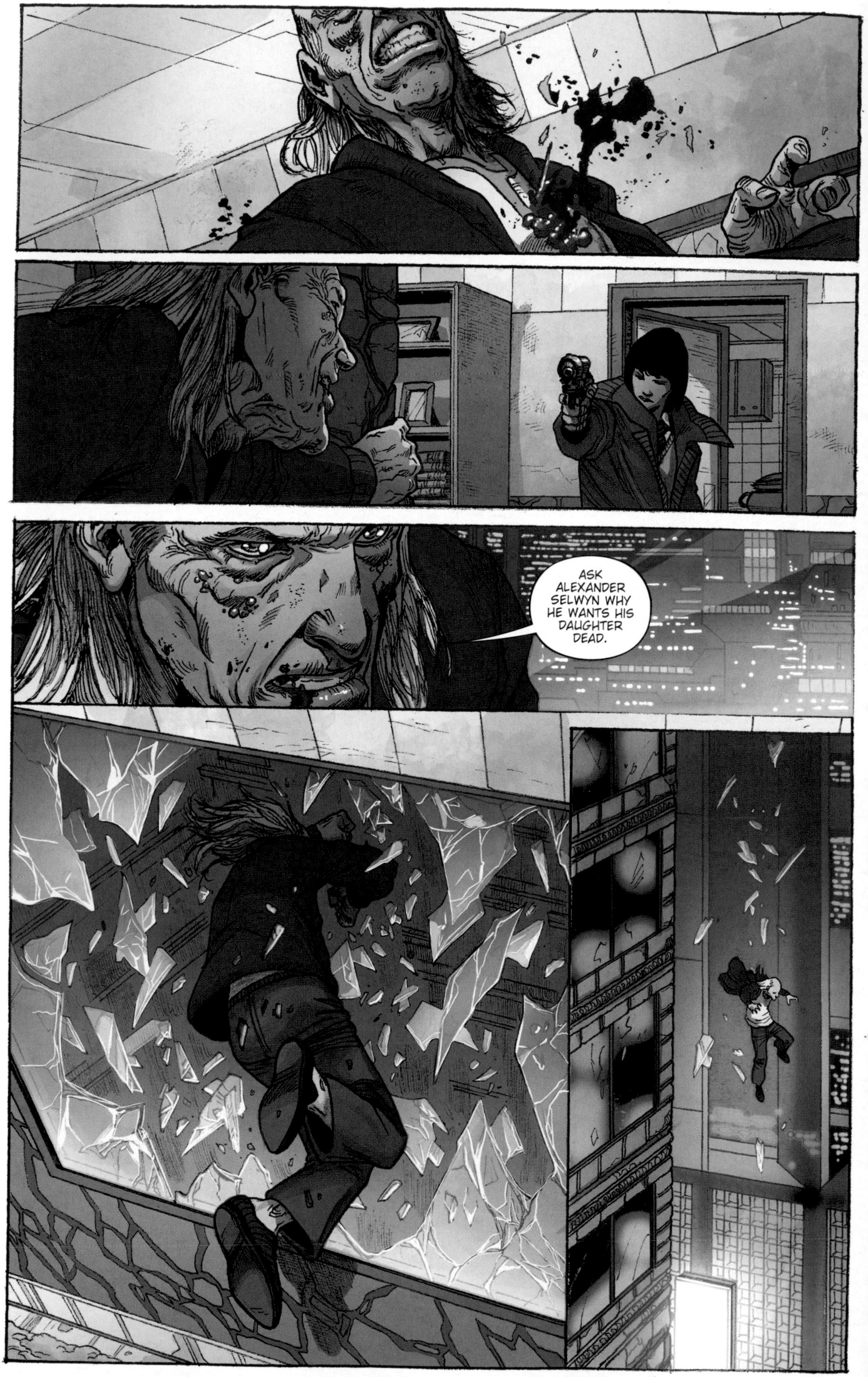
ASK ALEXANDER SELWYN WHY HE WANTS HIS DAUGHTER DEAD.

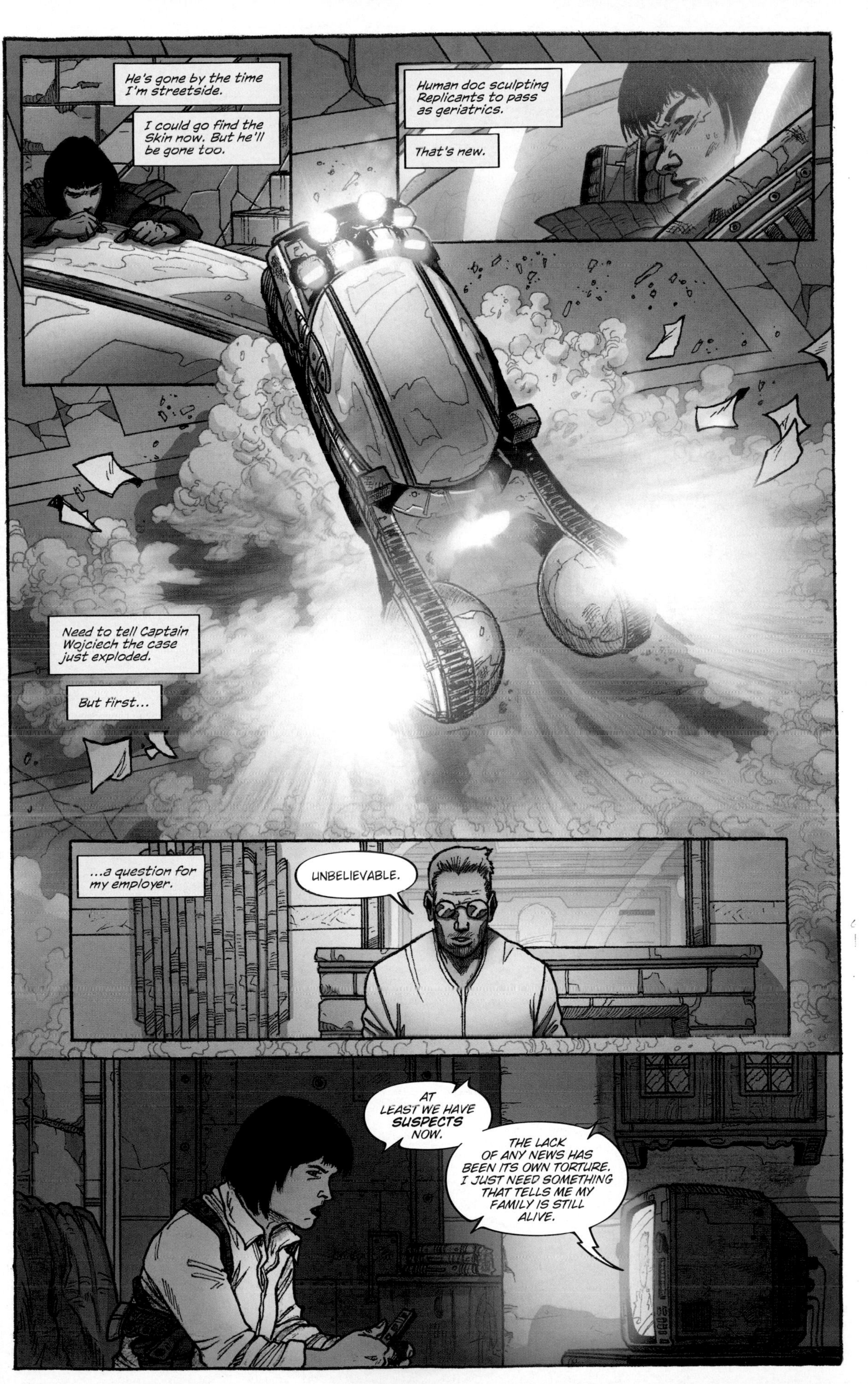
He's gone by the time I'm streetside.
I could go find the Skin now. But he'll be gone too.
Human doc sculpting Replicants to pass as geriatrics.
That's new.
Need to tell Captain Wojciech the case just exploded.
But first...
...a question for my employer.
UNBELIEVABLE.
AT LEAST WE HAVE **SUSPECTS** NOW.
THE LACK OF ANY NEWS HAS BEEN ITS OWN TORTURE. I JUST NEED SOMETHING THAT TELLS ME MY FAMILY IS STILL ALIVE.

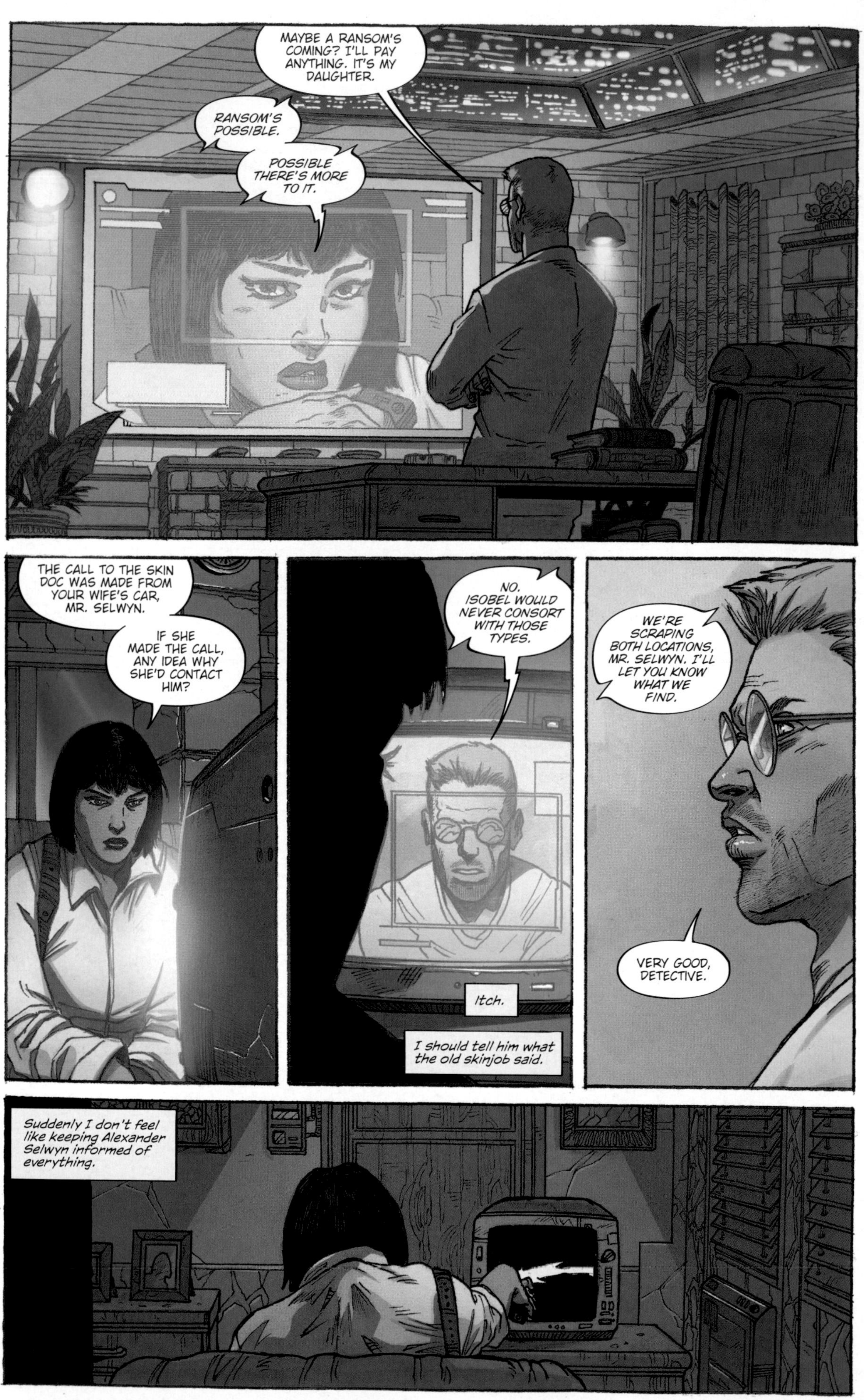

MAYBE A RANSOM'S COMING? I'LL PAY ANYTHING. IT'S MY DAUGHTER.
RANSOM'S POSSIBLE.
POSSIBLE THERE'S MORE TO IT.
THE CALL TO THE SKIN DOC WAS MADE FROM YOUR WIFE'S CAR, MR. SELWYN.
IF SHE MADE THE CALL, ANY IDEA WHY SHE'D CONTACT HIM?
NO. ISOBEL WOULD NEVER CONSORT WITH THOSE TYPES.
Itch.
I should tell him what the old skinjob said.
WE'RE SCRAPING BOTH LOCATIONS, MR. SELWYN. I'LL LET YOU KNOW WHAT WE FIND.
VERY GOOD, DETECTIVE.
Suddenly I don't feel like keeping Alexander Selwyn informed of everything.

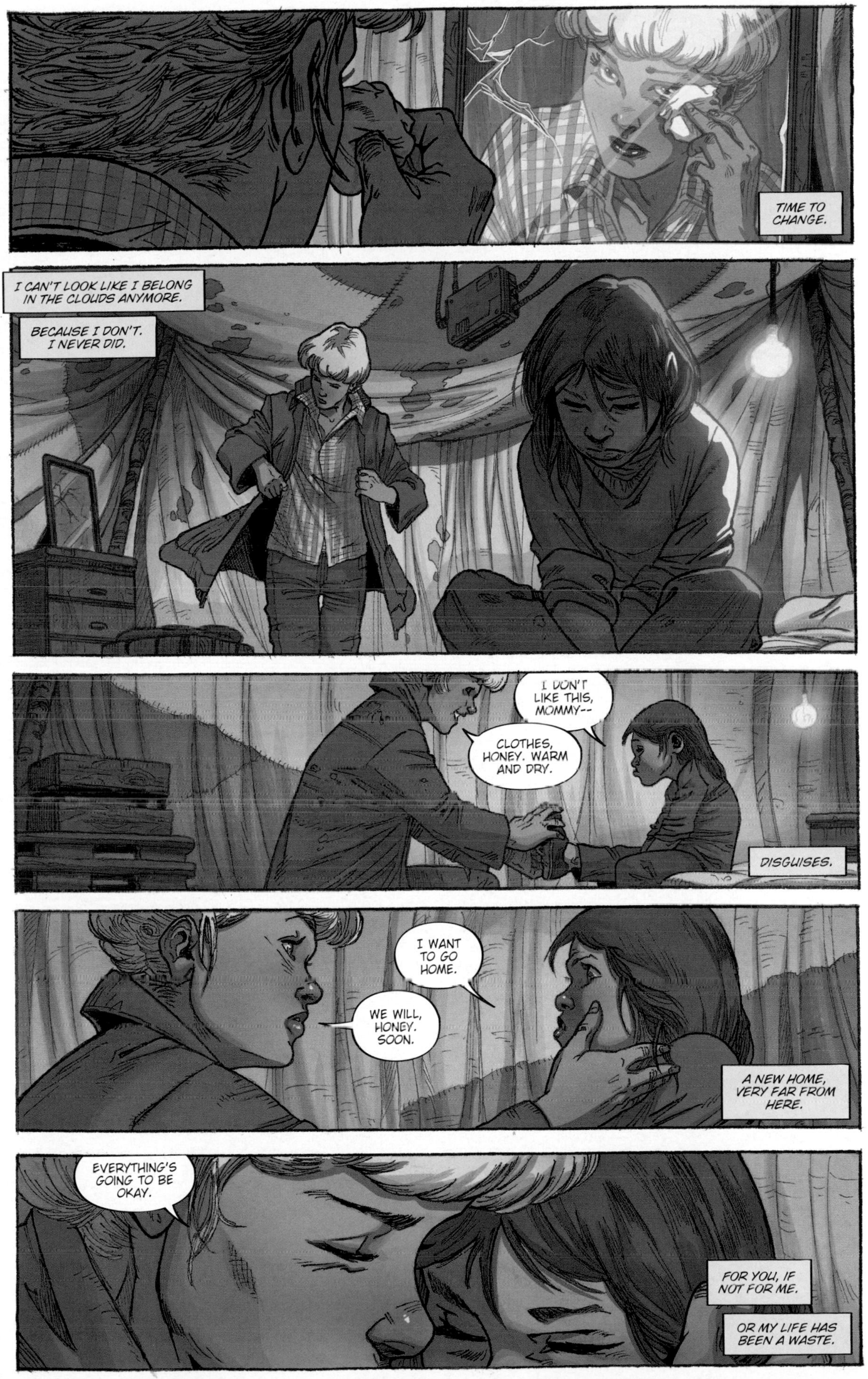
TIME TO CHANGE.
I CAN'T LOOK LIKE I BELONG IN THE CLOUDS ANYMORE.
BECAUSE I DON'T. I NEVER DID.
I DON'T LIKE THIS, MOMMY--
CLOTHES, HONEY. WARM AND DRY.
DISGUISES.
I WANT TO GO HOME.
WE WILL, HONEY. SOON.
A NEW HOME, VERY FAR FROM HERE.
EVERYTHING'S GOING TO BE OKAY.
FOR YOU, IF NOT FOR ME.
OR MY LIFE HAS BEEN A WASTE.

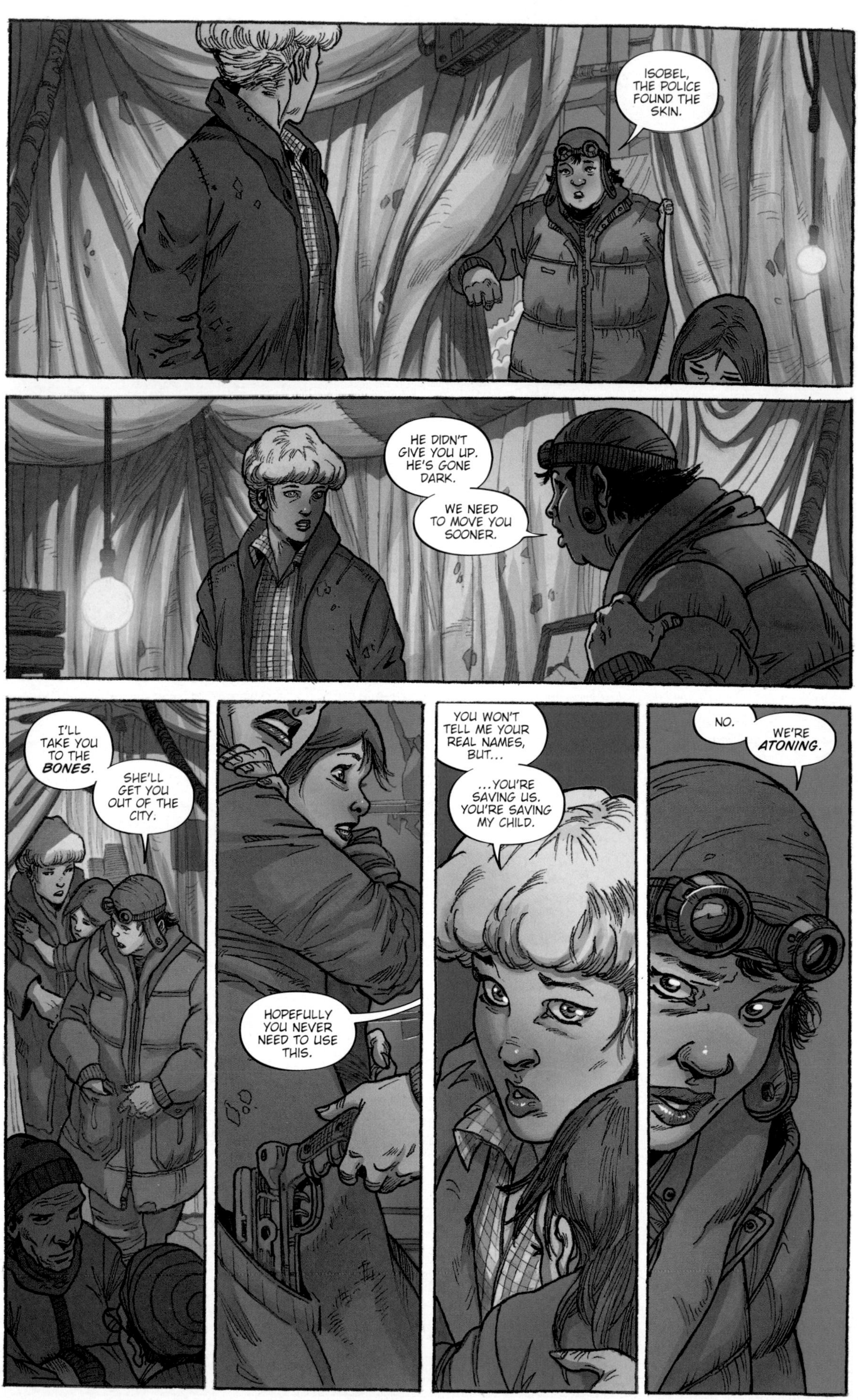
ISOBEL, THE POLICE FOUND THE SKIN.
HE DIDN'T GIVE YOU UP. HE'S GONE DARK.
WE NEED TO MOVE YOU SOONER.
I'LL TAKE YOU TO THE *BONES*.
SHE'LL GET YOU OUT OF THE CITY.
HOPEFULLY YOU NEVER NEED TO USE THIS.
YOU WON'T TELL ME YOUR REAL NAMES, BUT...
...YOU'RE SAVING US. YOU'RE SAVING MY CHILD.
NO.
WE'RE *ATONING*.

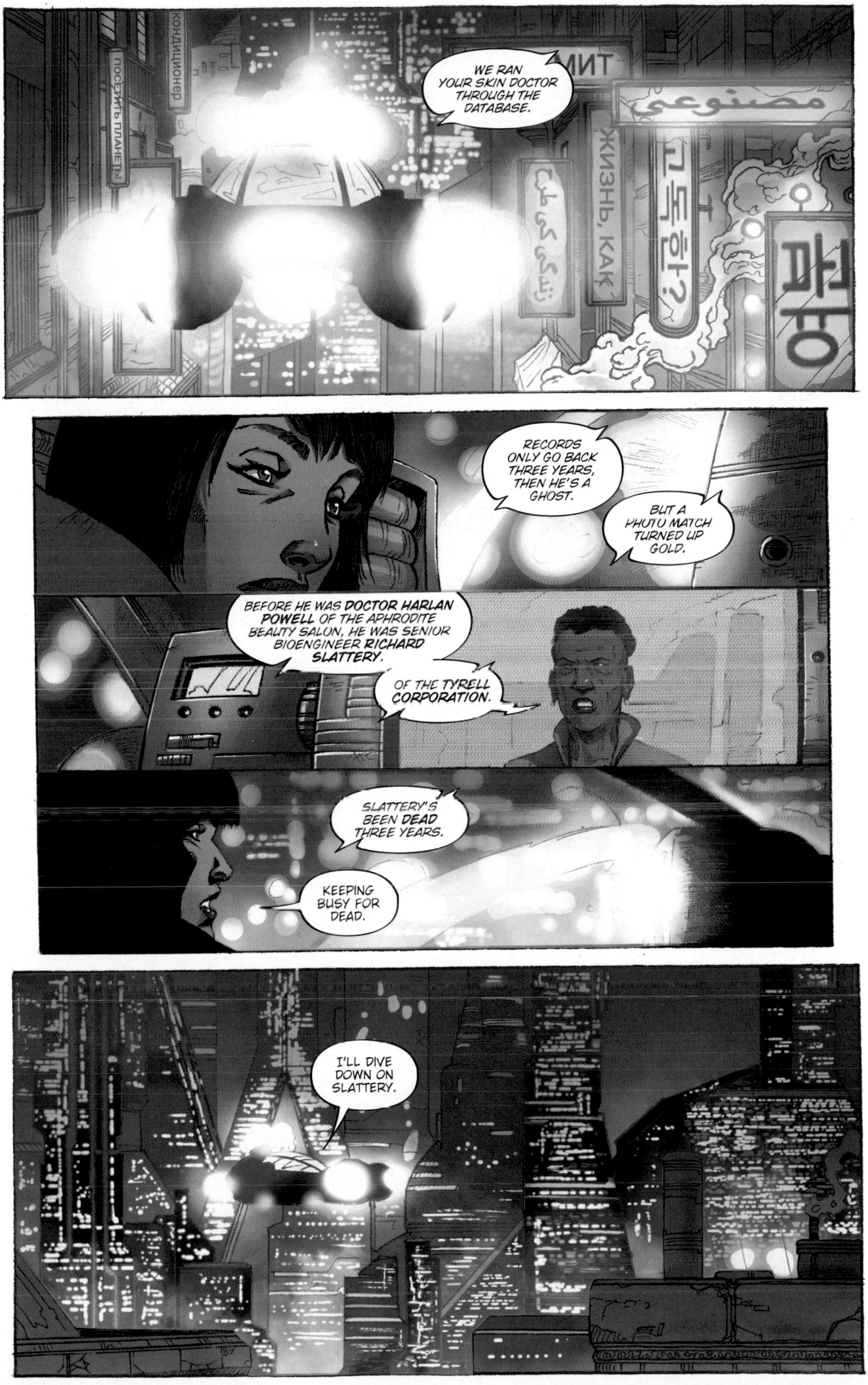
WE RAN YOUR SKIN DOCTOR THROUGH THE DATABASE.
RECORDS ONLY GO BACK THREE YEARS, THEN HE'S A GHOST.
BUT A PHOTO MATCH TURNED UP GOLD.
BEFORE HE WAS DOCTOR HARLAN POWELL OF THE APHRODITE BEAUTY SALON, HE WAS SENIOR BIOENGINEER RICHARD SLATTERY.
OF THE TYRELL CORPORATION.
SLATTERY'S BEEN DEAD THREE YEARS.
KEEPING BUSY FOR DEAD.
I'LL DIVE DOWN ON SLATTERY.

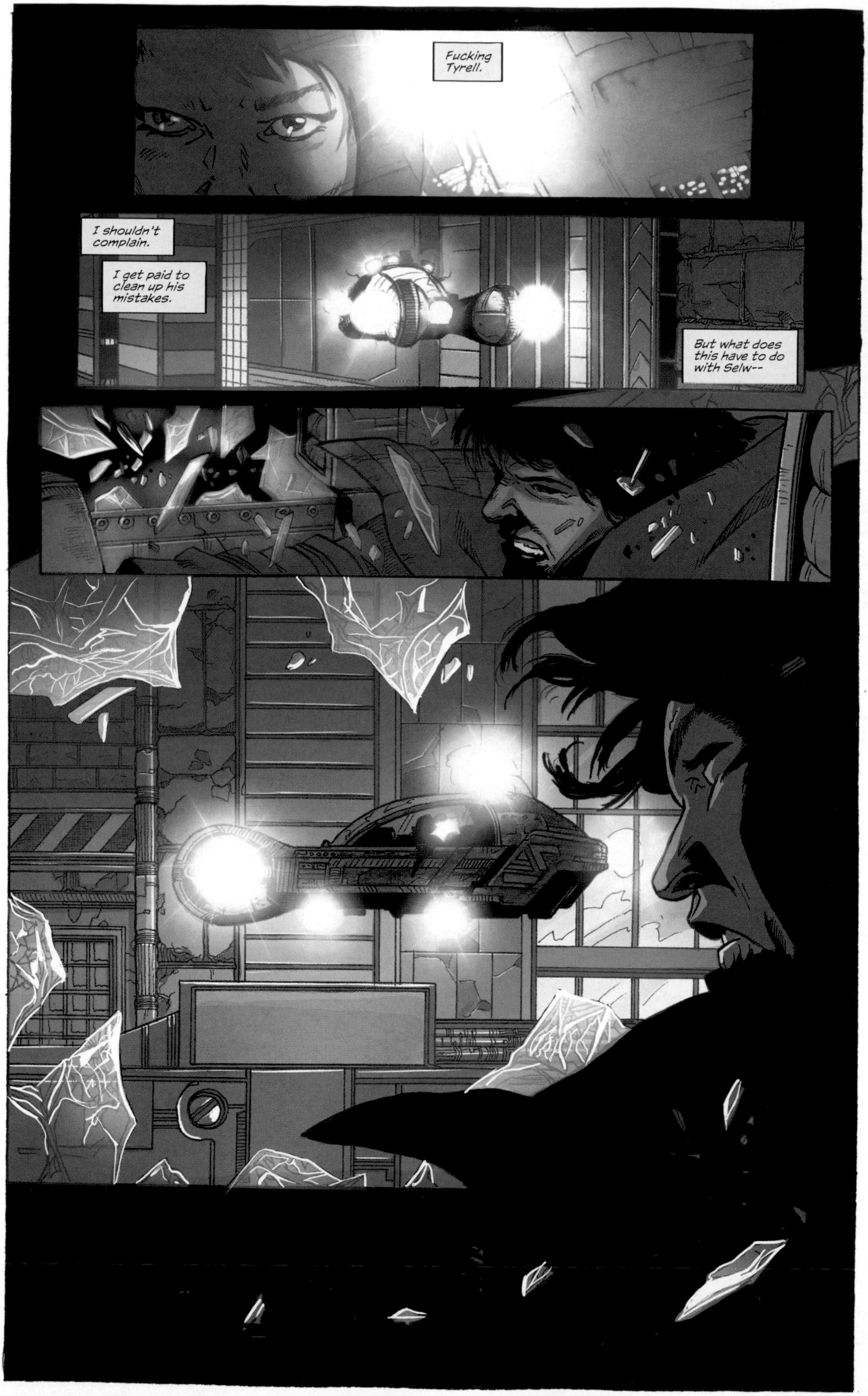

Fucking Tyrell.
I shouldn't complain.
I get paid to clean up his mistakes.
But what does this have to do with Selw--

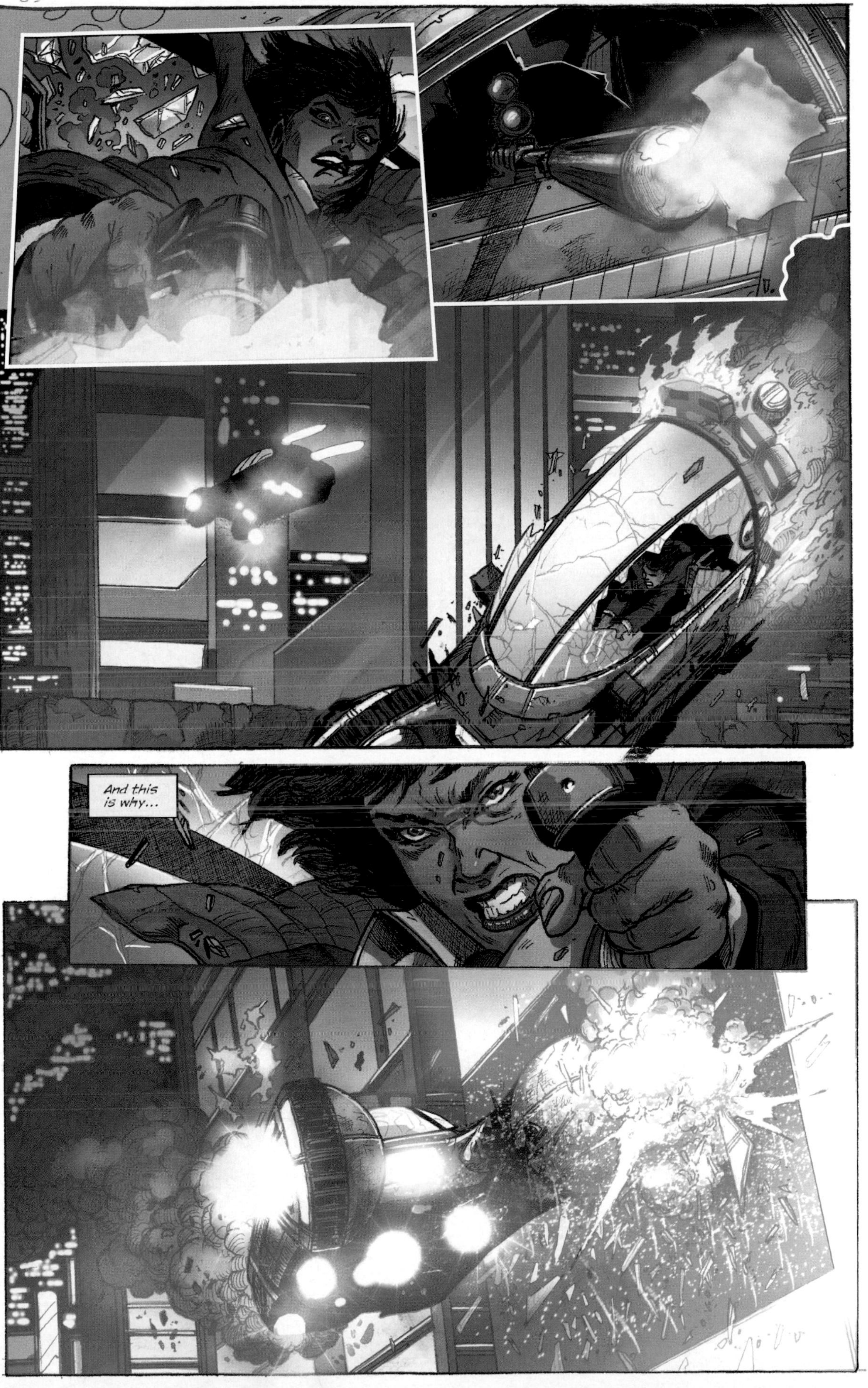
And this is why...

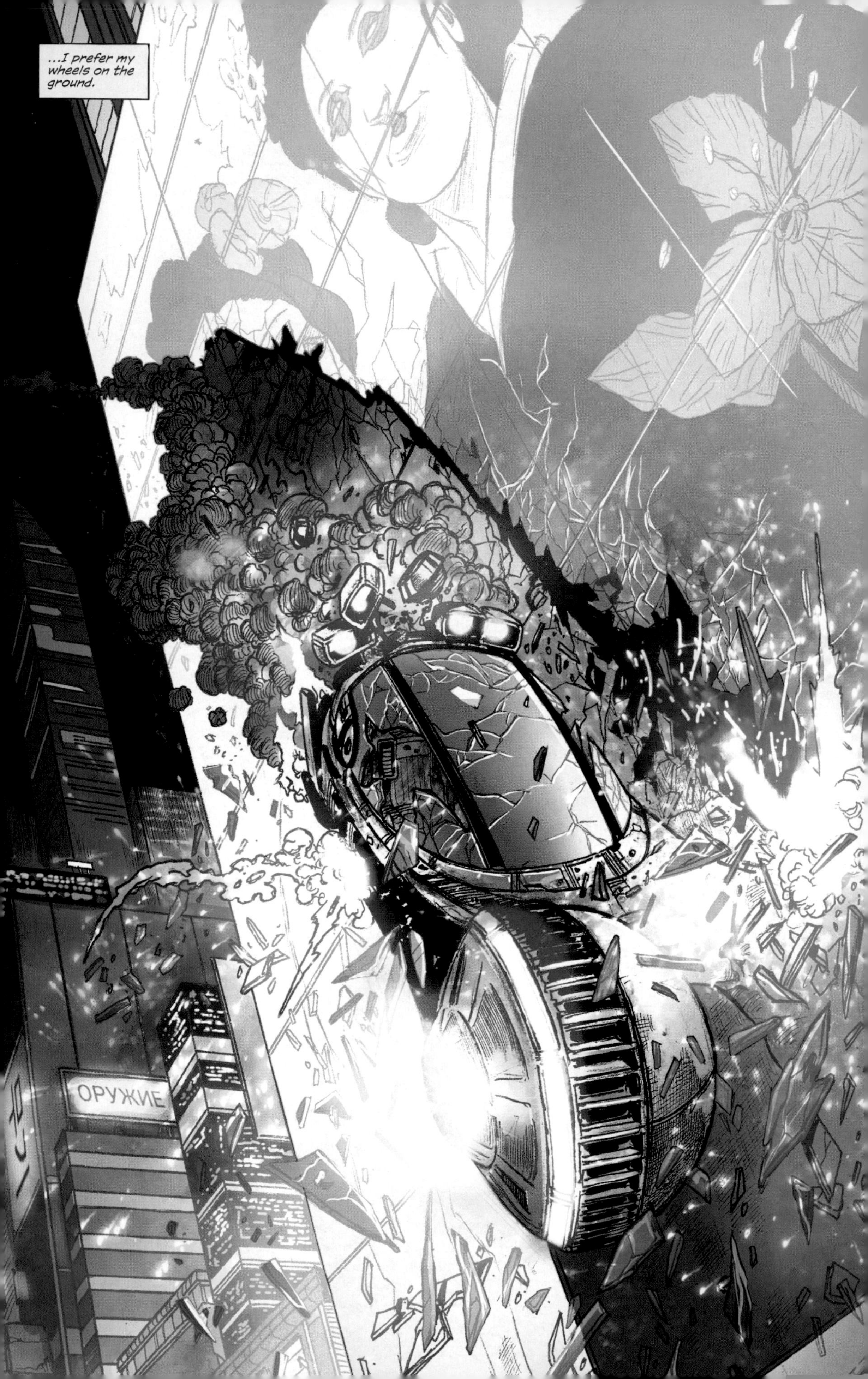
...I prefer my wheels on the ground.
ОРУЖИЕ

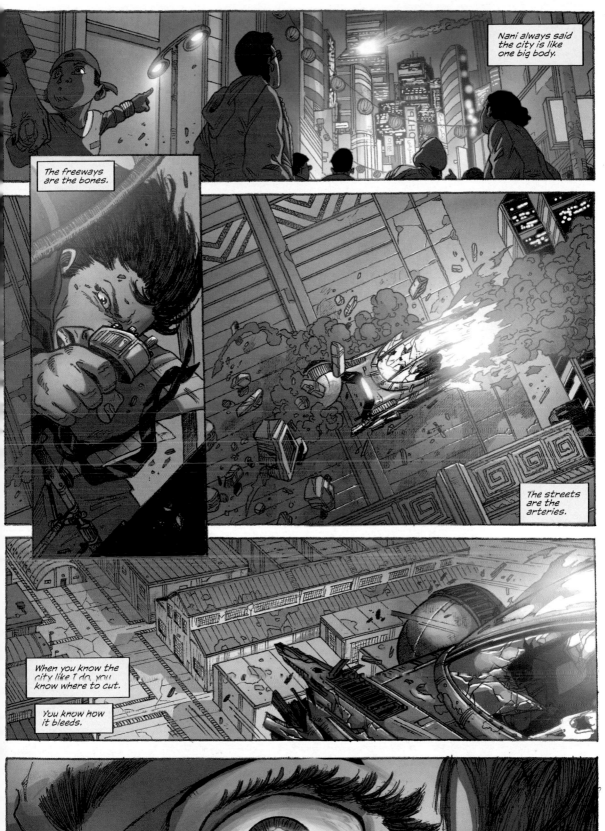

Nani always said the city is like one big body.

The freeways are the bones.

The streets are the arteries.

When you know the city like I do, you know where to cut.

You know how it bleeds.

You'd be proud of me now, Nani.

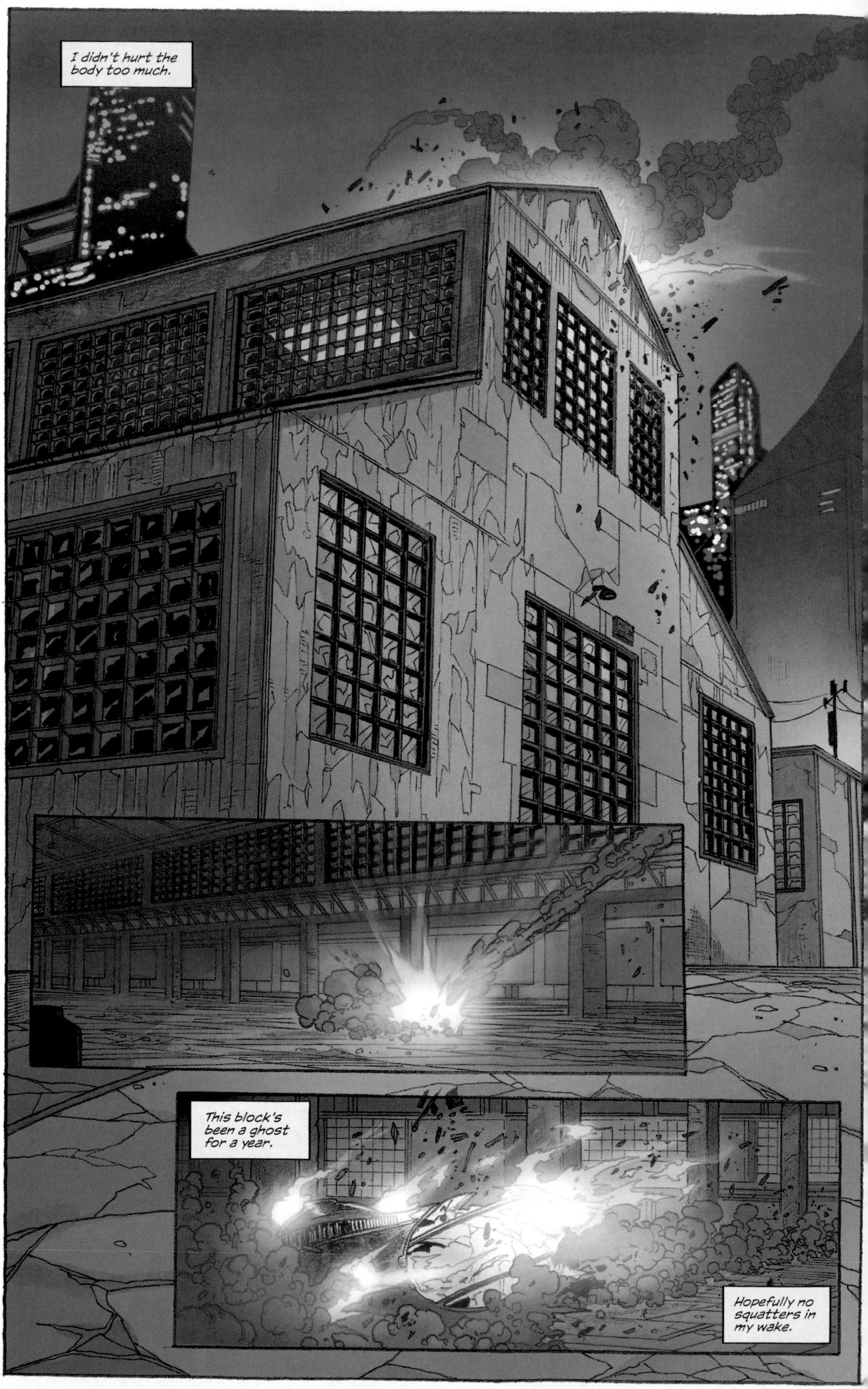
I didn't hurt the body too much.
This block's been a ghost for a year.
Hopefully no squatters in my wake.

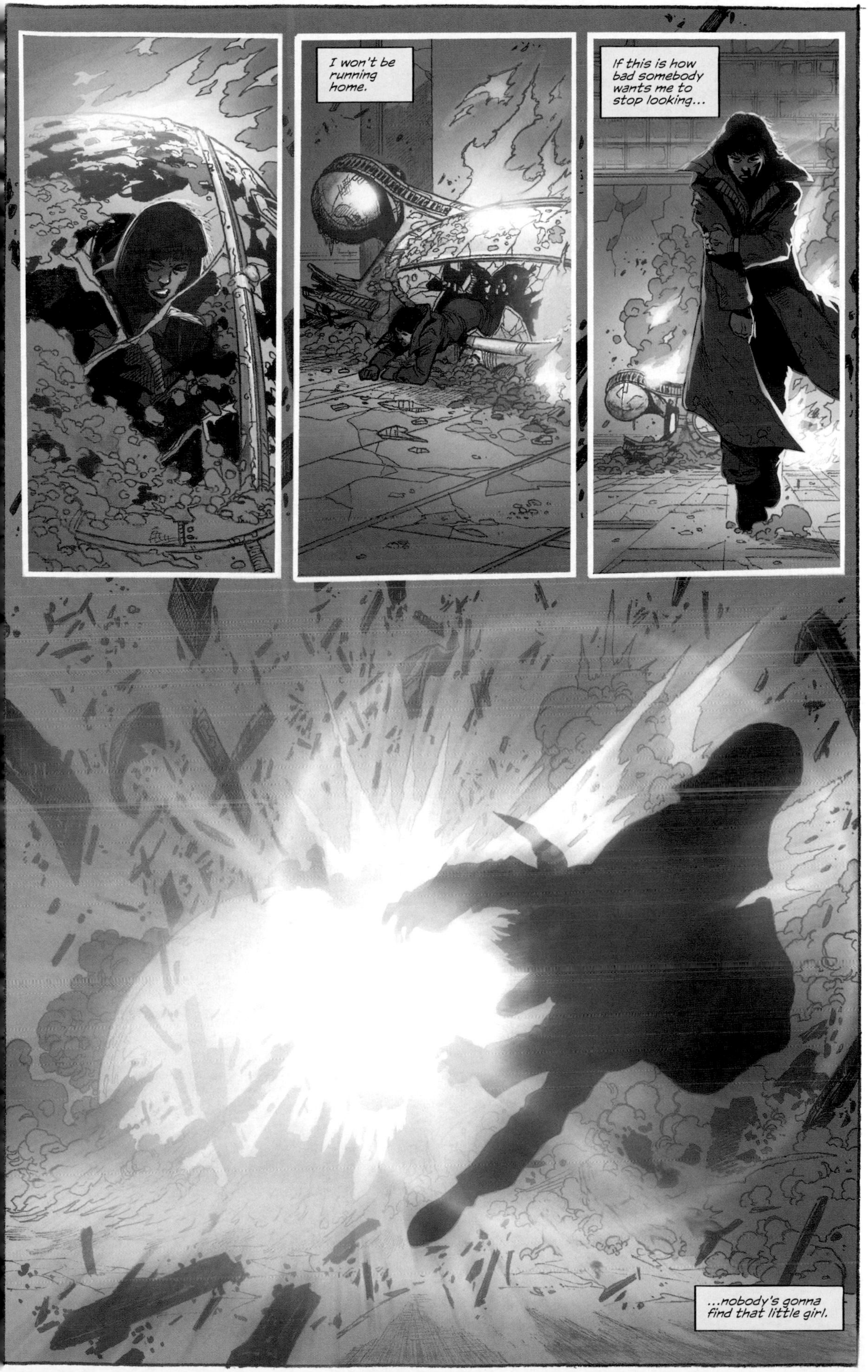
I won't be running home.
If this is how bad somebody wants me to stop looking...
...nobody's gonna find that little girl.

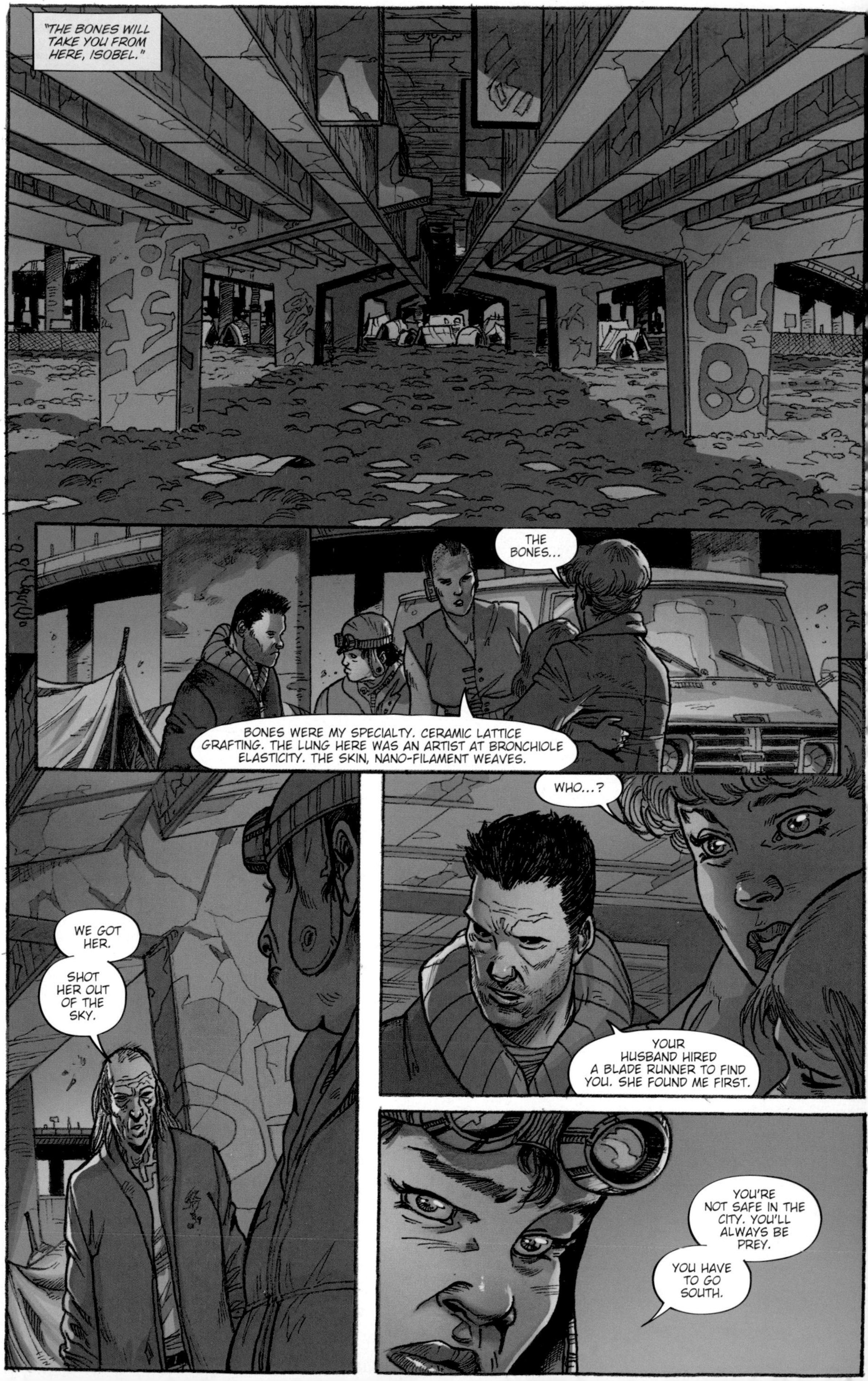

"THE BONES WILL TAKE YOU FROM HERE, ISOBEL."
THE BONES...
BONES WERE MY SPECIALTY. CERAMIC LATTICE GRAFTING. THE LUNG HERE WAS AN ARTIST AT BRONCHIOLE ELASTICITY. THE SKIN, NANO-FILAMENT WEAVES.
WE GOT HER.
SHOT HER OUT OF THE SKY.
WHO...?
YOUR HUSBAND HIRED A BLADE RUNNER TO FIND YOU. SHE FOUND ME FIRST.
YOU'RE NOT SAFE IN THE CITY. YOU'LL ALWAYS BE PREY.
YOU HAVE TO GO SOUTH.

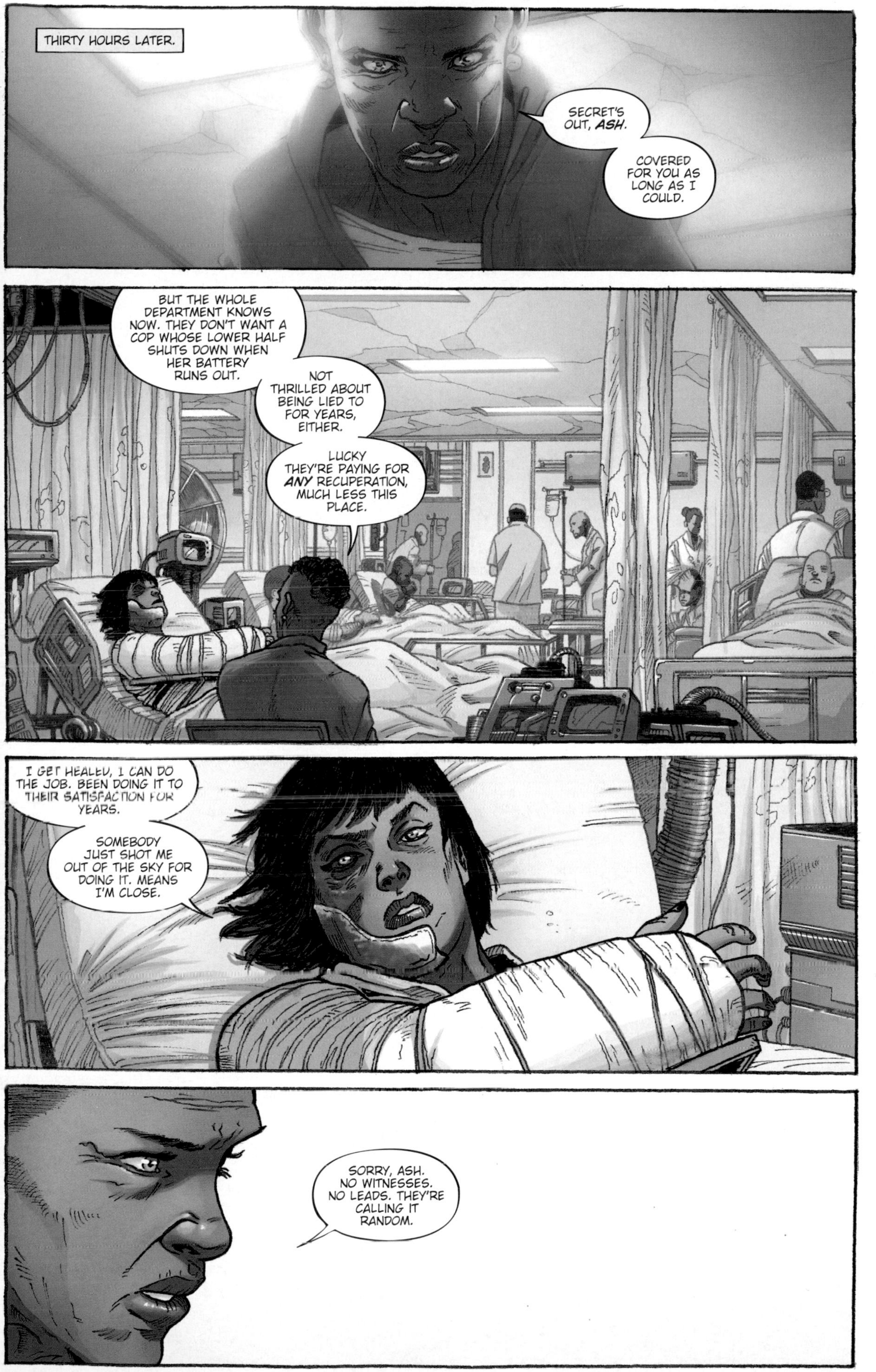
THIRTY HOURS LATER.
SECRET'S OUT, ASH.
COVERED FOR YOU AS LONG AS I COULD.
BUT THE WHOLE DEPARTMENT KNOWS NOW. THEY DON'T WANT A COP WHOSE LOWER HALF SHUTS DOWN WHEN HER BATTERY RUNS OUT.
NOT THRILLED ABOUT BEING LIED TO FOR YEARS, EITHER.
LUCKY THEY'RE PAYING FOR ANY RECUPERATION, MUCH LESS THIS PLACE.
I GET HEALED, I CAN DO THE JOB. BEEN DOING IT TO THEIR SATISFACTION FOR YEARS.
SOMEBODY JUST SHOT ME OUT OF THE SKY FOR DOING IT. MEANS I'M CLOSE.
SORRY, ASH. NO WITNESSES. NO LEADS. THEY'RE CALLING IT RANDOM.

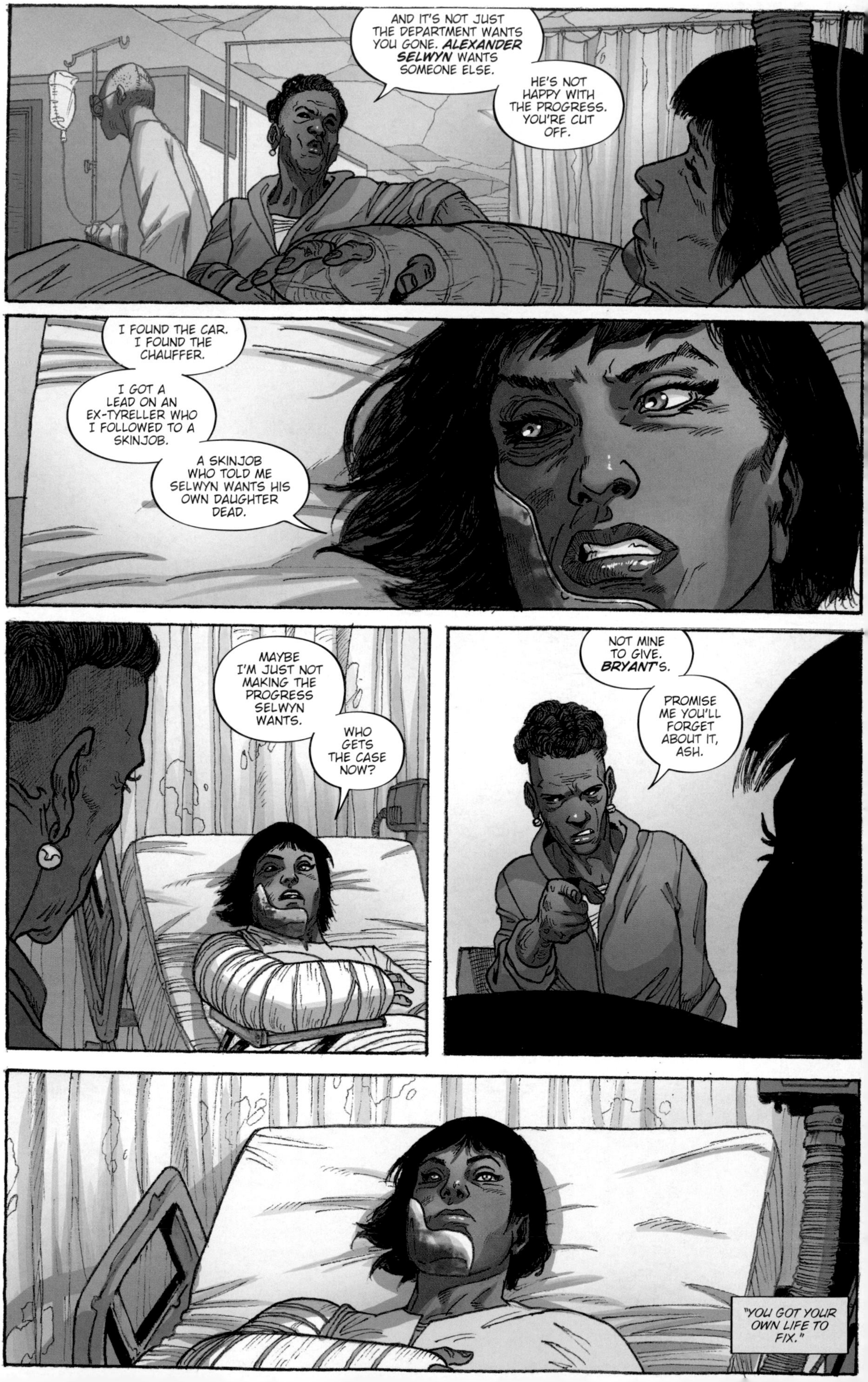
AND IT'S NOT JUST THE DEPARTMENT WANTS YOU GONE. ALEXANDER SELWYN WANTS SOMEONE ELSE.
HE'S NOT HAPPY WITH THE PROGRESS. YOU'RE CUT OFF.
I FOUND THE CAR. I FOUND THE CHAUFFER.
I GOT A LEAD ON AN EX-TYRELLER WHO I FOLLOWED TO A SKINJOB.
A SKINJOB WHO TOLD ME SELWYN WANTS HIS OWN DAUGHTER DEAD.
MAYBE I'M JUST NOT MAKING THE PROGRESS SELWYN WANTS.
WHO GETS THE CASE NOW?
NOT MINE TO GIVE. BRYANT'S.
PROMISE ME YOU'LL FORGET ABOUT IT, ASH.
"YOU GOT YOUR OWN LIFE TO FIX."

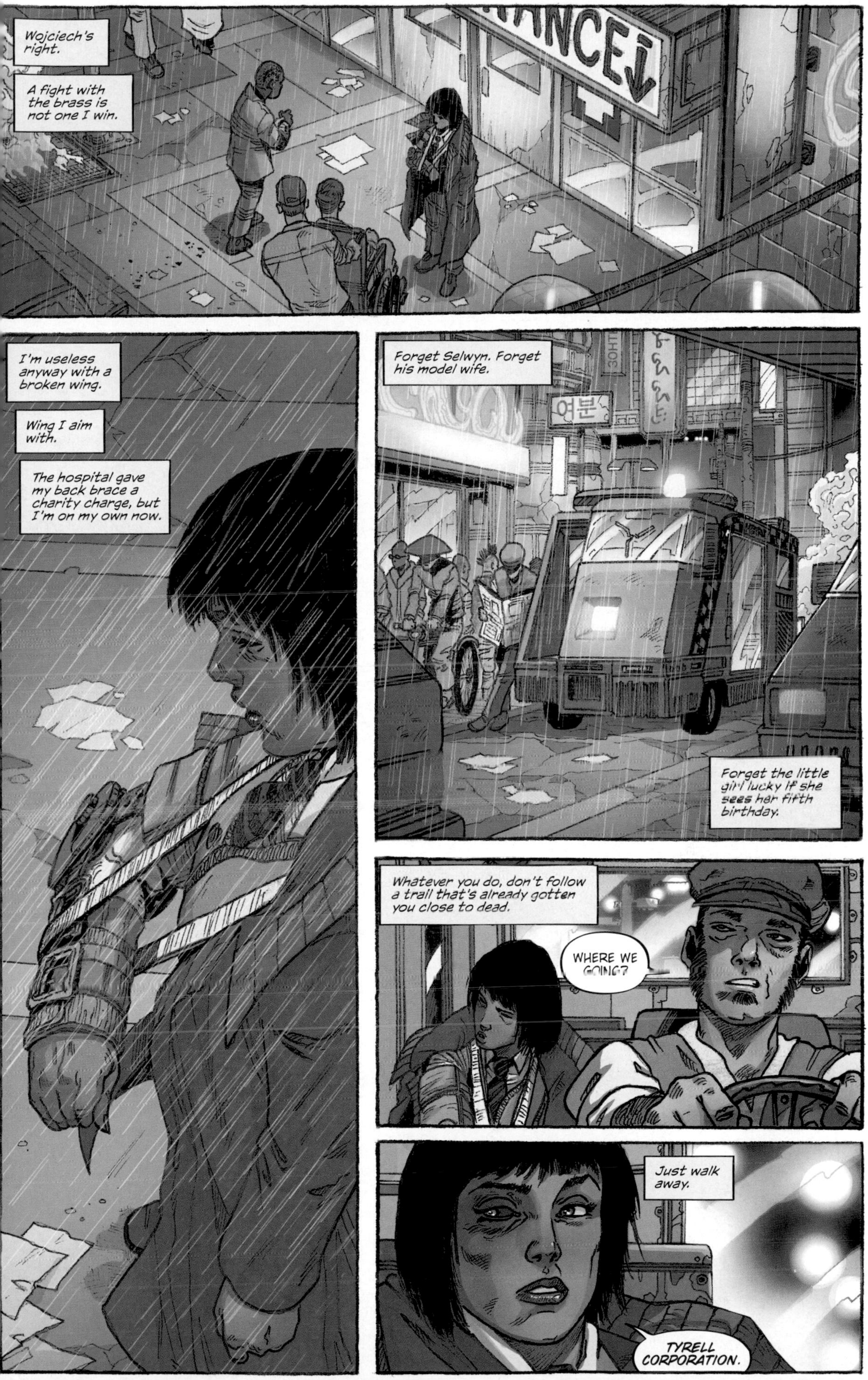
Wojciech's right.
A fight with the brass is not one I win.
I'm useless anyway with a broken wing.
Wing I aim with.
The hospital gave my back brace a charity charge, but I'm on my own now.
Forget Selwyn. Forget his model wife.
Forget the little girl lucky if she sees her fifth birthday.
Whatever you do, don't follow a trail that's already gotten you close to dead.
WHERE WE GOING?
Just walk away.
TYRELL CORPORATION.

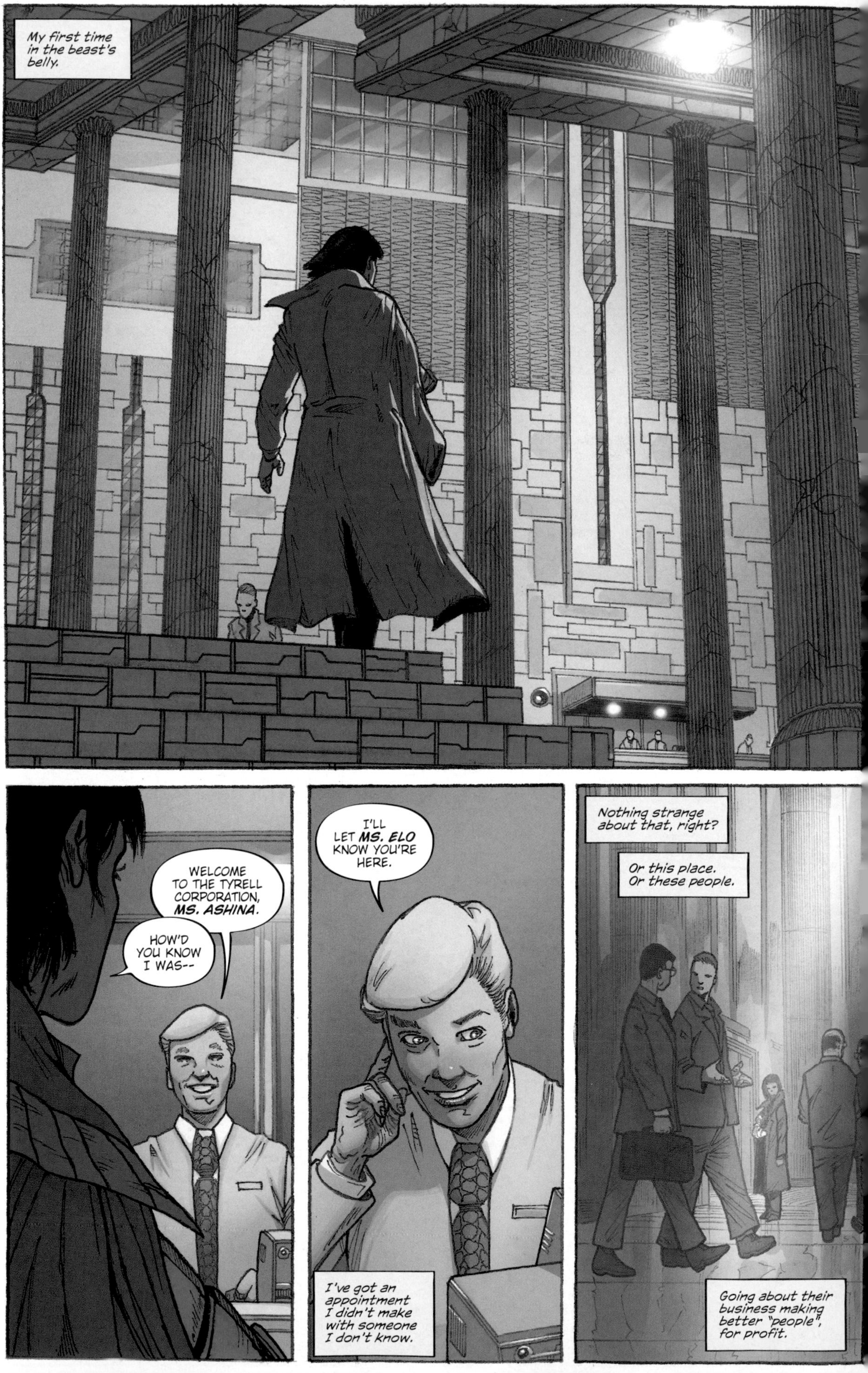
My first time in the beast's belly.
WELCOME TO THE TYRELL CORPORATION, **MS. ASHINA**.
HOW'D YOU KNOW I WAS--
I'LL LET **MS. ELO** KNOW YOU'RE HERE.
I've got an appointment I didn't make with someone I don't know.
Nothing strange about that, right?
Or this place. Or these people.
Going about their business making better "people", for profit.

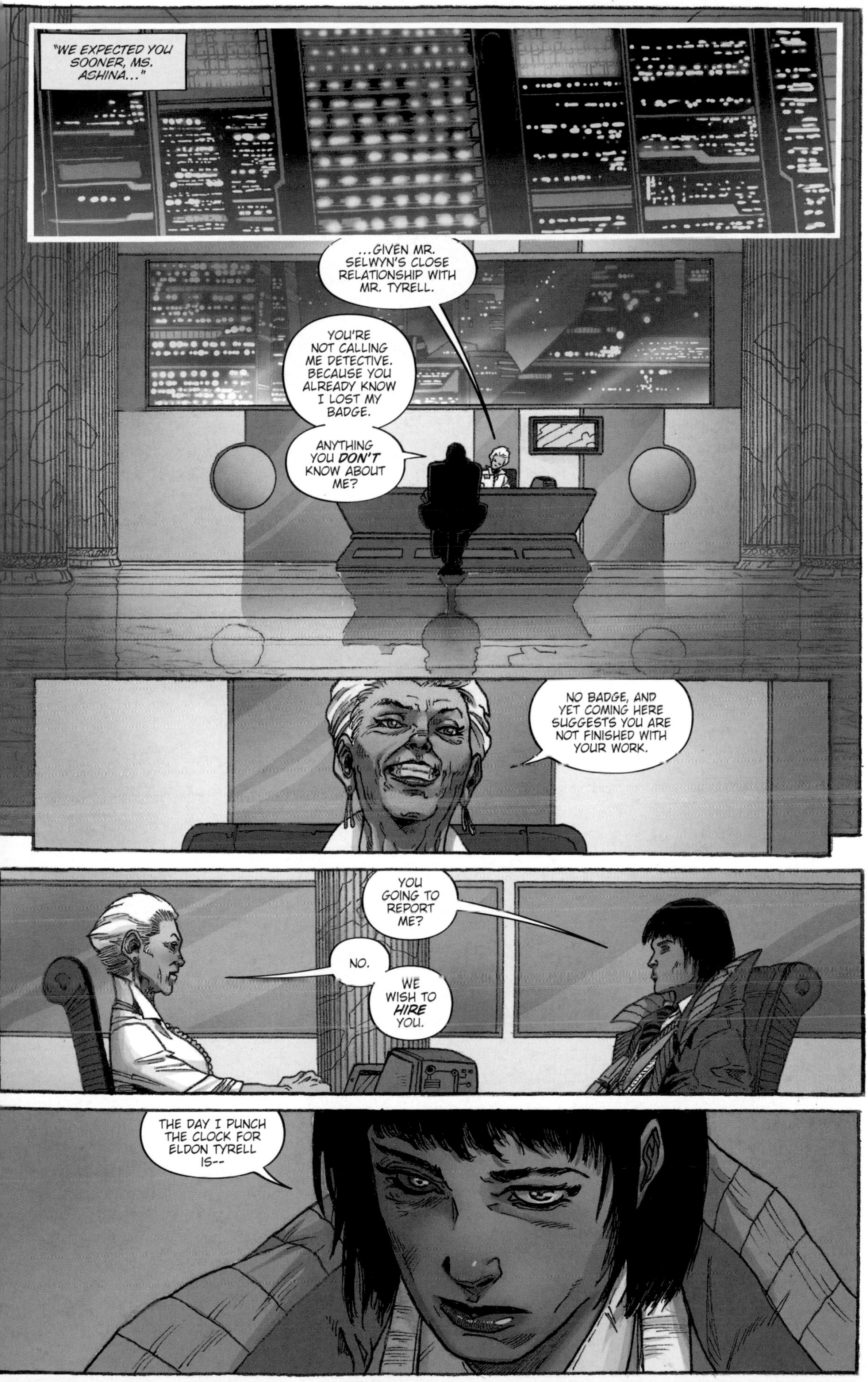
"WE EXPECTED YOU SOONER, MS. ASHINA..."
...GIVEN MR. SELWYN'S CLOSE RELATIONSHIP WITH MR. TYRELL.
YOU'RE NOT CALLING ME DETECTIVE. BECAUSE YOU ALREADY KNOW I LOST MY BADGE.
ANYTHING YOU DON'T KNOW ABOUT ME?
NO BADGE, AND YET COMING HERE SUGGESTS YOU ARE NOT FINISHED WITH YOUR WORK.
YOU GOING TO REPORT ME?
NO.
WE WISH TO HIRE YOU.
THE DAY I PUNCH THE CLOCK FOR ELDON TYRELL IS--

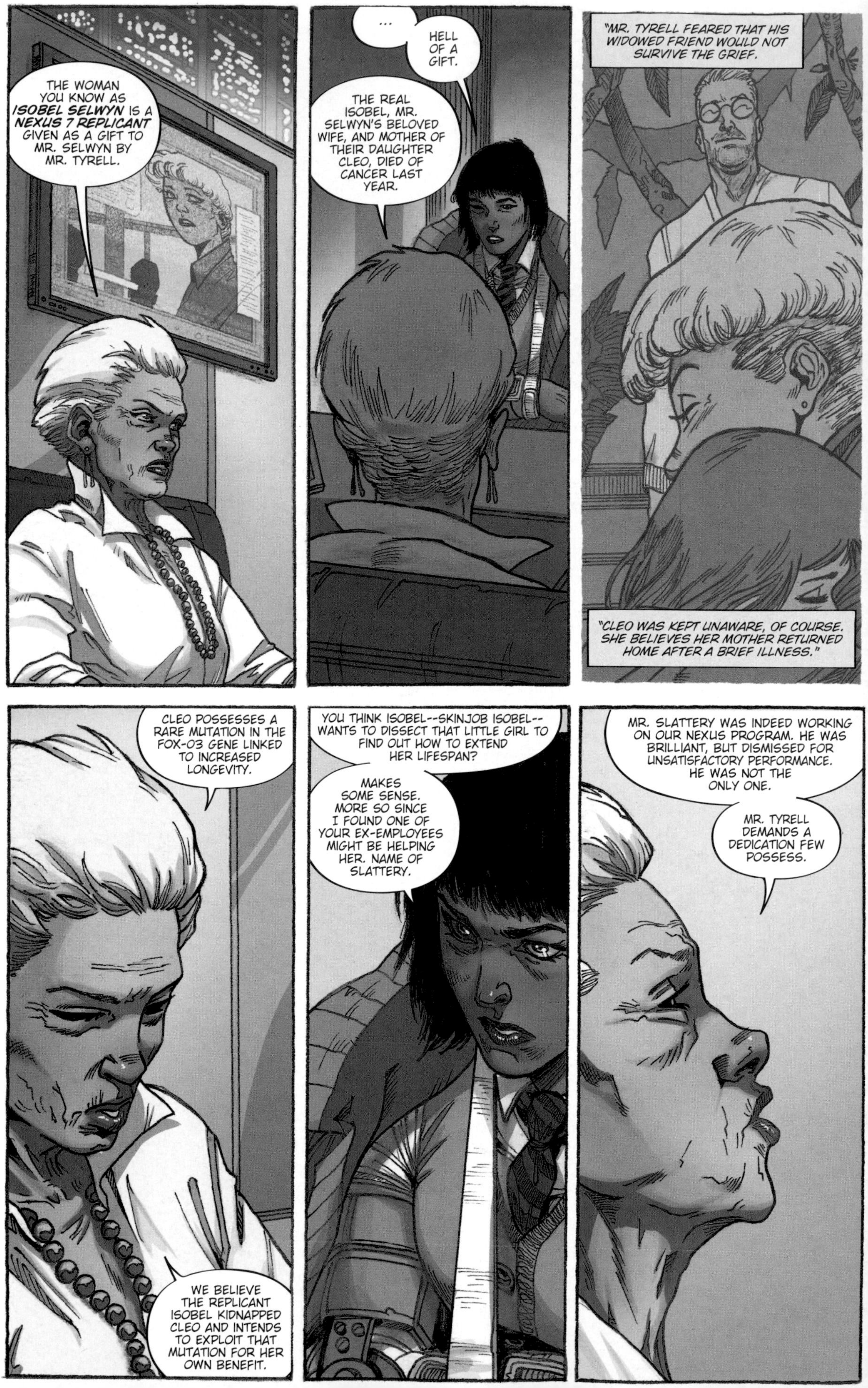
THE WOMAN YOU KNOW AS ISOBEL SELWYN IS A NEXUS 7 REPLICANT GIVEN AS A GIFT TO MR. SELWYN BY MR. TYRELL.
...
HELL OF A GIFT.
THE REAL ISOBEL, MR. SELWYN'S BELOVED WIFE, AND MOTHER OF THEIR DAUGHTER CLEO, DIED OF CANCER LAST YEAR.
"MR. TYRELL FEARED THAT HIS WIDOWED FRIEND WOULD NOT SURVIVE THE GRIEF.
"CLEO WAS KEPT UNAWARE, OF COURSE. SHE BELIEVES HER MOTHER RETURNED HOME AFTER A BRIEF ILLNESS."
CLEO POSSESSES A RARE MUTATION IN THE FOX-03 GENE LINKED TO INCREASED LONGEVITY.
WE BELIEVE THE REPLICANT ISOBEL KIDNAPPED CLEO AND INTENDS TO EXPLOIT THAT MUTATION FOR HER OWN BENEFIT.
YOU THINK ISOBEL--SKINJOB ISOBEL--WANTS TO DISSECT THAT LITTLE GIRL TO FIND OUT HOW TO EXTEND HER LIFESPAN?
MAKES SOME SENSE. MORE SO SINCE I FOUND ONE OF YOUR EX-EMPLOYEES MIGHT BE HELPING HER. NAME OF SLATTERY.
MR. SLATTERY WAS INDEED WORKING ON OUR NEXUS PROGRAM. HE WAS BRILLIANT, BUT DISMISSED FOR UNSATISFACTORY PERFORMANCE. HE WAS NOT THE ONLY ONE.
MR. TYRELL DEMANDS A DEDICATION FEW POSSESS.

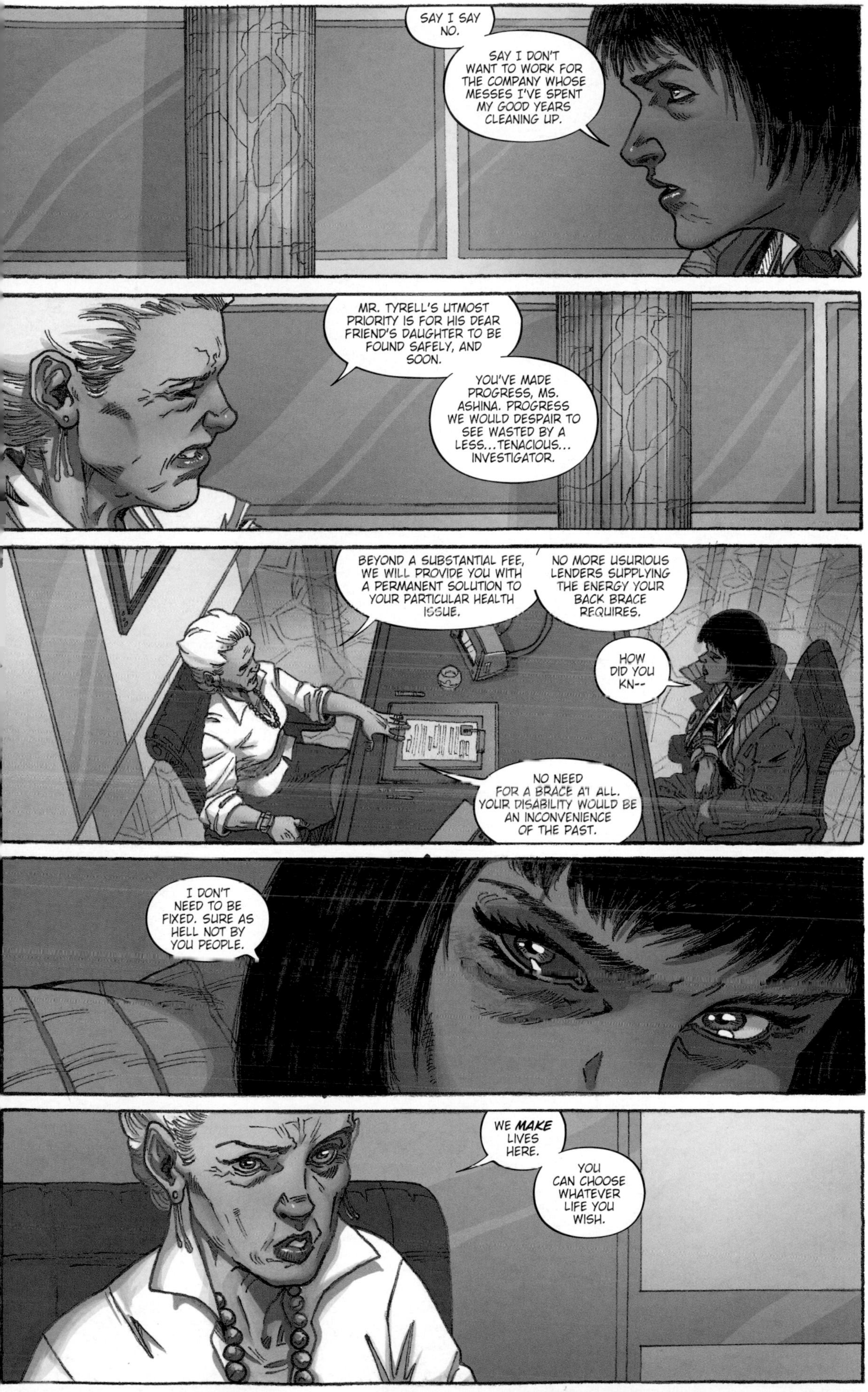
SAY I SAY NO.
SAY I DON'T WANT TO WORK FOR THE COMPANY WHOSE MESSES I'VE SPENT MY GOOD YEARS CLEANING UP.
MR. TYRELL'S UTMOST PRIORITY IS FOR HIS DEAR FRIEND'S DAUGHTER TO BE FOUND SAFELY, AND SOON.
YOU'VE MADE PROGRESS, MS. ASHINA. PROGRESS WE WOULD DESPAIR TO SEE WASTED BY A LESS...TENACIOUS... INVESTIGATOR.
BEYOND A SUBSTANTIAL FEE, WE WILL PROVIDE YOU WITH A PERMANENT SOLUTION TO YOUR PARTICULAR HEALTH ISSUE.
NO MORE USURIOUS LENDERS SUPPLYING THE ENERGY YOUR BACK BRACE REQUIRES.
HOW DID YOU KN--
NO NEED FOR A BRACE AT ALL. YOUR DISABILITY WOULD BE AN INCONVENIENCE OF THE PAST.
I DON'T NEED TO BE FIXED. SURE AS HELL NOT BY YOU PEOPLE.
WE MAKE LIVES HERE.
YOU CAN CHOOSE WHATEVER LIFE YOU WISH.

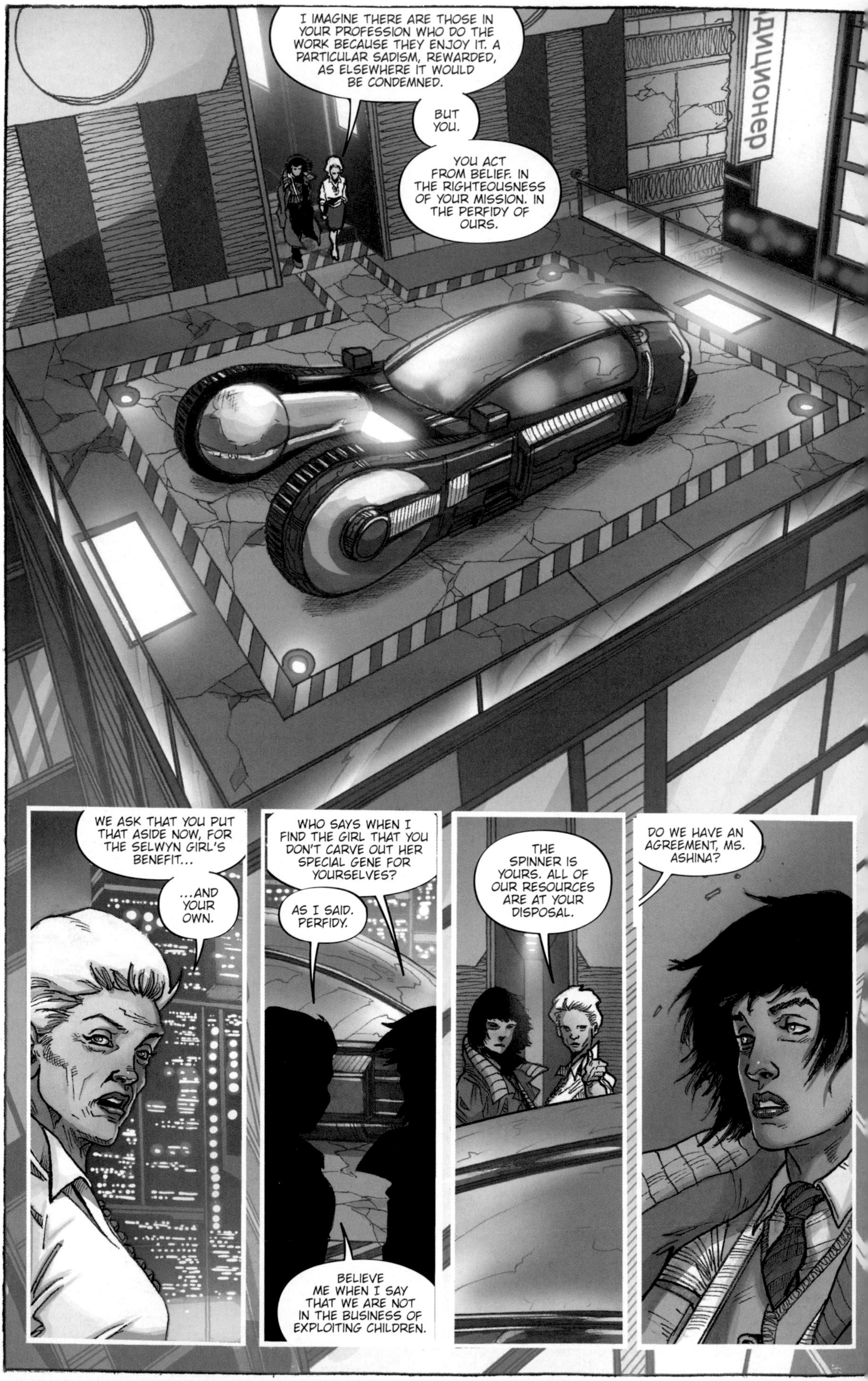
I IMAGINE THERE ARE THOSE IN YOUR PROFESSION WHO DO THE WORK BECAUSE THEY ENJOY IT. A PARTICULAR SADISM, REWARDED, AS ELSEWHERE IT WOULD BE CONDEMNED.
BUT YOU.
YOU ACT FROM BELIEF. IN THE RIGHTEOUSNESS OF YOUR MISSION. IN THE PERFIDY OF OURS.
WE ASK THAT YOU PUT THAT ASIDE NOW, FOR THE SELWYN GIRL'S BENEFIT...
...AND YOUR OWN.
WHO SAYS WHEN I FIND THE GIRL THAT YOU DON'T CARVE OUT HER SPECIAL GENE FOR YOURSELVES?
AS I SAID. PERFIDY.
BELIEVE ME WHEN I SAY THAT WE ARE NOT IN THE BUSINESS OF EXPLOITING CHILDREN.
THE SPINNER IS YOURS. ALL OF OUR RESOURCES ARE AT YOUR DISPOSAL.
DO WE HAVE AN AGREEMENT, MS. ASHINA?

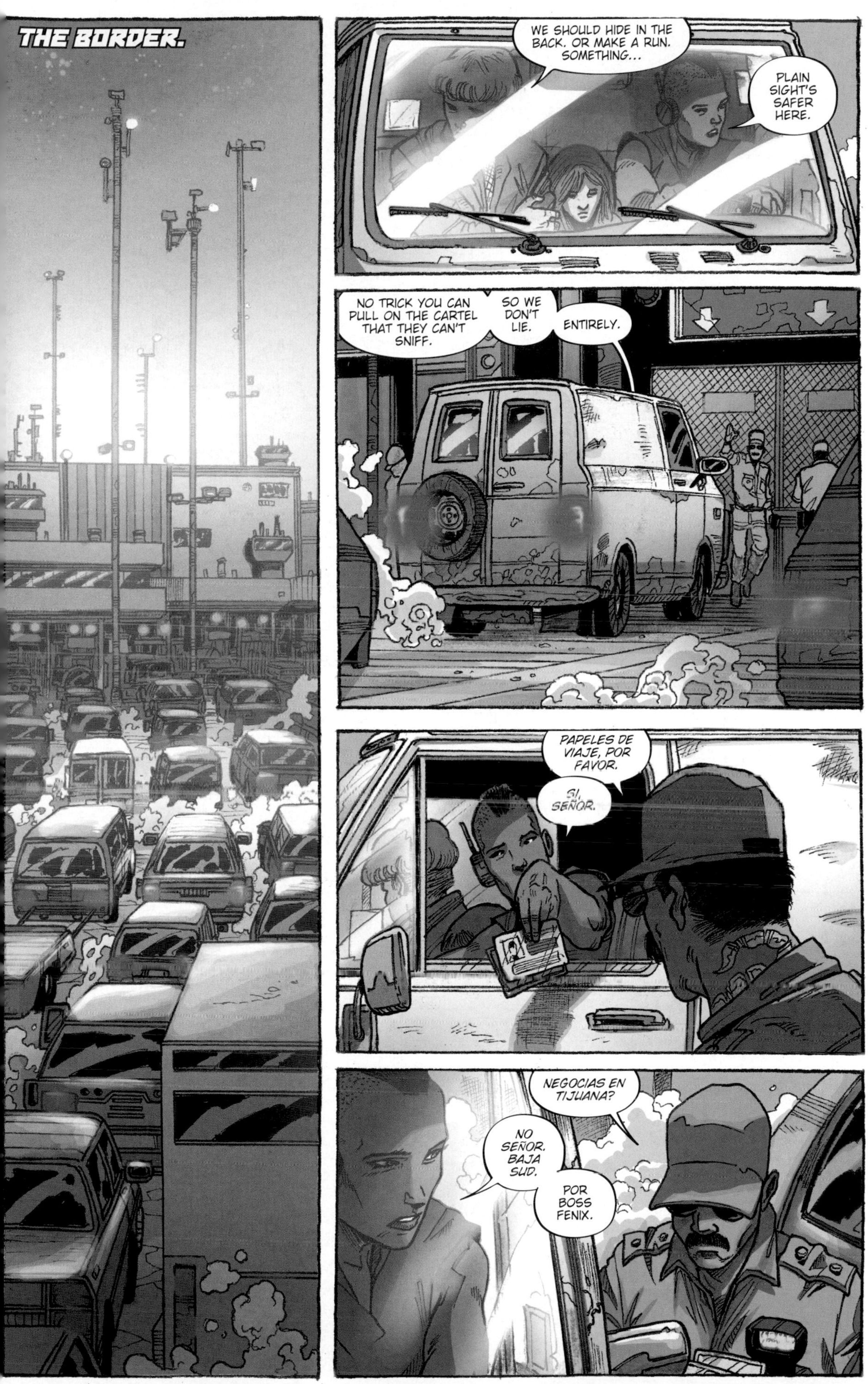
THE BORDER.
WE SHOULD HIDE IN THE BACK. OR MAKE A RUN. SOMETHING...
PLAIN SIGHT'S SAFER HERE.
NO TRICK YOU CAN PULL ON THE CARTEL THAT THEY CAN'T SNIFF.
SO WE DON'T LIE.
ENTIRELY.
PAPELES DE VIAJE, POR FAVOR.
SI, SEÑOR.
NEGOCIAS EN TIJUANA?
NO SEÑOR. BAJA SUD.
POR BOSS FENIX.

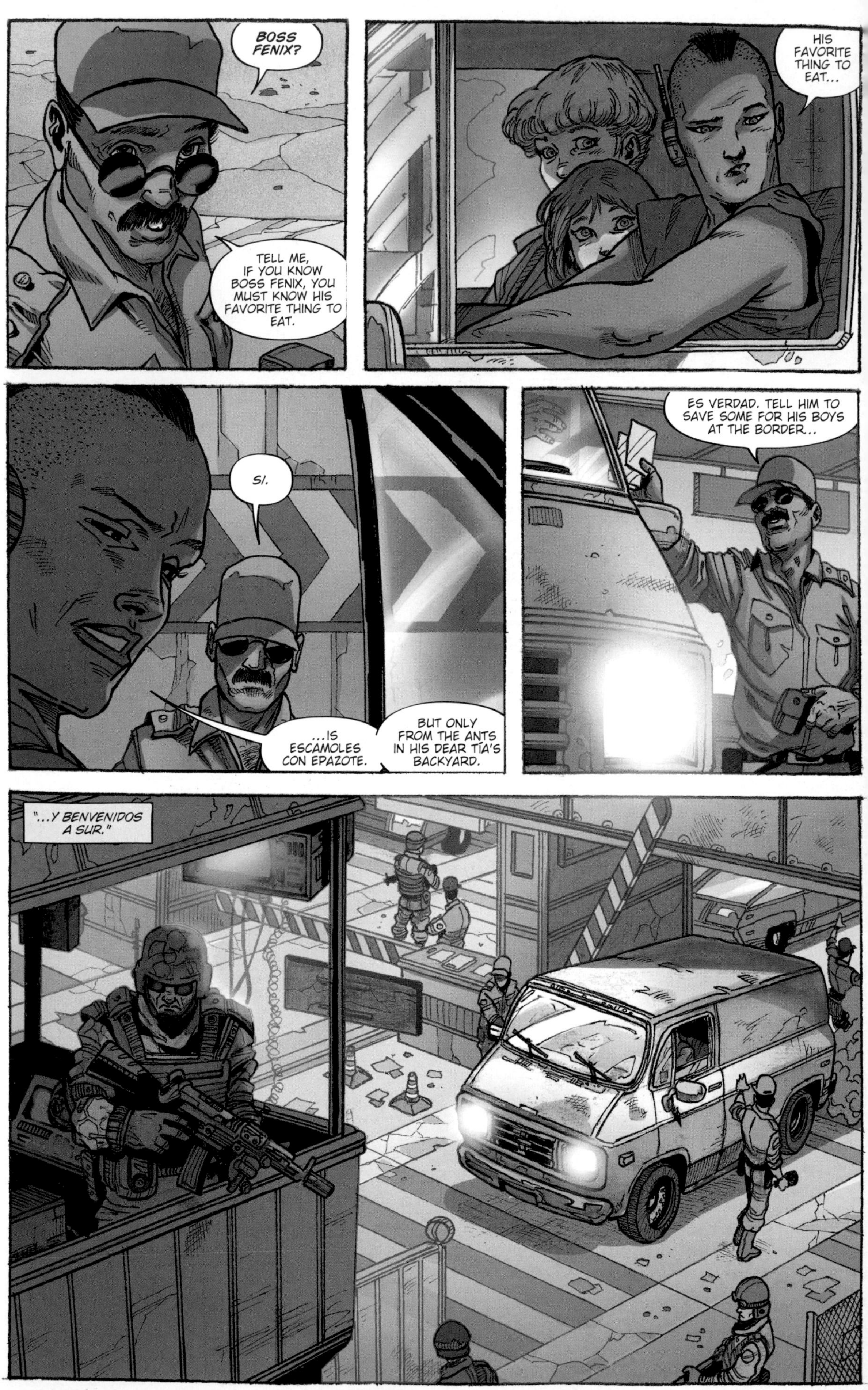
BOSS FENIX?
TELL ME, IF YOU KNOW BOSS FENIX, YOU MUST KNOW HIS FAVORITE THING TO EAT.
HIS FAVORITE THING TO EAT...
SÍ.
...IS ESCAMOLES CON EPAZOTE.
BUT ONLY FROM THE ANTS IN HIS DEAR TÍA'S BACKYARD.
ES VERDAD. TELL HIM TO SAVE SOME FOR HIS BOYS AT THE BORDER...
"...Y BENVENIDOS A SUR."

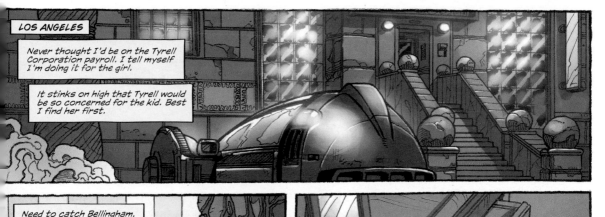

LOS ANGELES

Never thought I'd be on the Tyrell Corporation payroll. I tell myself I'm doing it for the girl.

It stinks on high that Tyrell would be so concerned for the kid. Best I find her first.

Need to catch Bellingham, the geriatric I tumbled with, so I'm back at the scene.

Could be was on his way to Isobel.

The old skinjob thinks he has an artist's soul.

Thinks he **has** a soul.

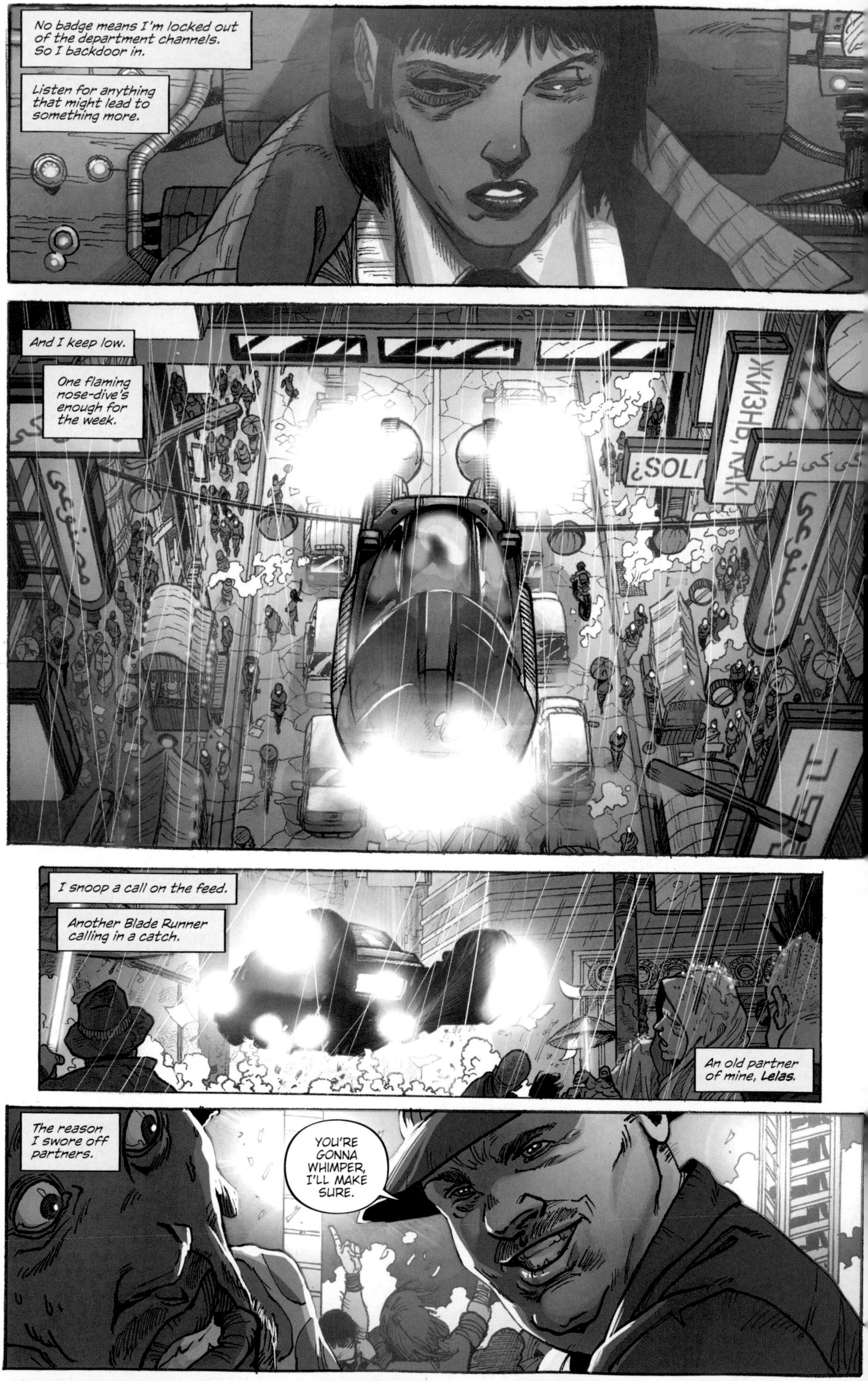
No badge means I'm locked out of the department channels. So I backdoor in.
Listen for anything that might lead to something more.
And I keep low.
One flaming nose-dive's enough for the week.
¿SOLI
ЖИЗНЬ, КАК
I snoop a call on the feed.
Another Blade Runner calling in a catch.
An old partner of mine, **Lelas**.
The reason I swore off partners.
YOU'RE GONNA WHIMPER, I'LL MAKE SURE.

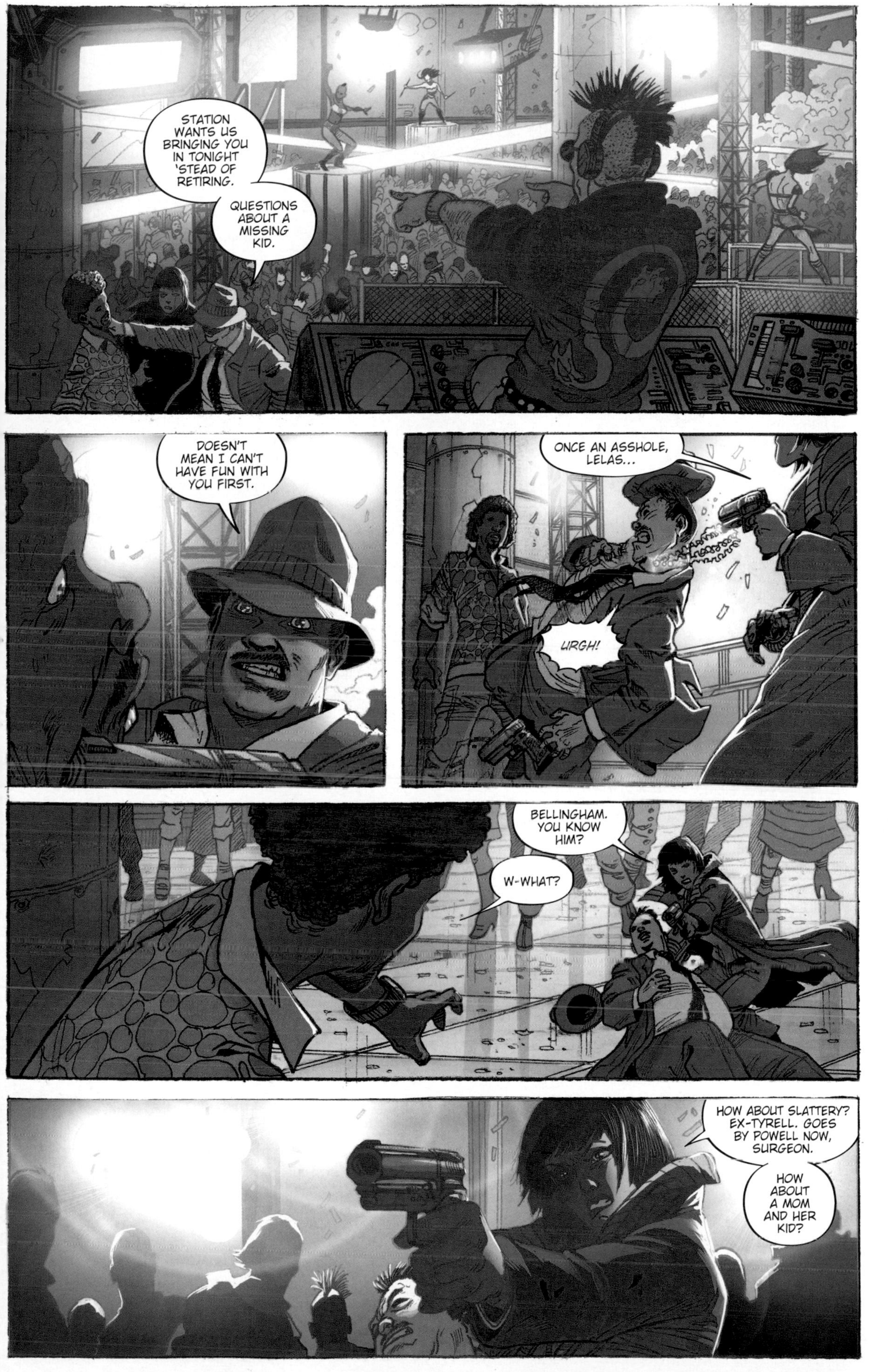

STATION WANTS US BRINGING YOU IN TONIGHT 'STEAD OF RETIRING.
QUESTIONS ABOUT A MISSING KID.
DOESN'T MEAN I CAN'T HAVE FUN WITH YOU FIRST.
ONCE AN ASSHOLE, LELAS...
URGH!
BELLINGHAM. YOU KNOW HIM?
W-WHAT?
HOW ABOUT SLATTERY? EX-TYRELL. GOES BY POWELL NOW, SURGEON.
HOW ABOUT A MOM AND HER KID?

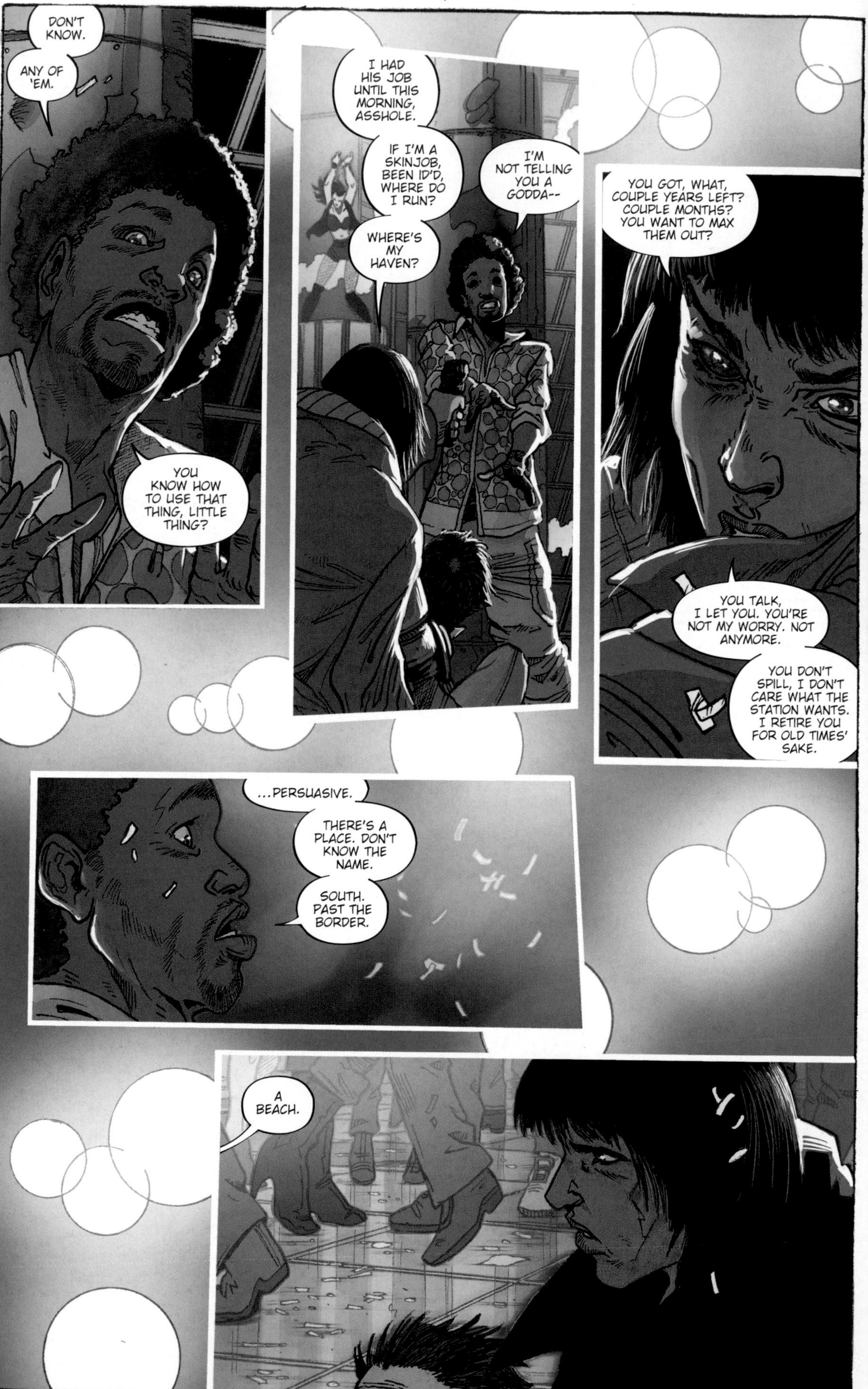
DON'T KNOW.
ANY OF 'EM.
YOU KNOW HOW TO USE THAT THING, LITTLE THING?
I HAD HIS JOB UNTIL THIS MORNING, ASSHOLE.
IF I'M A SKINJOB, BEEN ID'D, WHERE DO I RUN?
WHERE'S MY HAVEN?
I'M NOT TELLING YOU A GODDA--
YOU GOT, WHAT, COUPLE YEARS LEFT? COUPLE MONTHS? YOU WANT TO MAX THEM OUT?
YOU TALK, I LET YOU. YOU'RE NOT MY WORRY. NOT ANYMORE.
YOU DON'T SPILL, I DON'T CARE WHAT THE STATION WANTS. I RETIRE YOU FOR OLD TIMES' SAKE.
...PERSUASIVE.
THERE'S A PLACE. DON'T KNOW THE NAME.
SOUTH. PAST THE BORDER.
A BEACH.

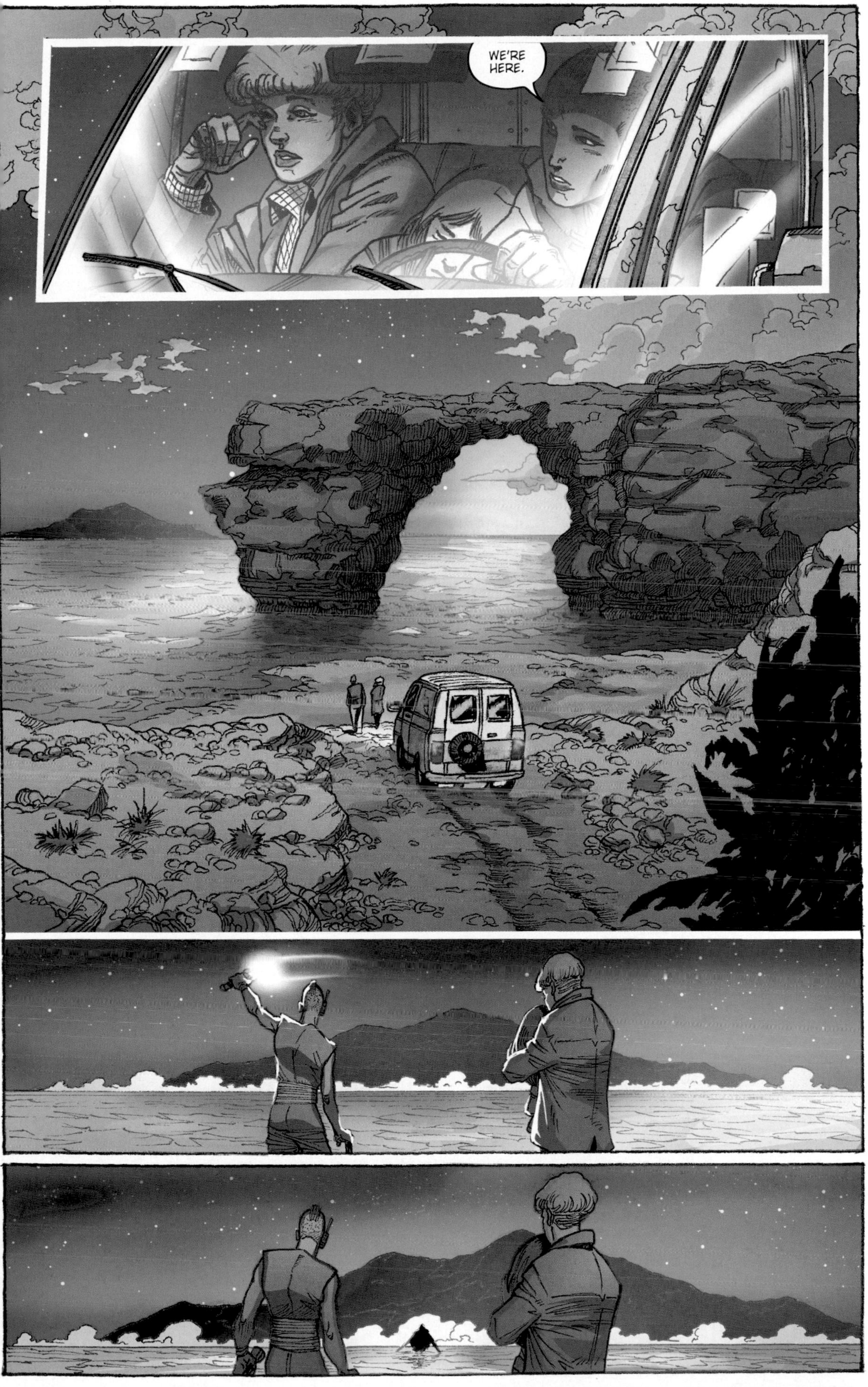
WE'RE HERE.

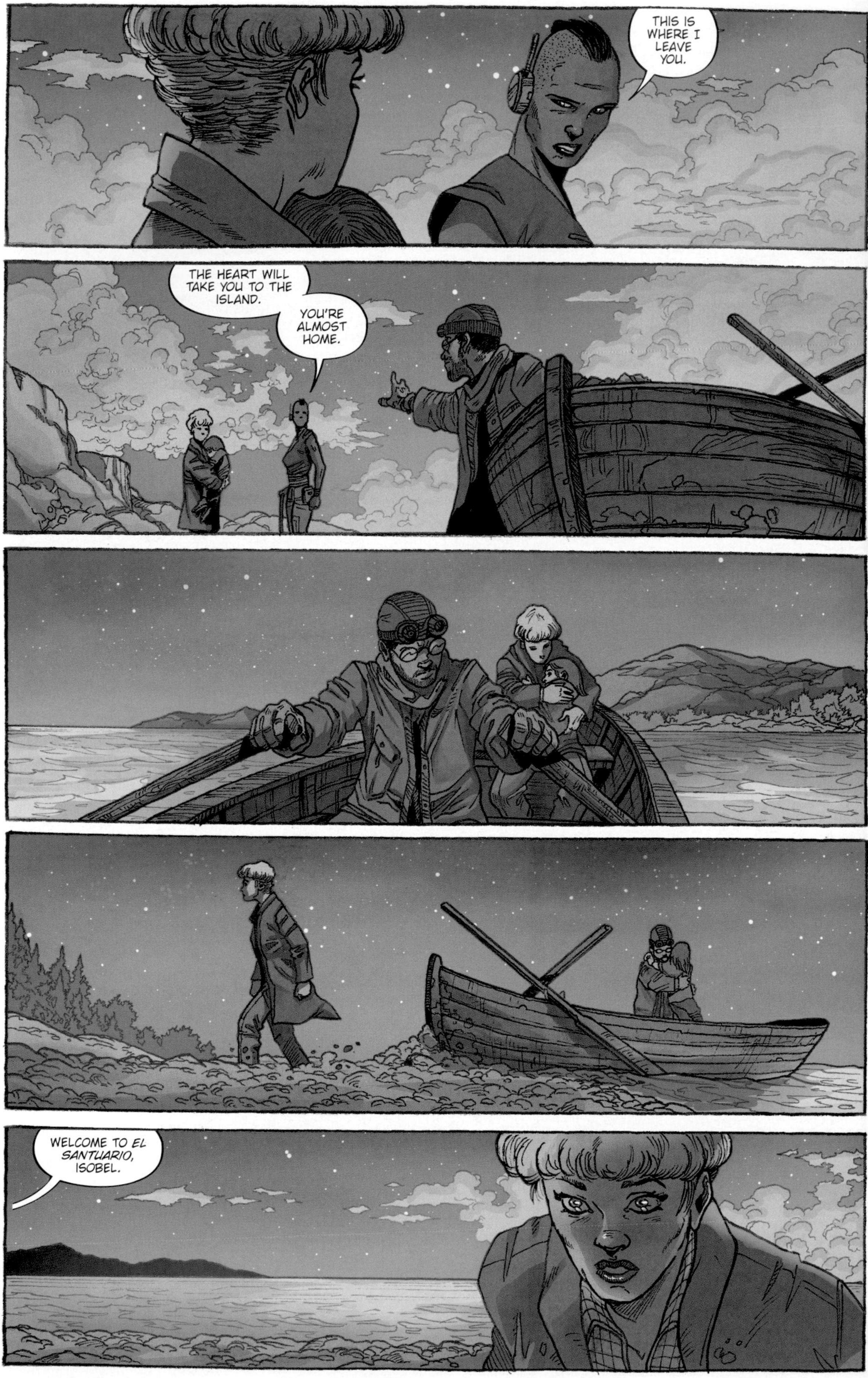
THIS IS WHERE I LEAVE YOU.
THE HEART WILL TAKE YOU TO THE ISLAND.
YOU'RE ALMOST HOME.
WELCOME TO EL SANTUARIO, ISOBEL.

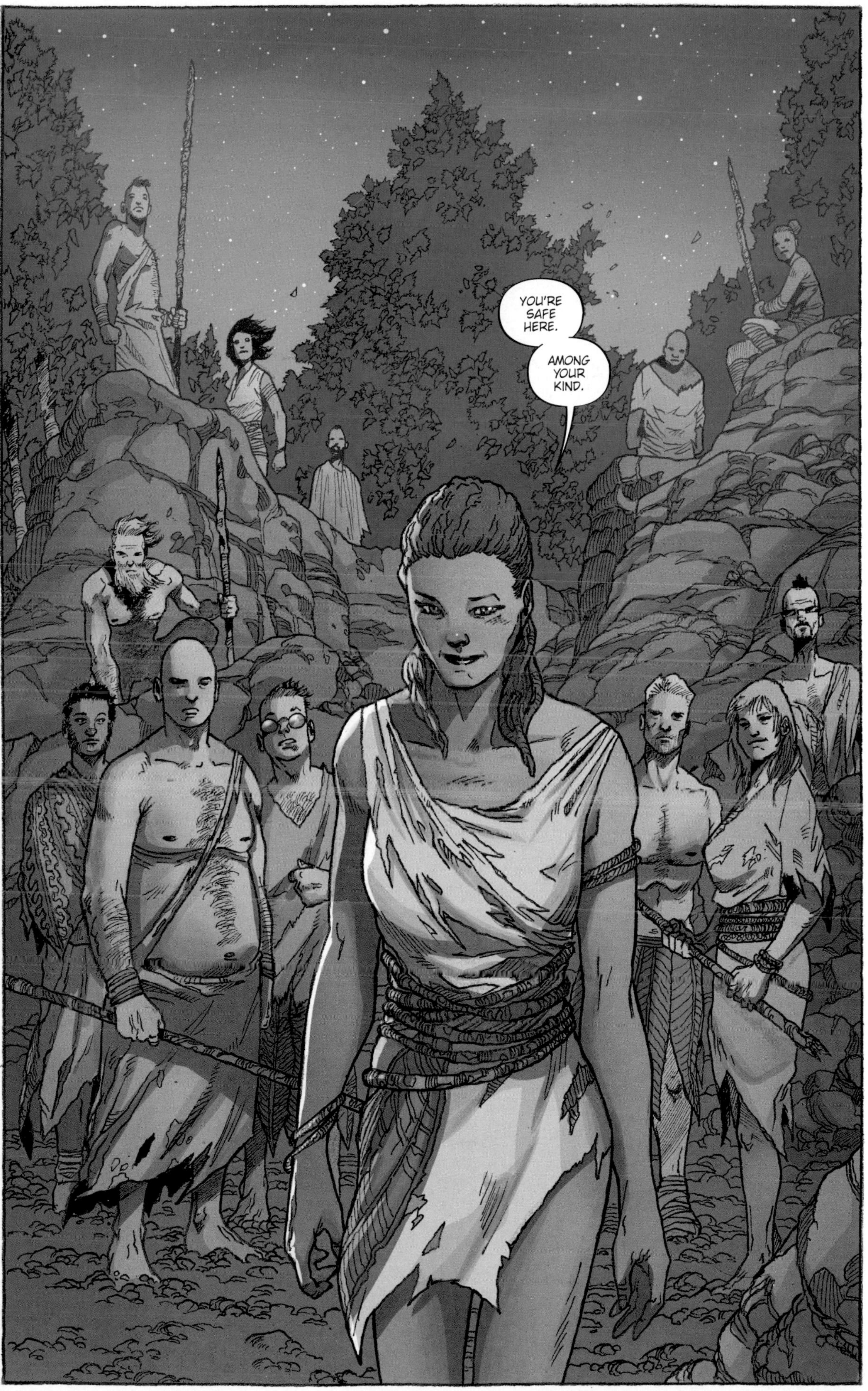
YOU'RE SAFE HERE.
AMONG YOUR KIND.

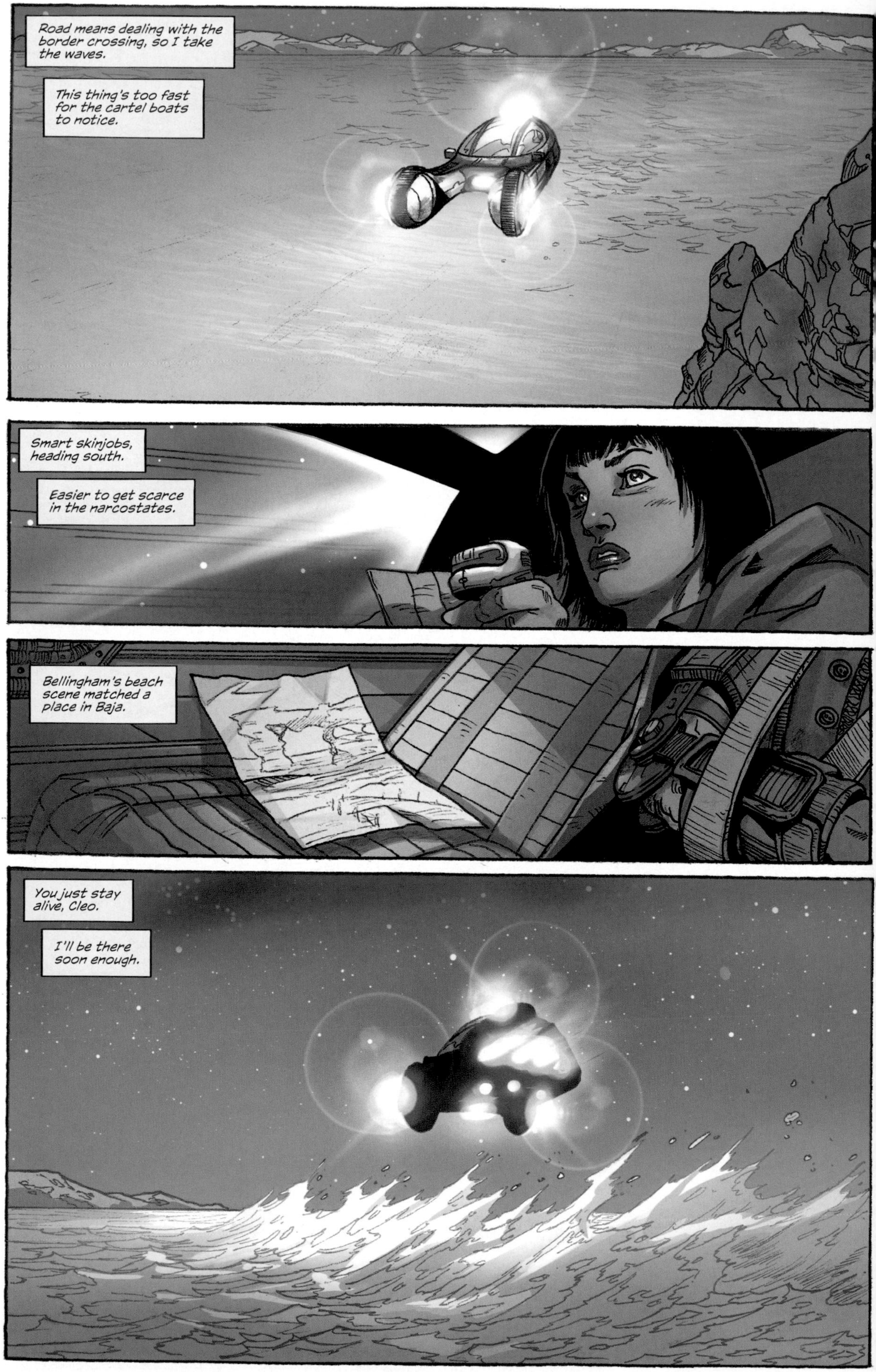
Road means dealing with the border crossing, so I take the waves.
This thing's too fast for the cartel boats to notice.
Smart skinjobs, heading south.
Easier to get scarce in the narcostates.
Bellingham's beach scene matched a place in Baja.
You just stay alive, Cleo.
I'll be there soon enough.

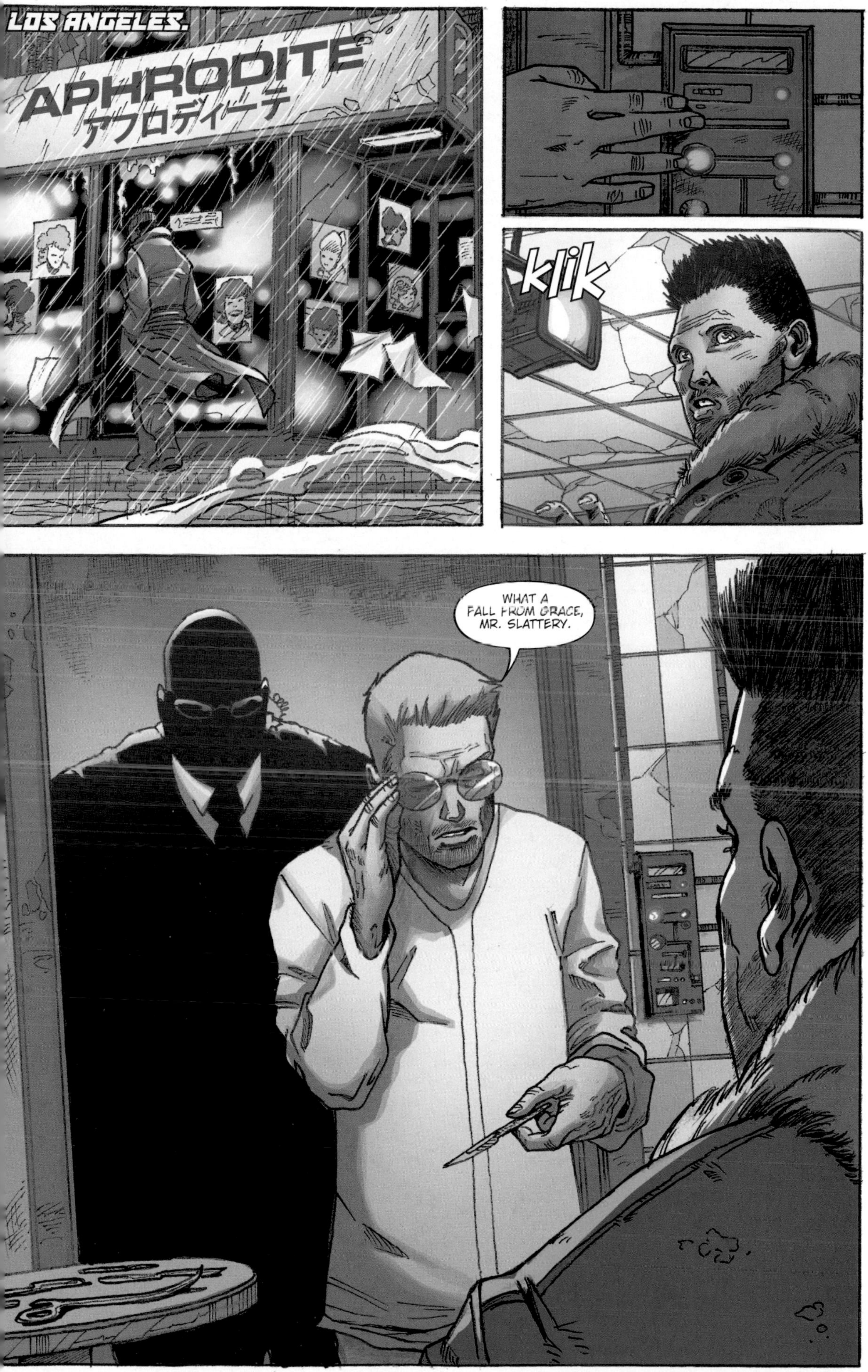
LOS ANGELES.
APHRODITE
アフロディーテ
klik
WHAT A FALL FROM GRACE, MR. SLATTERY.

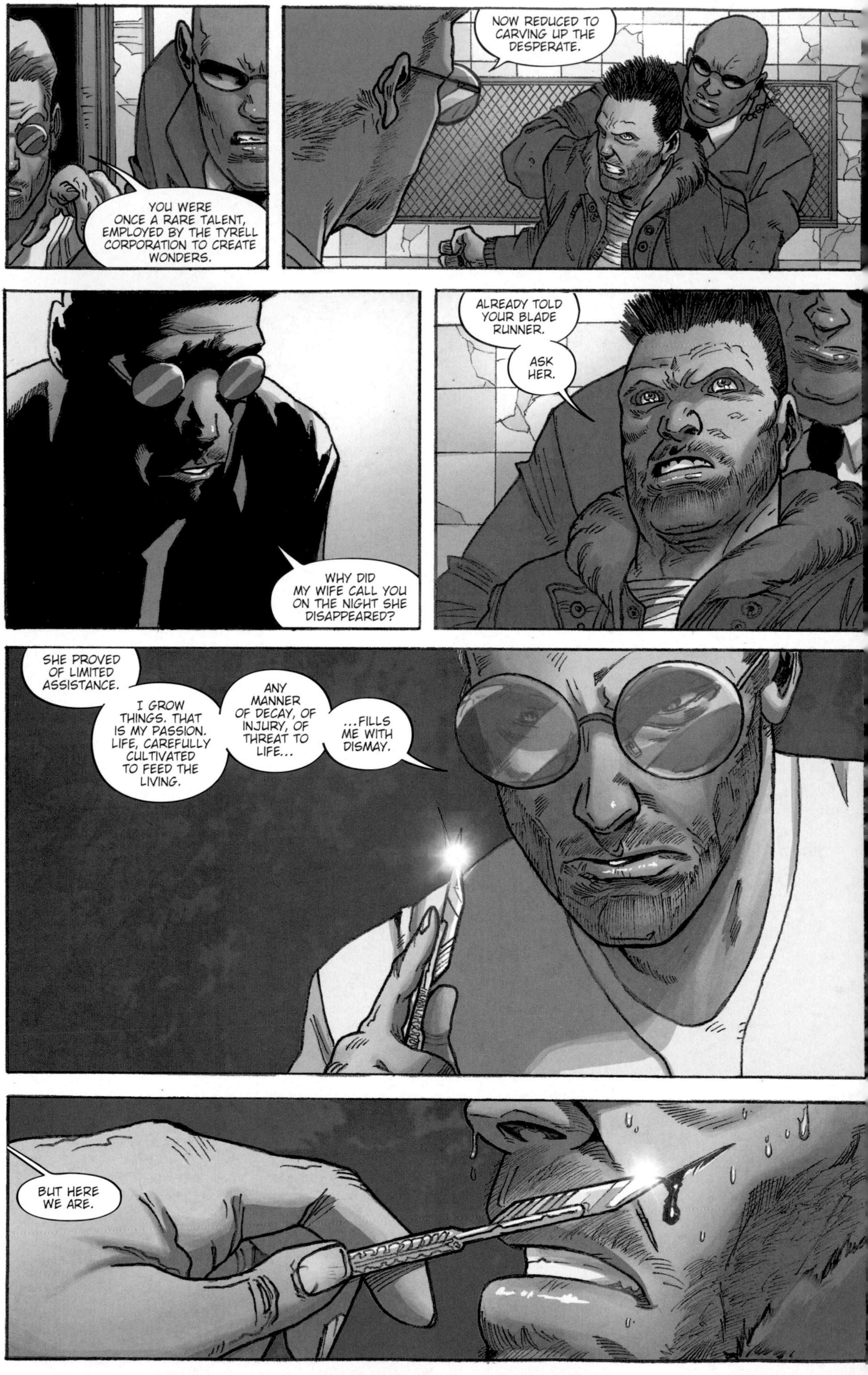
YOU WERE ONCE A RARE TALENT, EMPLOYED BY THE TYRELL CORPORATION TO CREATE WONDERS.
NOW REDUCED TO CARVING UP THE DESPERATE.
WHY DID MY WIFE CALL YOU ON THE NIGHT SHE DISAPPEARED?
ALREADY TOLD YOUR BLADE RUNNER.
ASK HER.
SHE PROVED OF LIMITED ASSISTANCE.
I GROW THINGS. THAT IS MY PASSION. LIFE, CAREFULLY CULTIVATED TO FEED THE LIVING.
ANY MANNER OF DECAY, OF INJURY, OF THREAT TO LIFE...
...FILLS ME WITH DISMAY.
BUT HERE WE ARE.

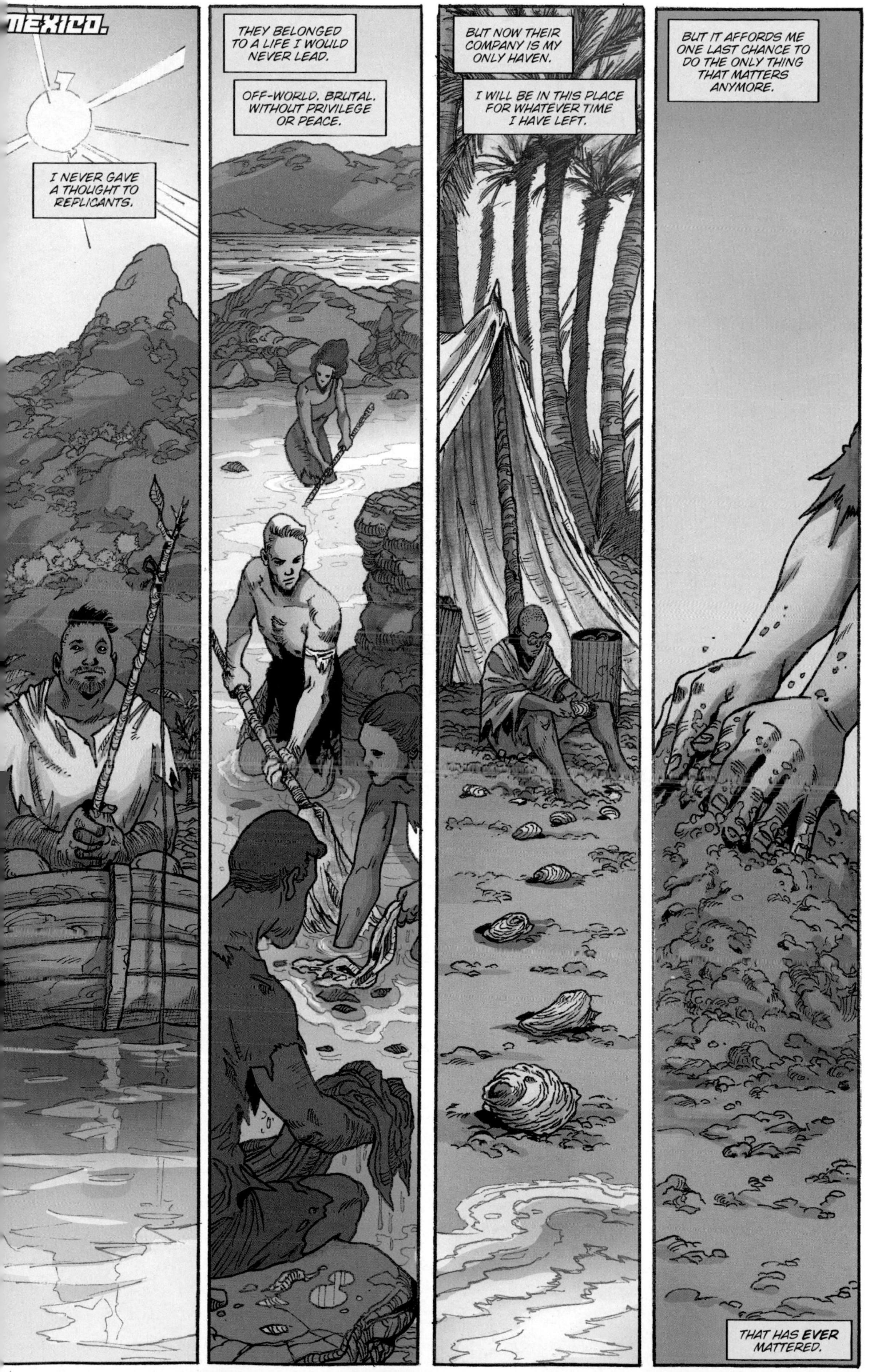
MEXICO.
I NEVER GAVE A THOUGHT TO REPLICANTS.
THEY BELONGED TO A LIFE I WOULD NEVER LEAD.
OFF-WORLD. BRUTAL. WITHOUT PRIVILEGE OR PEACE.
BUT NOW THEIR COMPANY IS MY ONLY HAVEN.
I WILL BE IN THIS PLACE FOR WHATEVER TIME I HAVE LEFT.
BUT IT AFFORDS ME ONE LAST CHANCE TO DO THE ONLY THING THAT MATTERS ANYMORE.
THAT HAS EVER MATTERED.

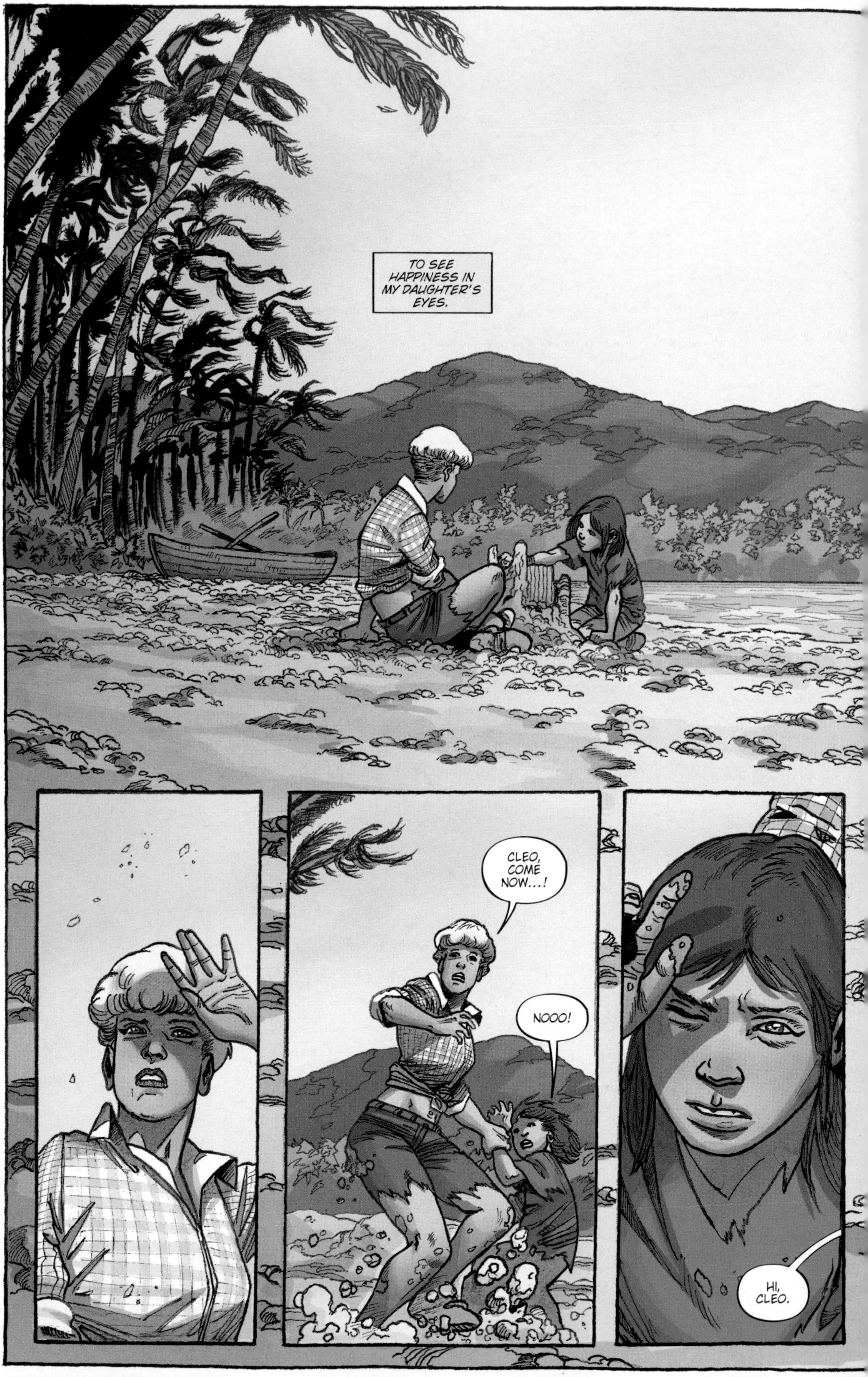
TO SEE HAPPINESS IN MY DAUGHTER'S EYES.
CLEO, COME NOW...!
NOOO!
HI, CLEO.

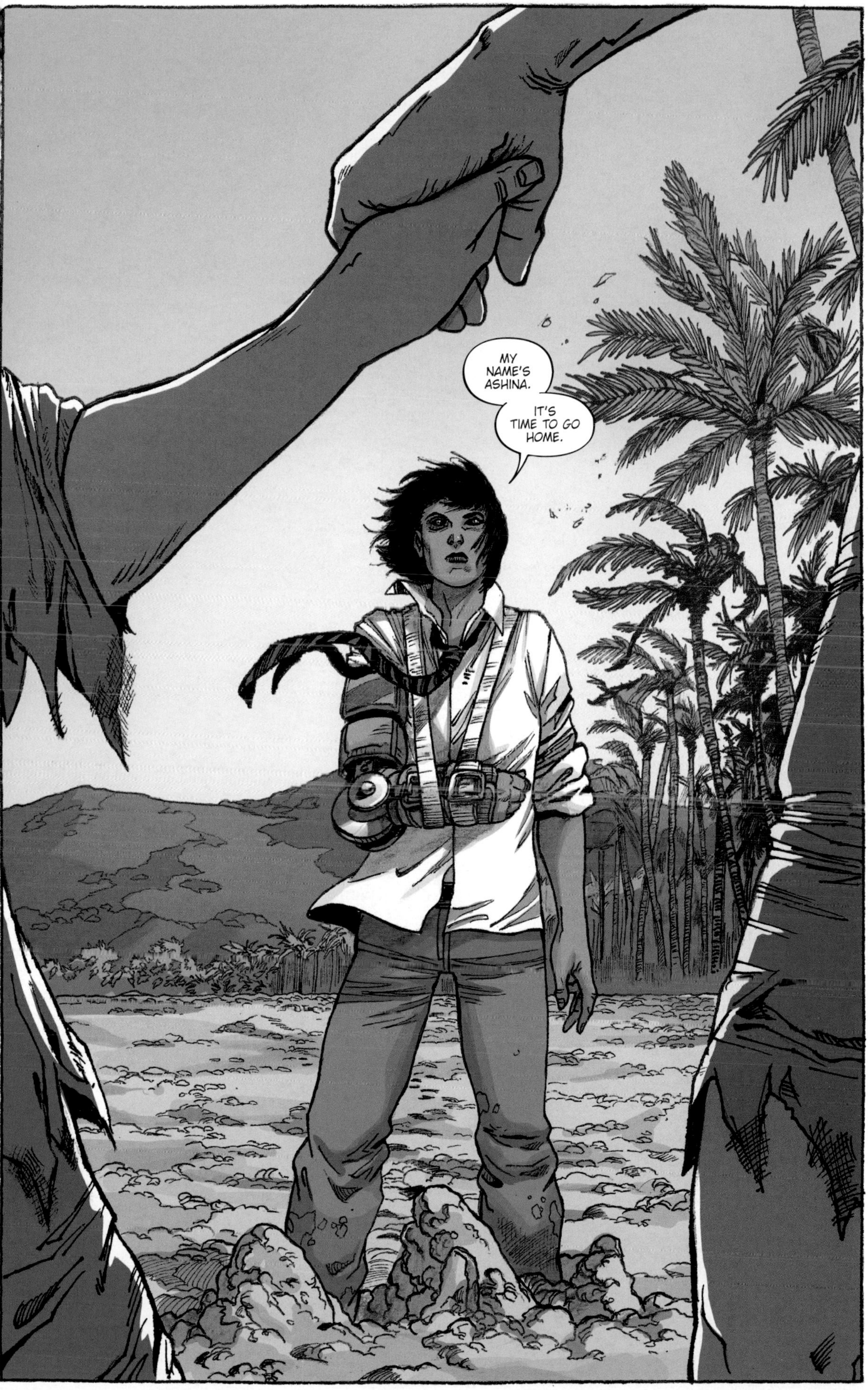
MY NAME'S ASHINA.
IT'S TIME TO GO HOME.

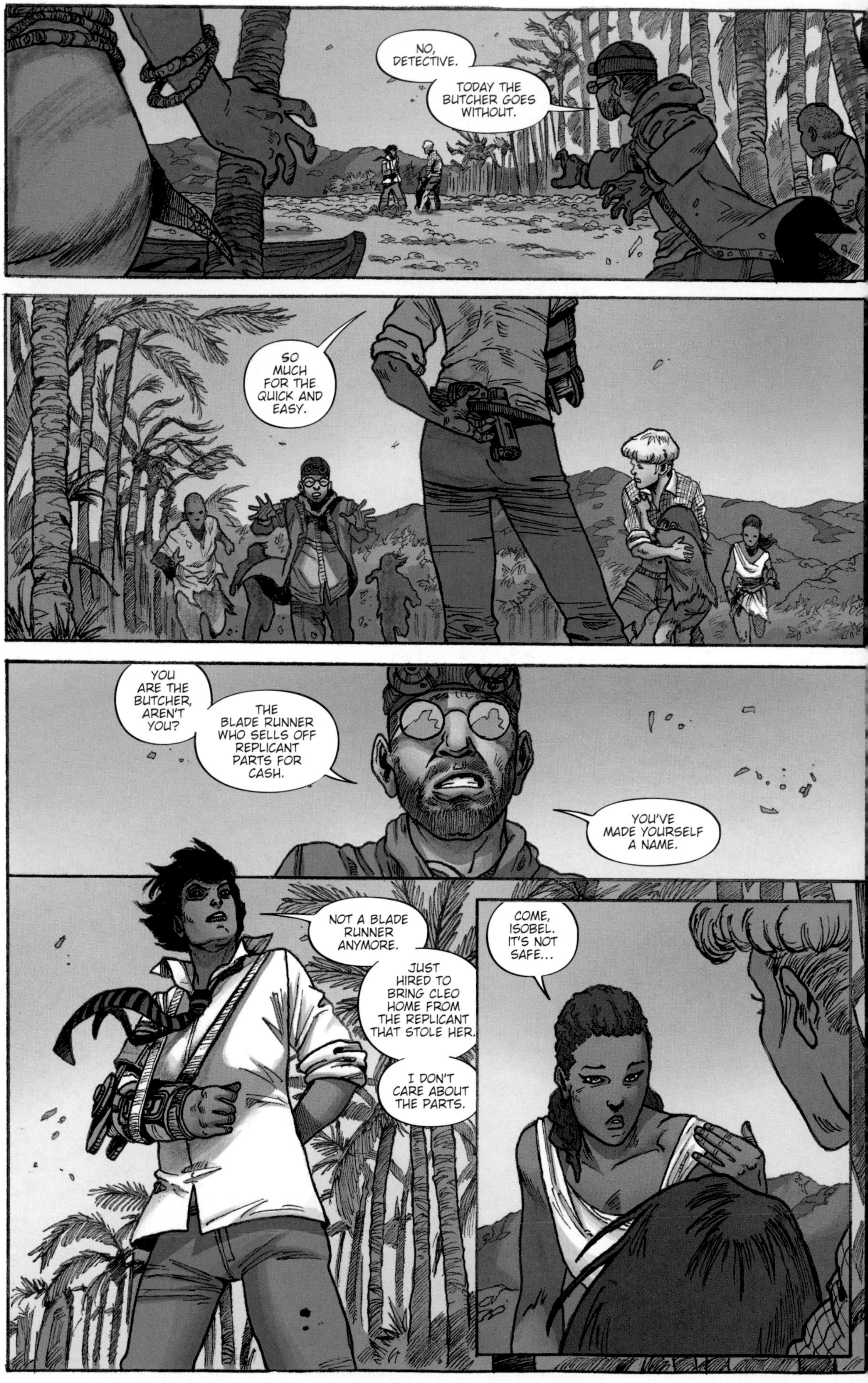
NO, DETECTIVE.
TODAY THE BUTCHER GOES WITHOUT.
SO MUCH FOR THE QUICK AND EASY.
YOU ARE THE BUTCHER, AREN'T YOU?
THE BLADE RUNNER WHO SELLS OFF REPLICANT PARTS FOR CASH.
YOU'VE MADE YOURSELF A NAME.
NOT A BLADE RUNNER ANYMORE.
JUST HIRED TO BRING CLEO HOME FROM THE REPLICANT THAT STOLE HER.
I DON'T CARE ABOUT THE PARTS.
COME, ISOBEL. IT'S NOT SAFE...

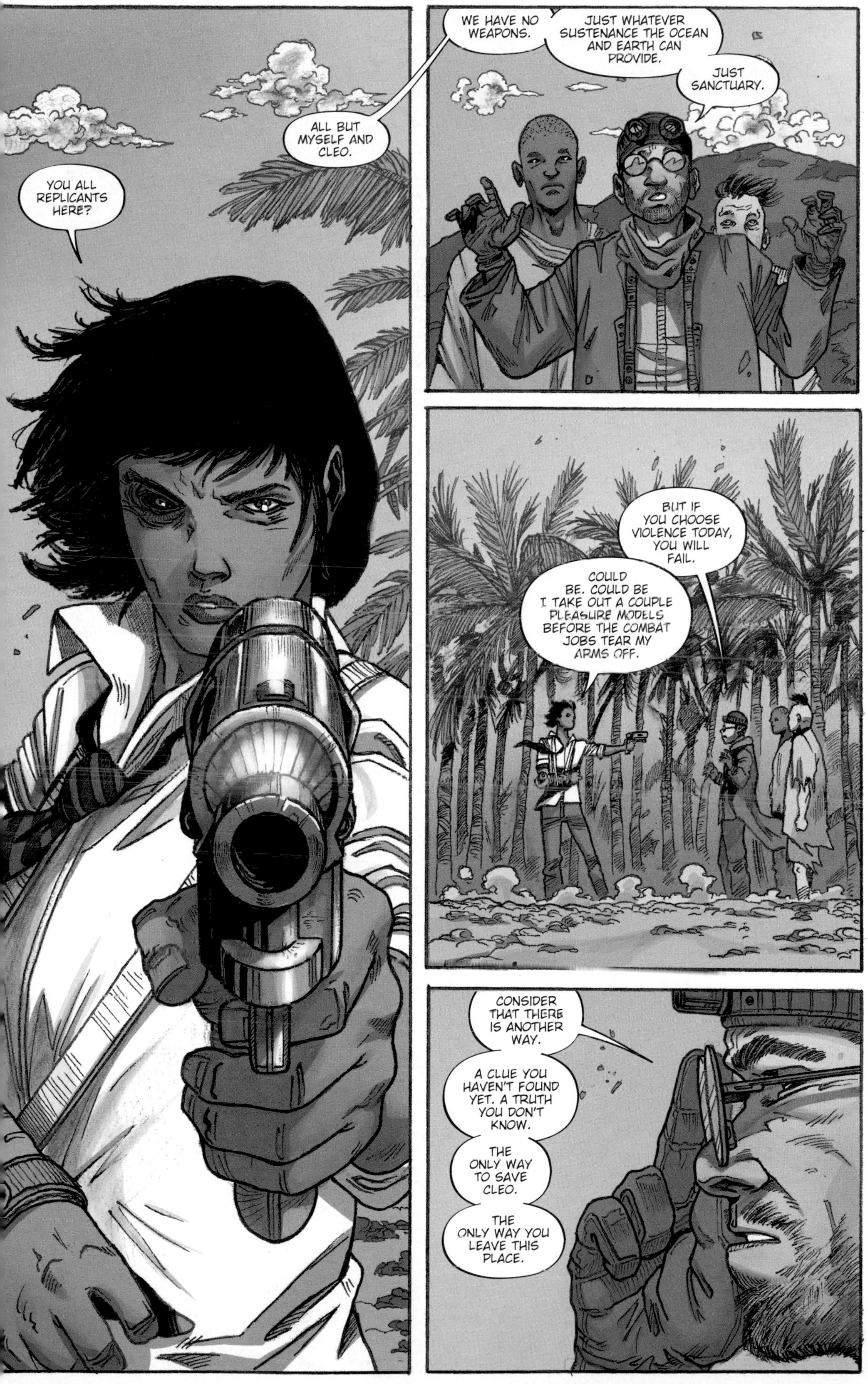
YOU ALL REPLICANTS HERE?
ALL BUT MYSELF AND CLEO.
WE HAVE NO WEAPONS.
JUST WHATEVER SUSTENANCE THE OCEAN AND EARTH CAN PROVIDE.
JUST SANCTUARY.
BUT IF YOU CHOOSE VIOLENCE TODAY, YOU WILL FAIL.
COULD BE. COULD BE I TAKE OUT A COUPLE PLEASURE MODELS BEFORE THE COMBAT JOBS TEAR MY ARMS OFF.
CONSIDER THAT THERE IS ANOTHER WAY.
A CLUE YOU HAVEN'T FOUND YET. A TRUTH YOU DON'T KNOW.
THE ONLY WAY TO SAVE CLEO.
THE ONLY WAY YOU LEAVE THIS PLACE.

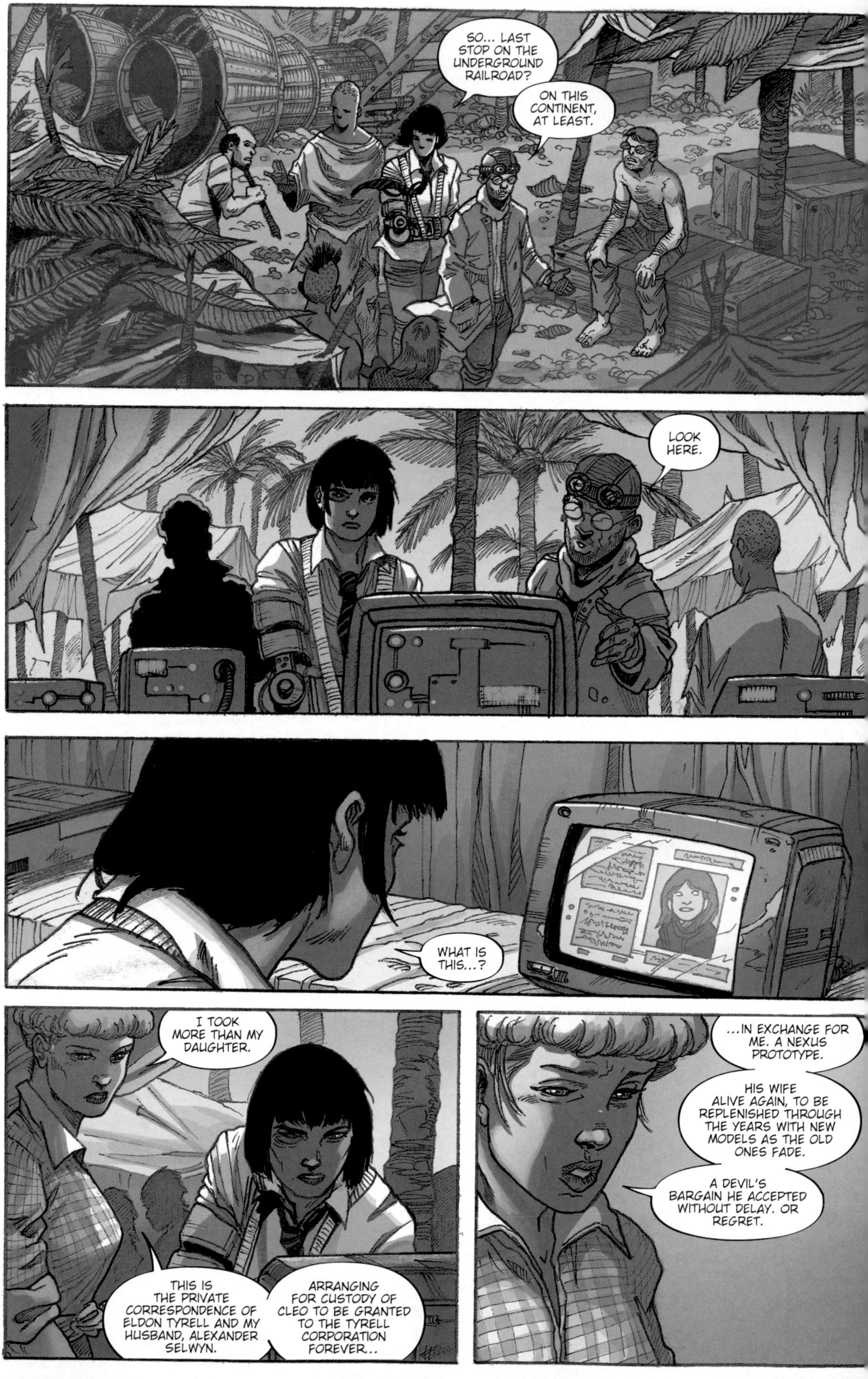
SO... LAST STOP ON THE UNDERGROUND RAILROAD?
ON THIS CONTINENT, AT LEAST.
LOOK HERE.
WHAT IS THIS...?
I TOOK MORE THAN MY DAUGHTER.
THIS IS THE PRIVATE CORRESPONDENCE OF ELDON TYRELL AND MY HUSBAND, ALEXANDER SELWYN.
ARRANGING FOR CUSTODY OF CLEO TO BE GRANTED TO THE TYRELL CORPORATION FOREVER...
...IN EXCHANGE FOR ME. A NEXUS PROTOTYPE.
HIS WIFE ALIVE AGAIN, TO BE REPLENISHED THROUGH THE YEARS WITH NEW MODELS AS THE OLD ONES FADE.
A DEVIL'S BARGAIN HE ACCEPTED WITHOUT DELAY. OR REGRET.

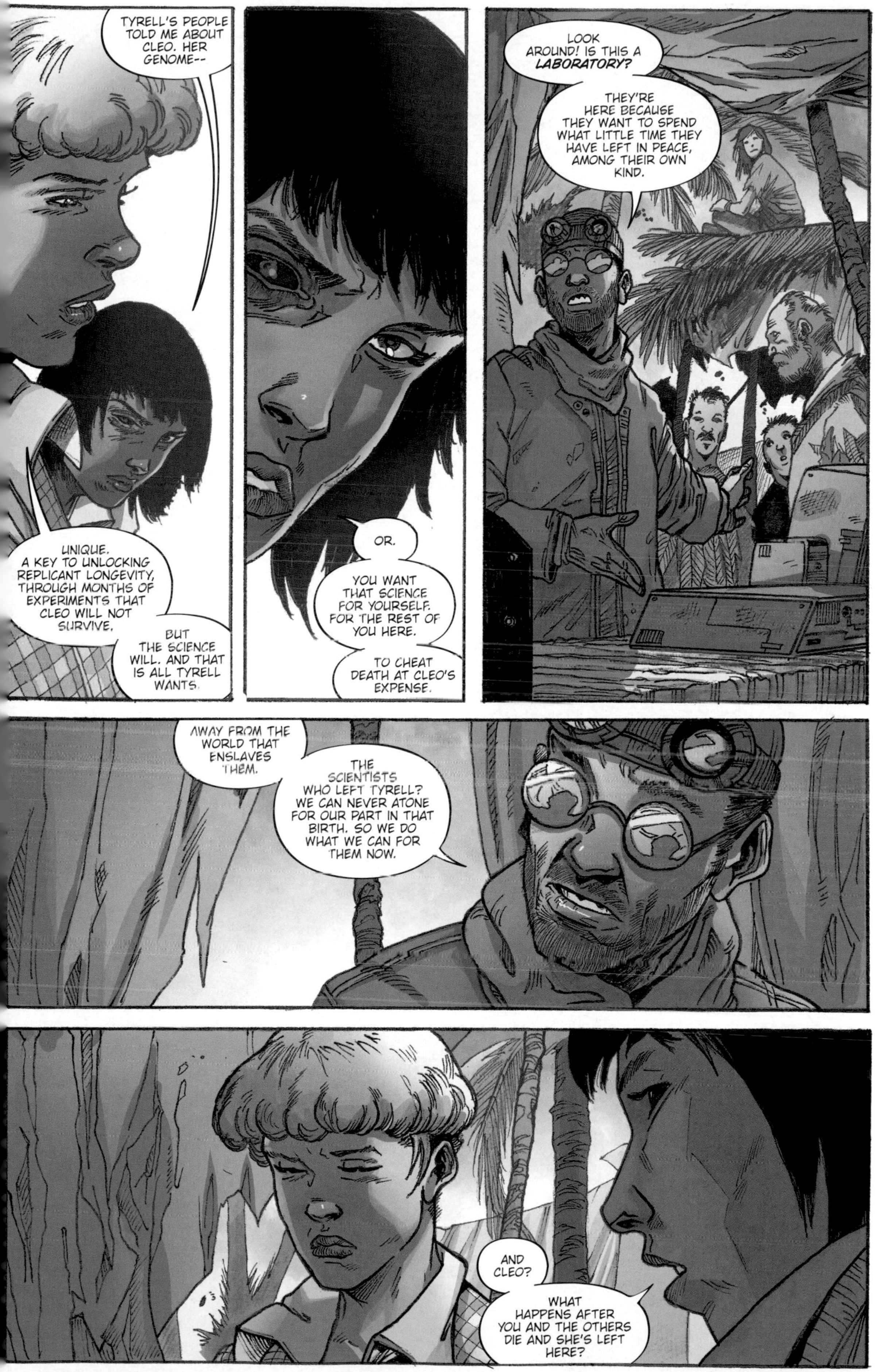
TYRELL'S PEOPLE TOLD ME ABOUT CLEO. HER GENOME--
UNIQUE. A KEY TO UNLOCKING REPLICANT LONGEVITY, THROUGH MONTHS OF EXPERIMENTS THAT CLEO WILL NOT SURVIVE.
BUT THE SCIENCE WILL. AND THAT IS ALL TYRELL WANTS.
OR.
YOU WANT THAT SCIENCE FOR YOURSELF. FOR THE REST OF YOU HERE.
TO CHEAT DEATH AT CLEO'S EXPENSE.
LOOK AROUND! IS THIS A ***LABORATORY?***
THEY'RE HERE BECAUSE THEY WANT TO SPEND WHAT LITTLE TIME THEY HAVE LEFT IN PEACE, AMONG THEIR OWN KIND.
AWAY FROM THE WORLD THAT ENSLAVES THEM.
THE SCIENTISTS WHO LEFT TYRELL? WE CAN NEVER ATONE FOR OUR PART IN THAT BIRTH. SO WE DO WHAT WE CAN FOR THEM NOW.
AND CLEO?
WHAT HAPPENS AFTER YOU AND THE OTHERS DIE AND SHE'S LEFT HERE?

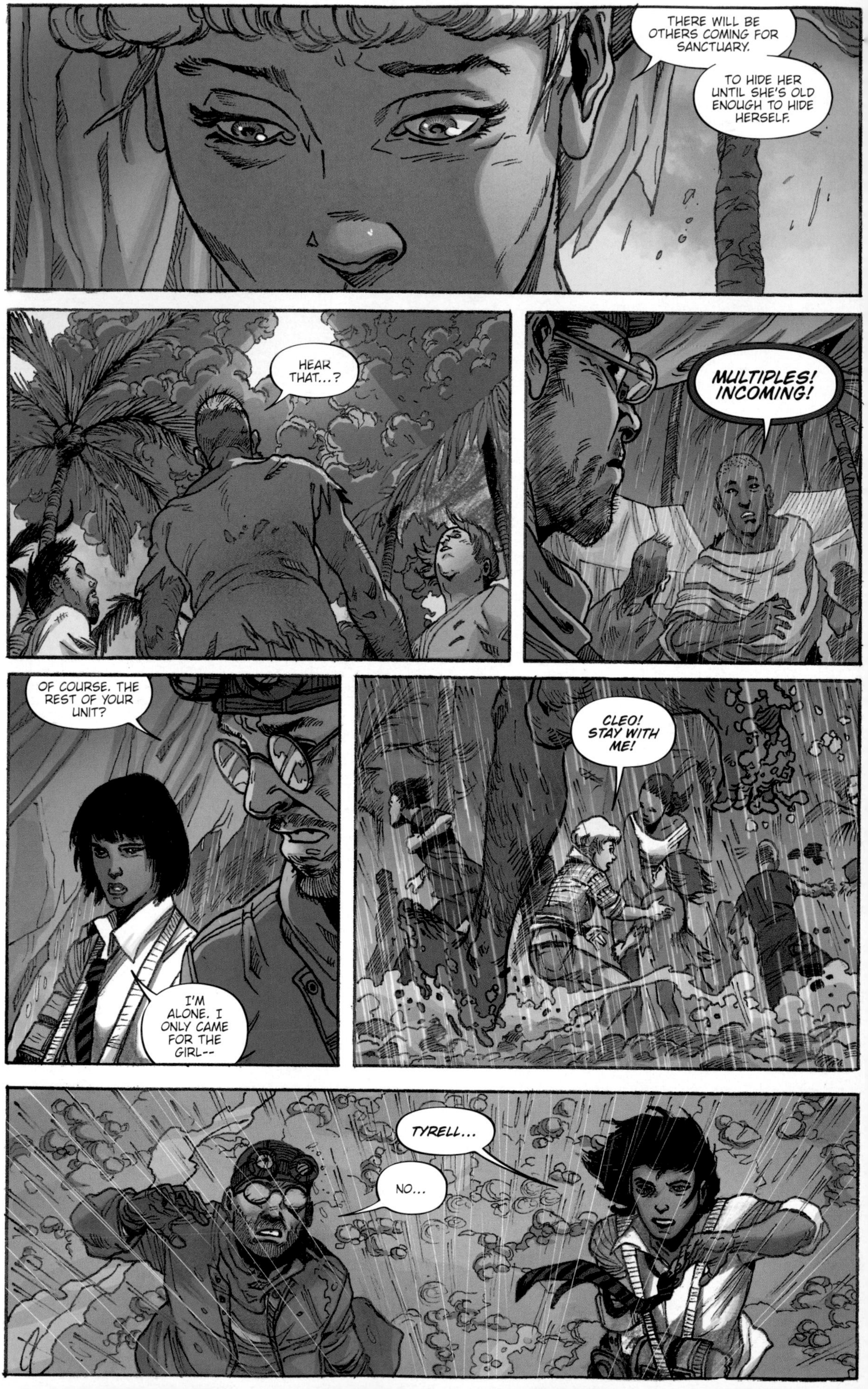
THERE WILL BE OTHERS COMING FOR SANCTUARY.
TO HIDE HER UNTIL SHE'S OLD ENOUGH TO HIDE HERSELF.
HEAR THAT...?
MULTIPLES! INCOMING!
OF COURSE. THE REST OF YOUR UNIT?
I'M ALONE. I ONLY CAME FOR THE GIRL--
CLEO! STAY WITH ME!
TYRELL...
NO...

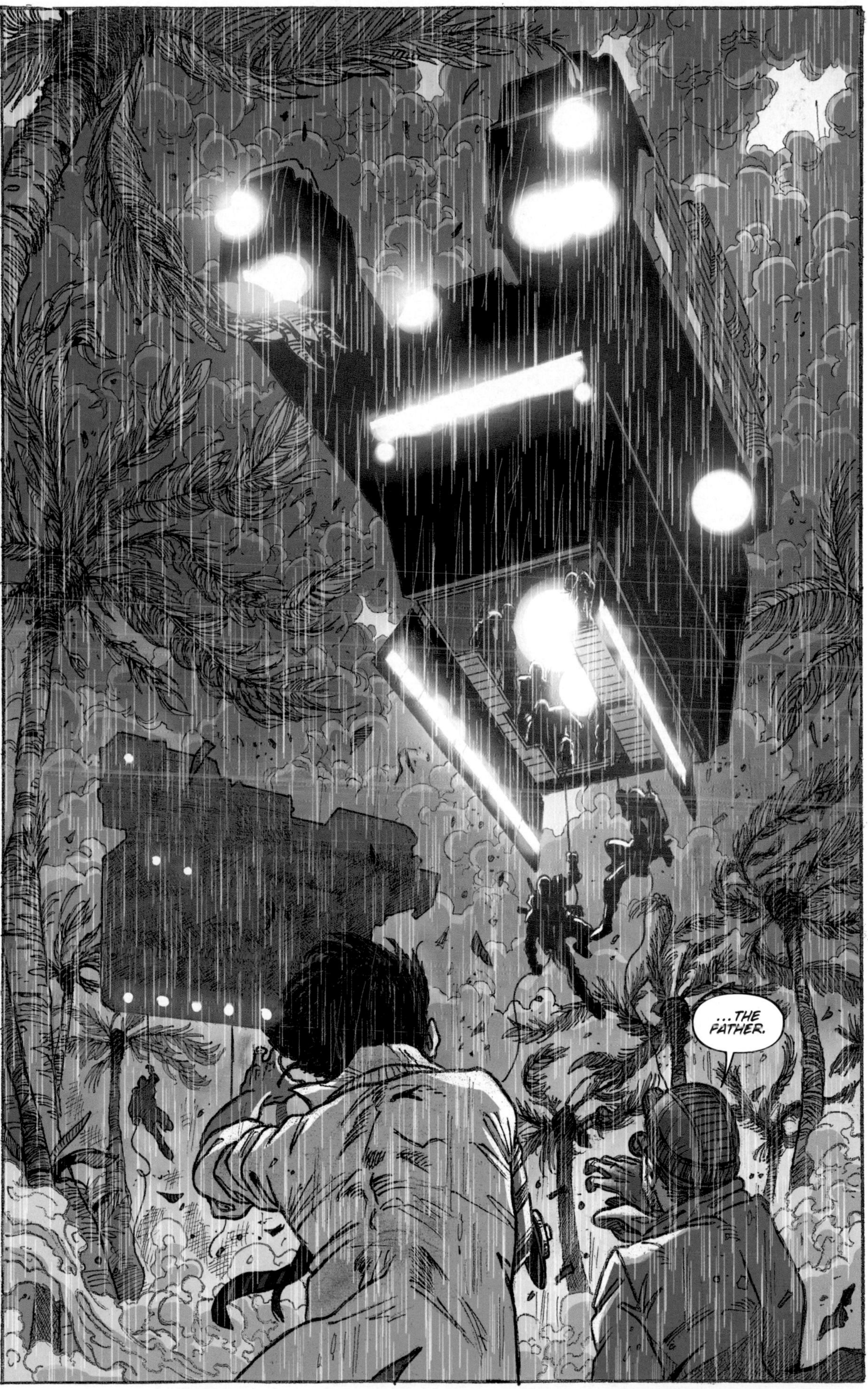
...THE FATHER.

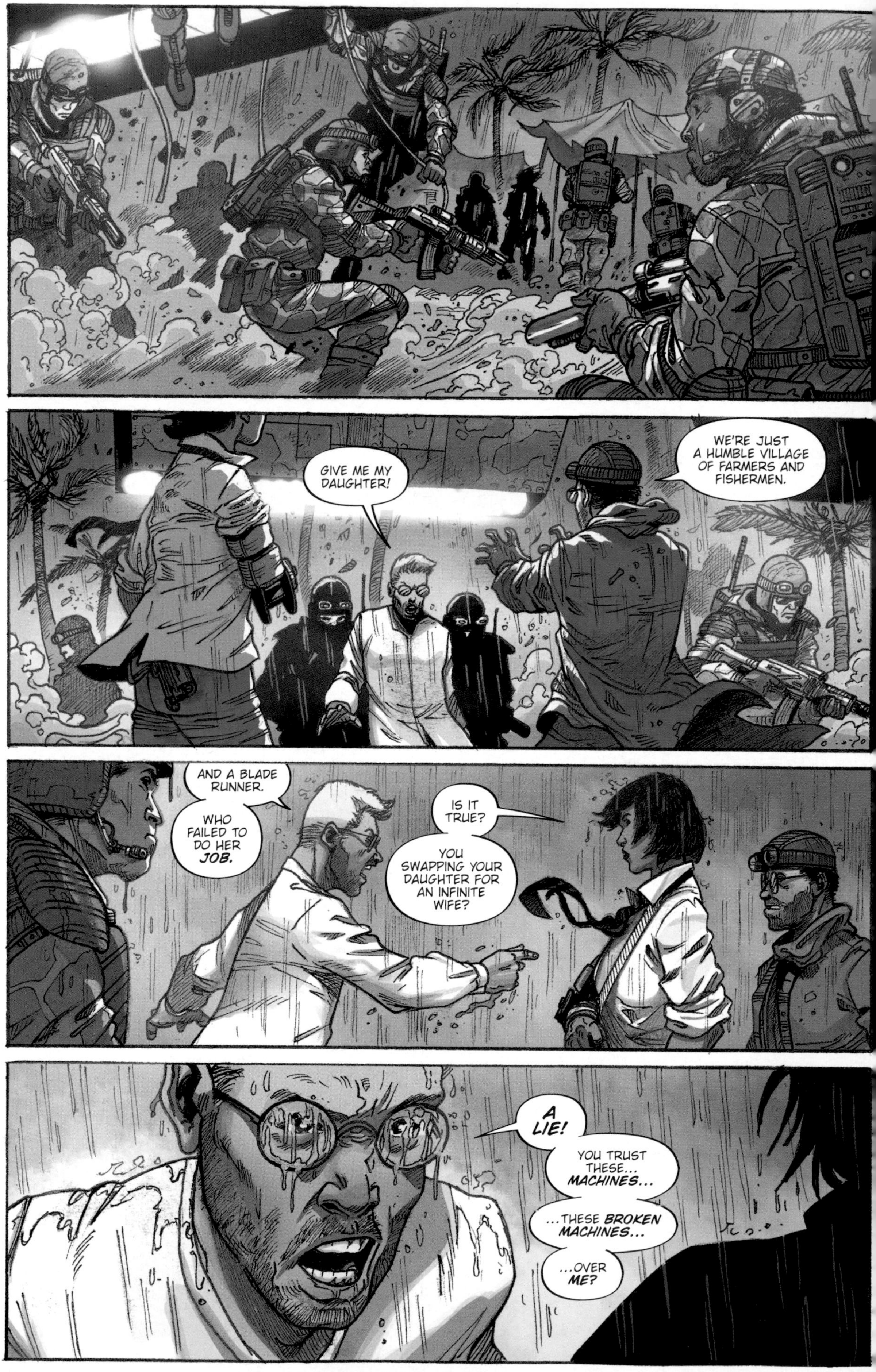

GIVE ME MY DAUGHTER!
WE'RE JUST A HUMBLE VILLAGE OF FARMERS AND FISHERMEN.
AND A BLADE RUNNER.
WHO FAILED TO DO HER JOB.
IS IT TRUE?
YOU SWAPPING YOUR DAUGHTER FOR AN INFINITE WIFE?
A LIE!
YOU TRUST THESE... MACHINES...
...THESE BROKEN MACHINES...
...OVER ME?

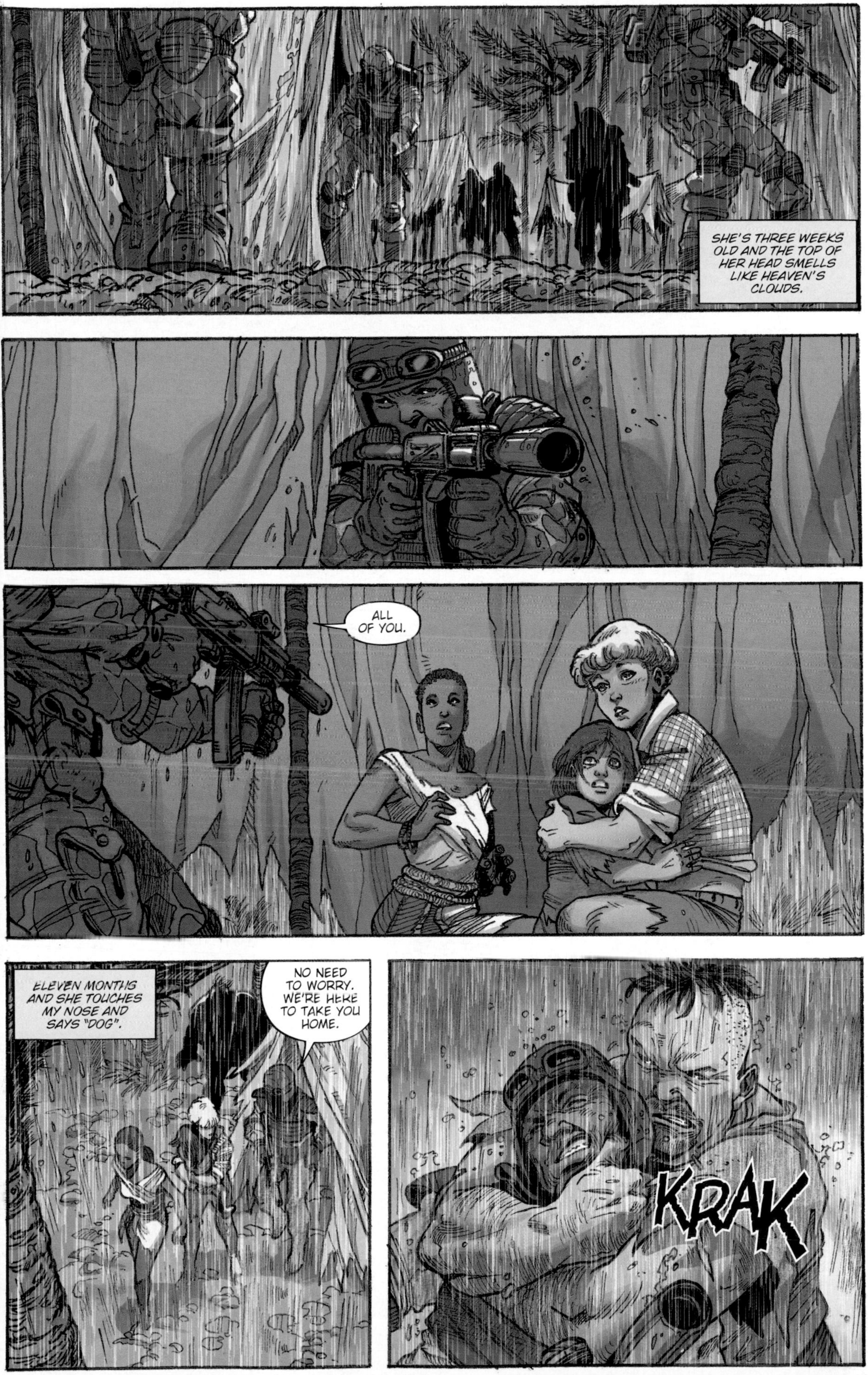
SHE'S THREE WEEKS OLD AND THE TOP OF HER HEAD SMELLS LIKE HEAVEN'S CLOUDS.
ALL OF YOU.
ELEVEN MONTHS AND SHE TOUCHES MY NOSE AND SAYS "DOG".
NO NEED TO WORRY. WE'RE HERE TO TAKE YOU HOME.
KRAK

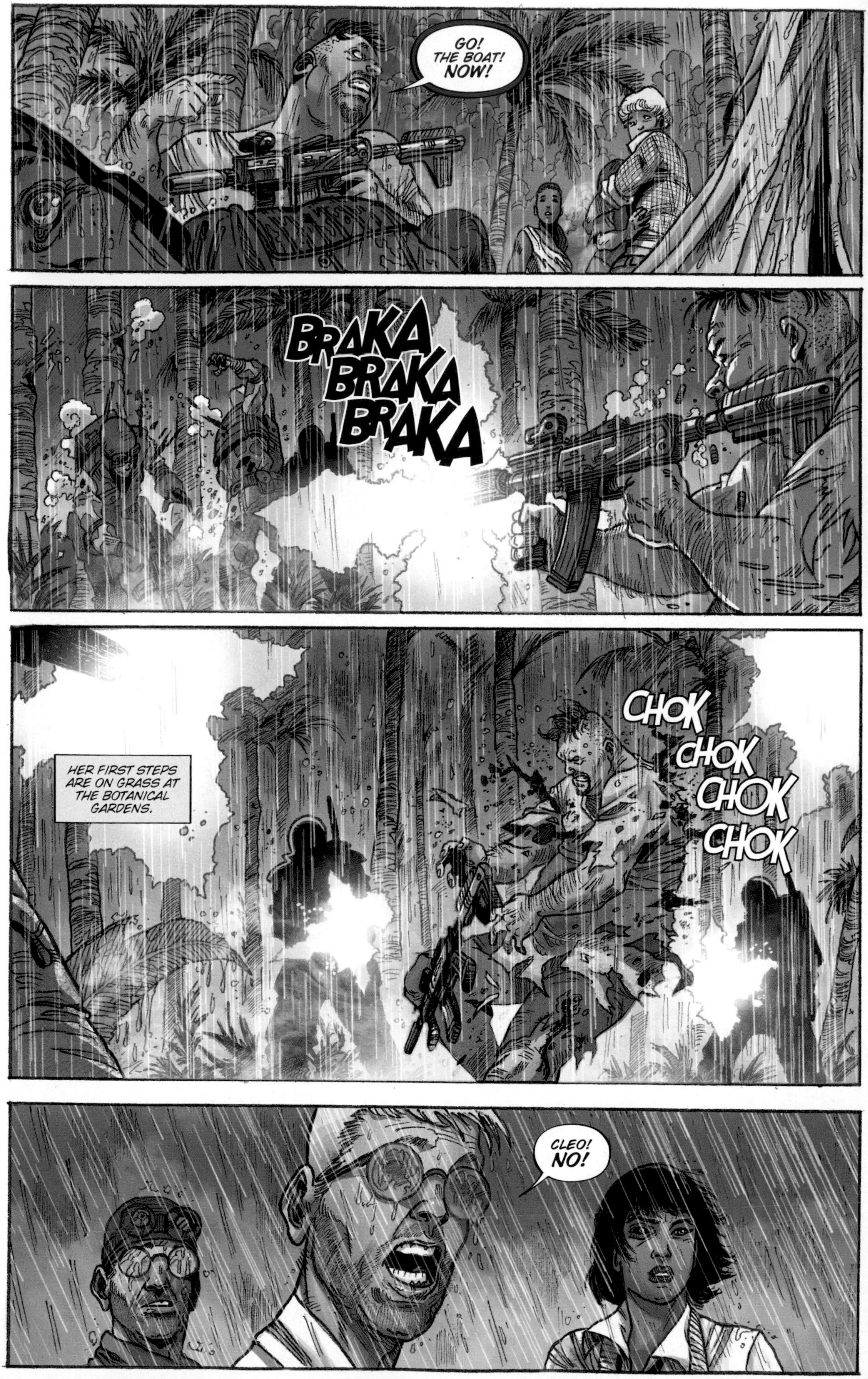
GO! THE BOAT! NOW!
BRAKA BRAKA BRAKA
HER FIRST STEPS ARE ON GRASS AT THE BOTANICAL GARDENS.
CHOK CHOK CHOK CHOK
CLEO! NO!

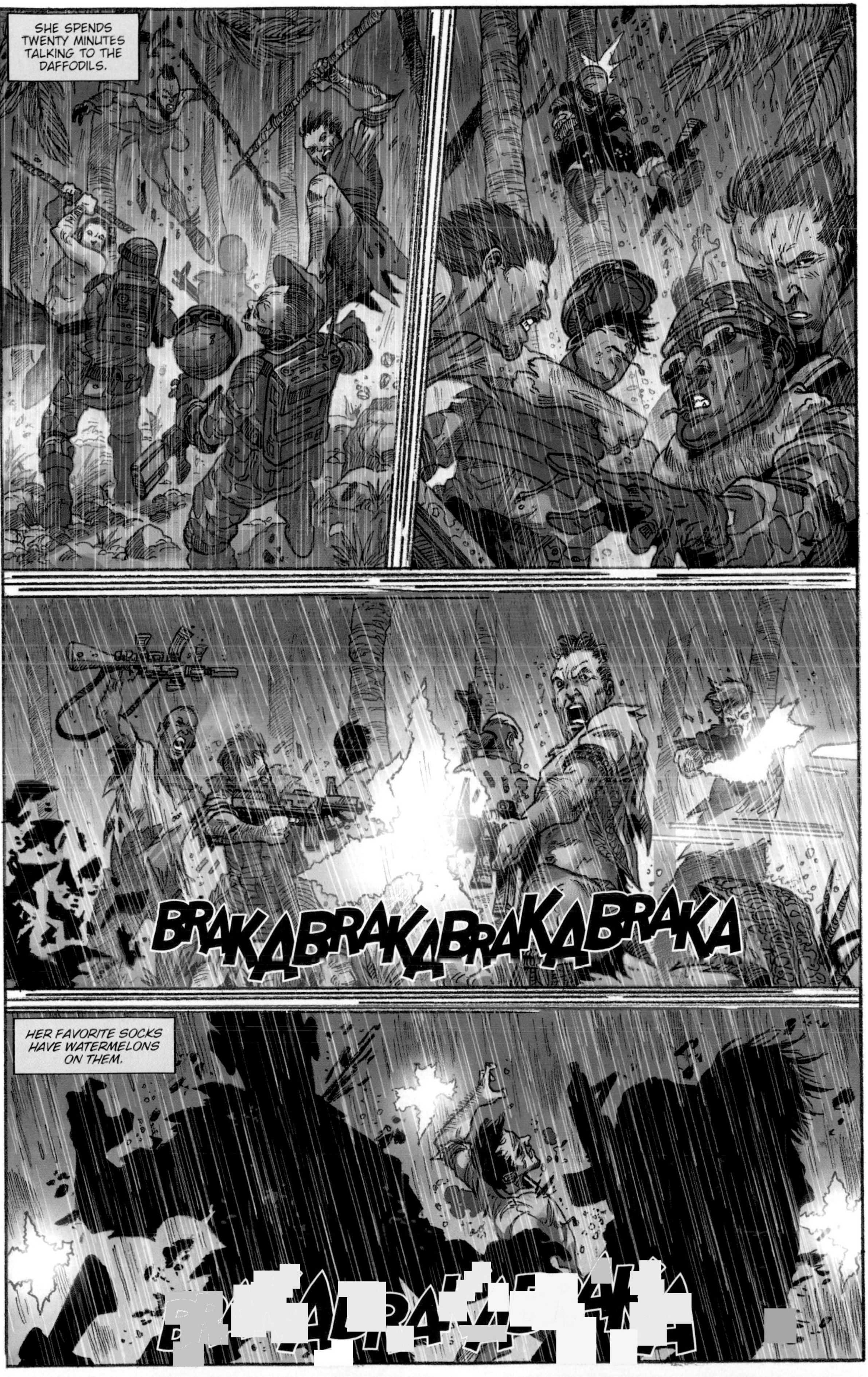
SHE SPENDS TWENTY MINUTES TALKING TO THE DAFFODILS.
BRAKABRAKABRAKABRAKA
HER FAVORITE SOCKS HAVE WATERMELONS ON THEM.

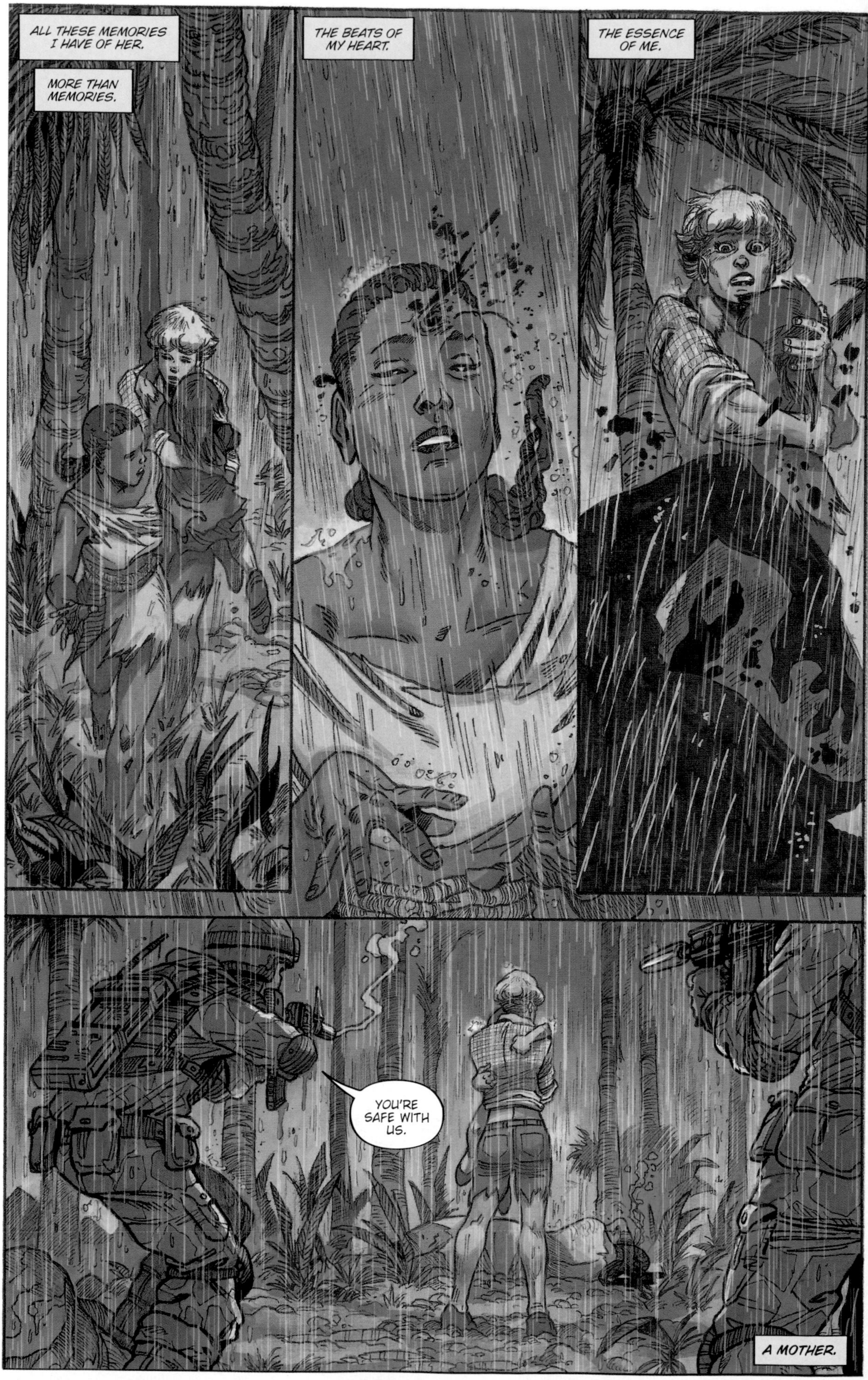
ALL THESE MEMORIES I HAVE OF HER.
MORE THAN MEMORIES.
THE BEATS OF MY HEART.
THE ESSENCE OF ME.
YOU'RE SAFE WITH US.
A MOTHER.

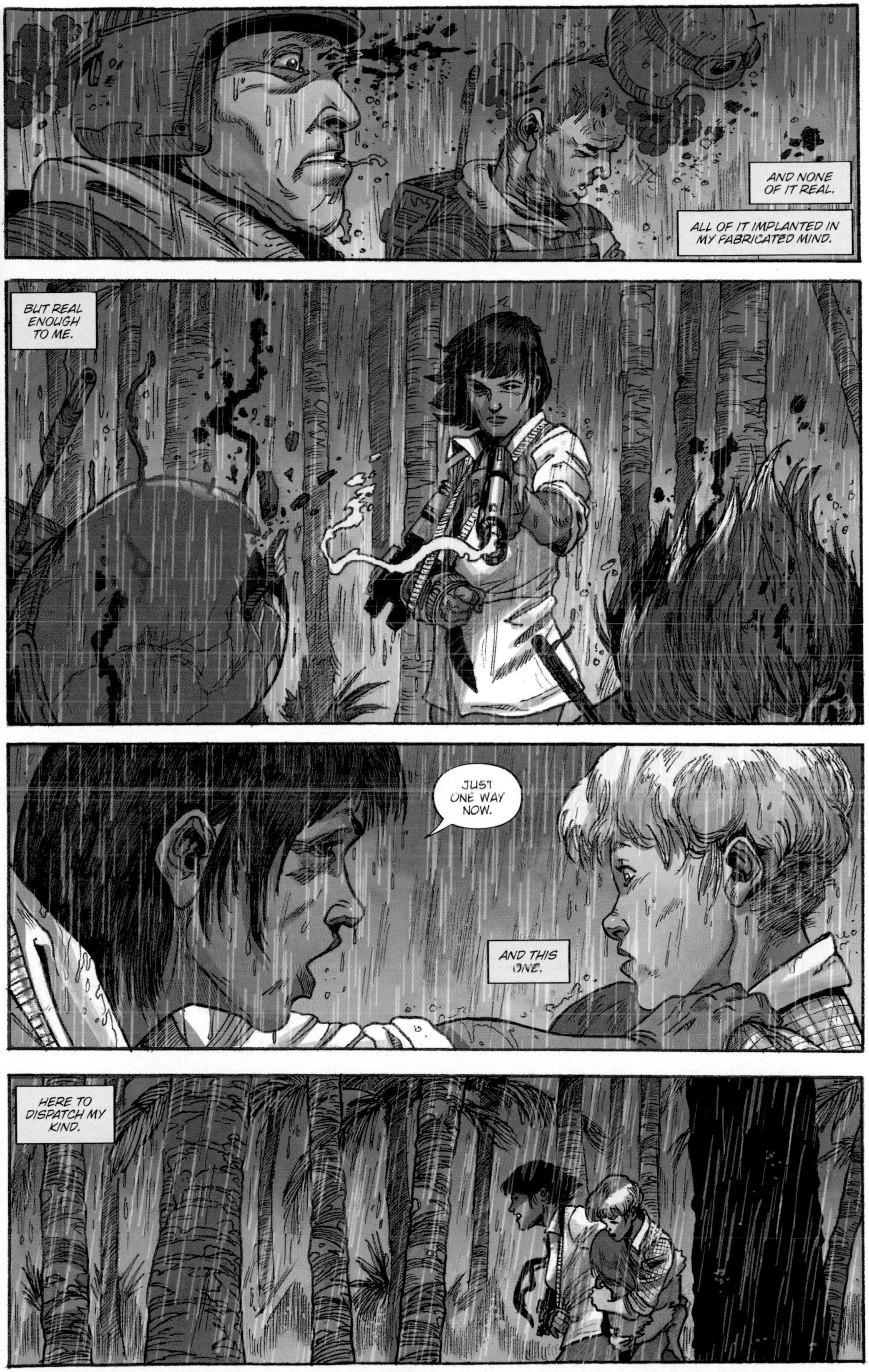
AND NONE OF IT REAL.
ALL OF IT IMPLANTED IN MY FABRICATED MIND.
BUT REAL ENOUGH TO ME.
JUST ONE WAY NOW.
AND THIS ONE.
HERE TO DISPATCH MY KIND.

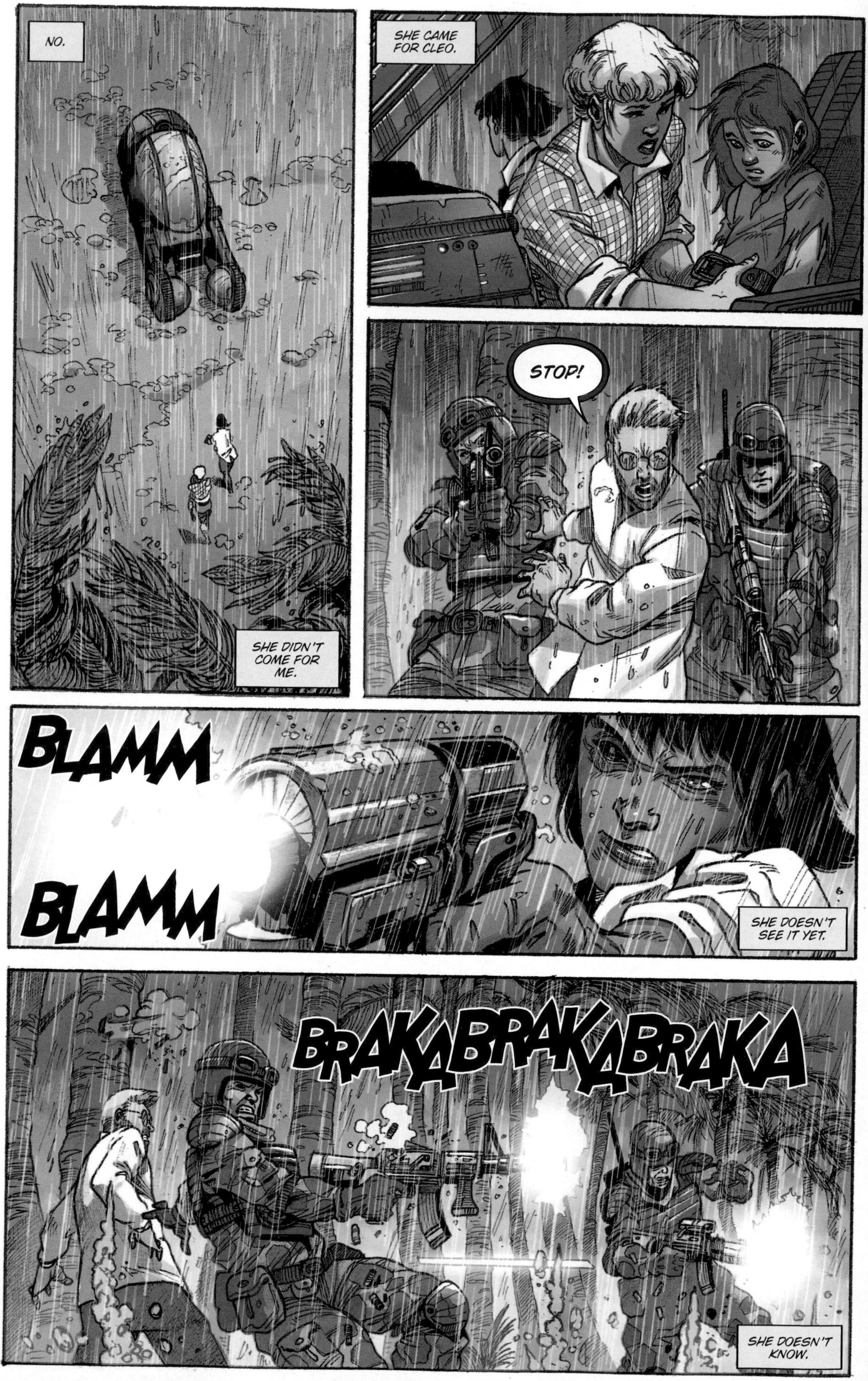
NO.
SHE DIDN'T COME FOR ME.
SHE CAME FOR CLEO.
STOP!
BLAMM
BLAMM
SHE DOESN'T SEE IT YET.
BRAKABRAKABRAKA
SHE DOESN'T KNOW.

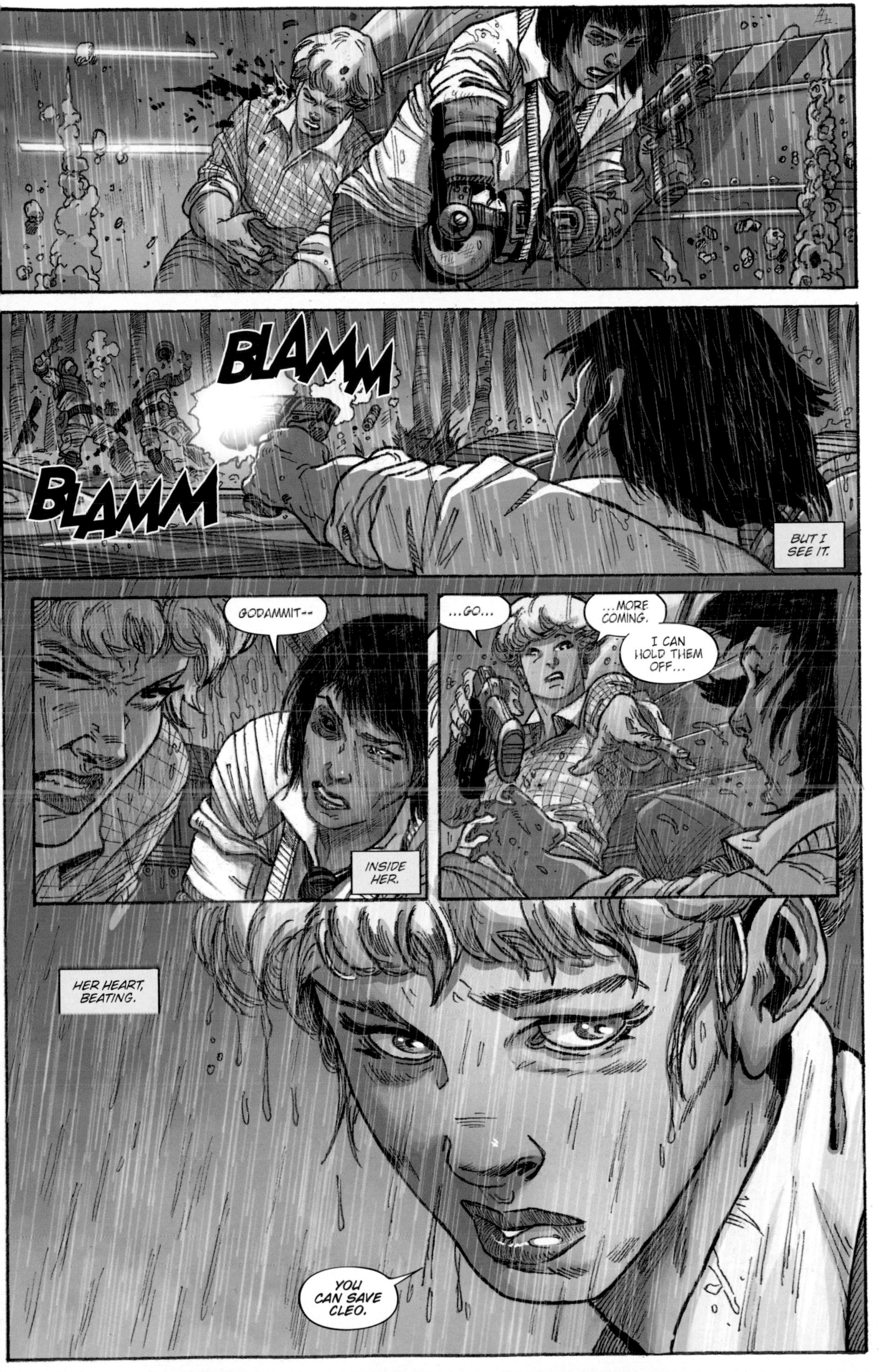

BLAMM
BLAMM
BUT I SEE IT.
GODAMMIT--
INSIDE HER.
...GO...
...MORE COMING.
I CAN HOLD THEM OFF...
HER HEART, BEATING.
YOU CAN SAVE CLEO.

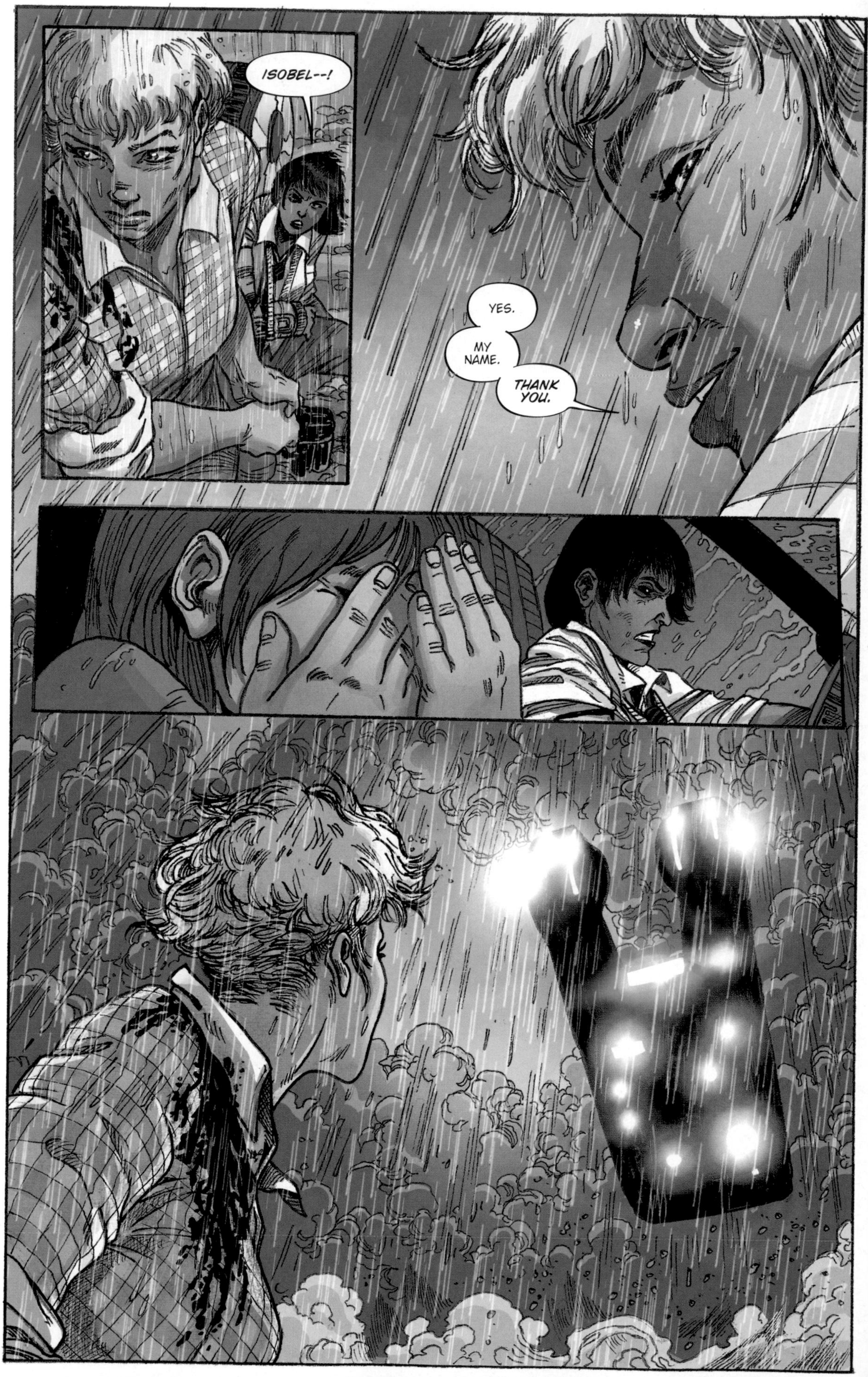
ISOBEL--!
YES.
MY NAME.
THANK YOU.

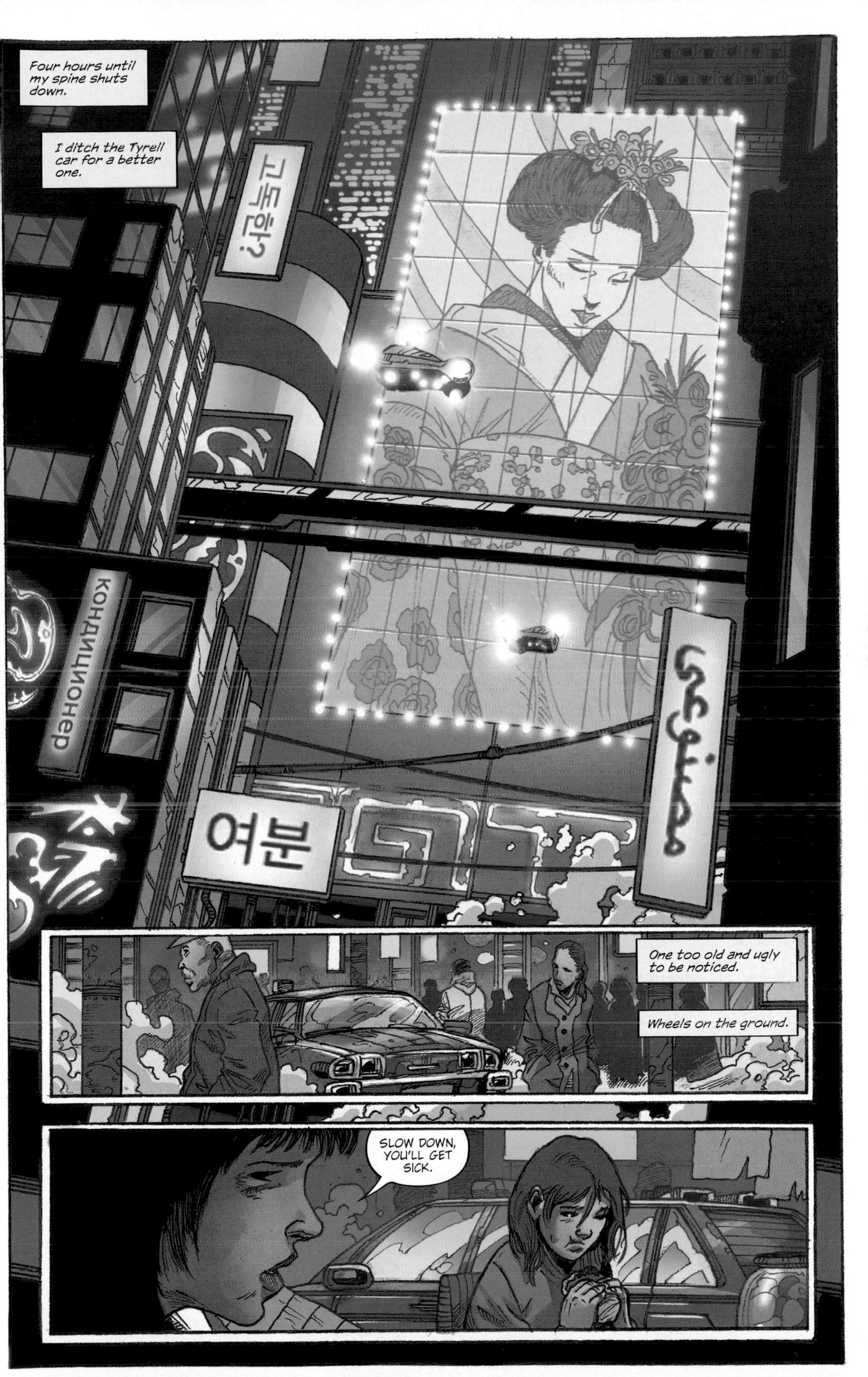

Four hours until my spine shuts down.
I ditch the Tyrell car for a better one.
여분
One too old and ugly to be noticed.
Wheels on the ground.
SLOW DOWN, YOU'LL GET SICK.

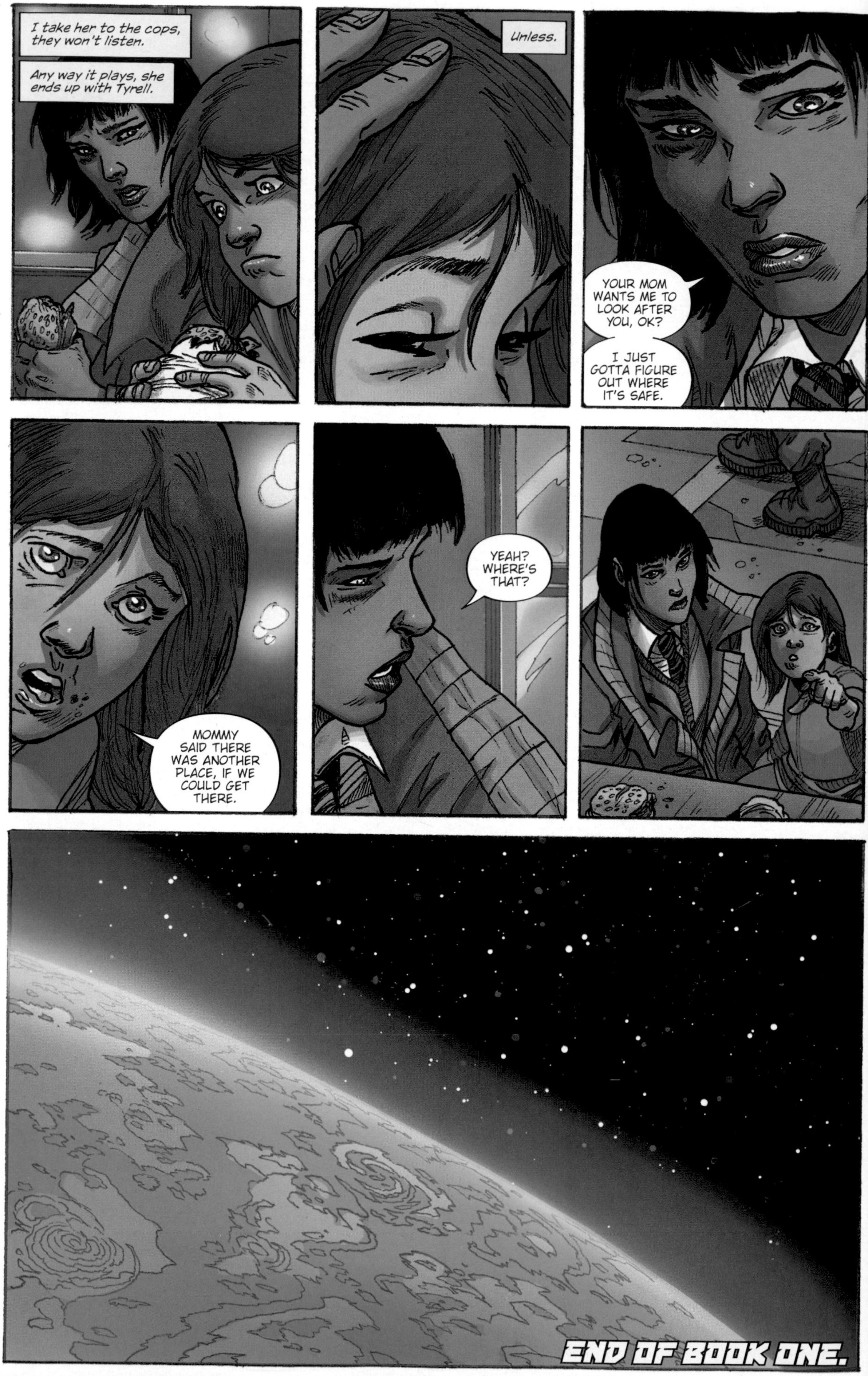
I take her to the cops, they won't listen.
Any way it plays, she ends up with Tyrell.
Unless.
YOUR MOM WANTS ME TO LOOK AFTER YOU, OK?
I JUST GOTTA FIGURE OUT WHERE IT'S SAFE.
MOMMY SAID THERE WAS ANOTHER PLACE, IF WE COULD GET THERE.
YEAH? WHERE'S THAT?
END OF BOOK ONE.

# COVER GALLERY

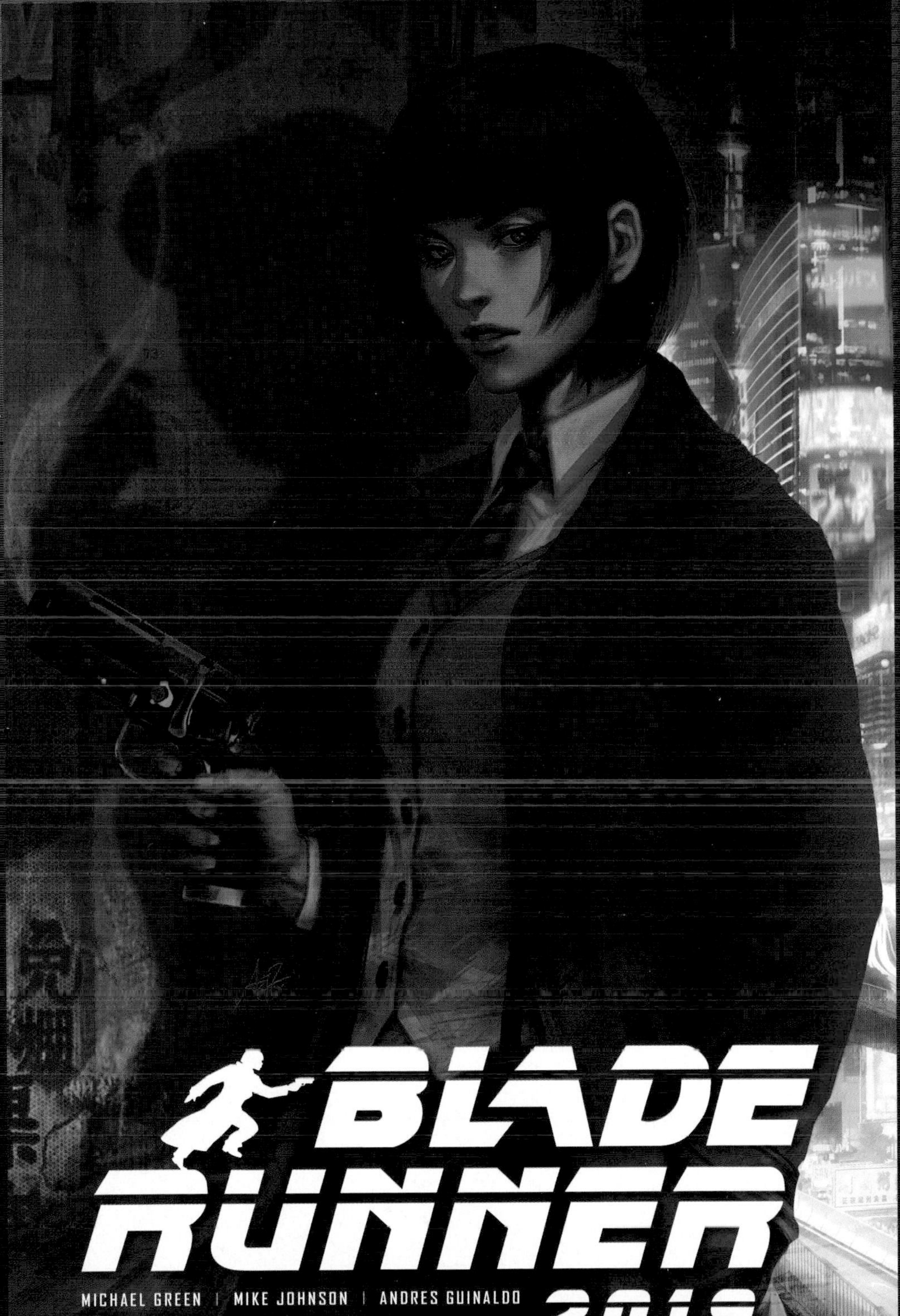
BLADE RUNNER
MICHAEL GREEN | MIKE JOHNSON | ANDRES GUINALDO
2019

BLADE RUNNER 2019
ISSUE ONE

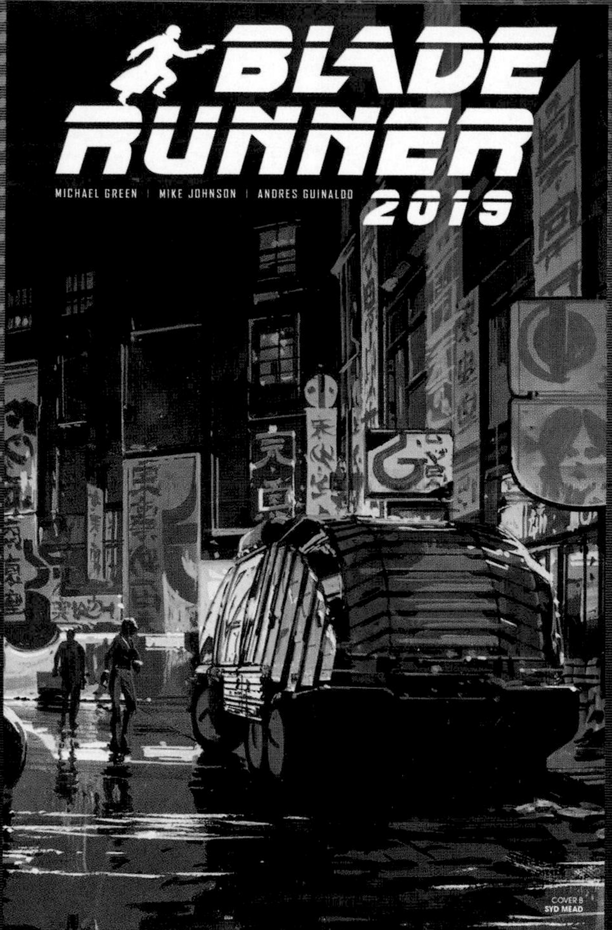
BLADE RUNNER
MICHAEL GREEN | MIKE JOHNSON | ANDRES GUINALDO
2019
COVER B
SYD MEAD

COVER B
SYD MEAD

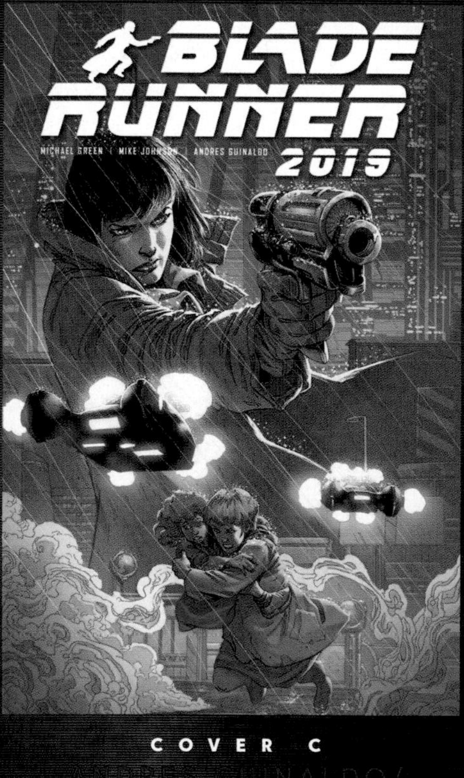
BLADE RUNNER
MICHAEL GREEN | MIKE JOHNSON | ANDRES GUINALDO
2019

COVER C
ANDRES GUINALDO/
MARCO LESKO

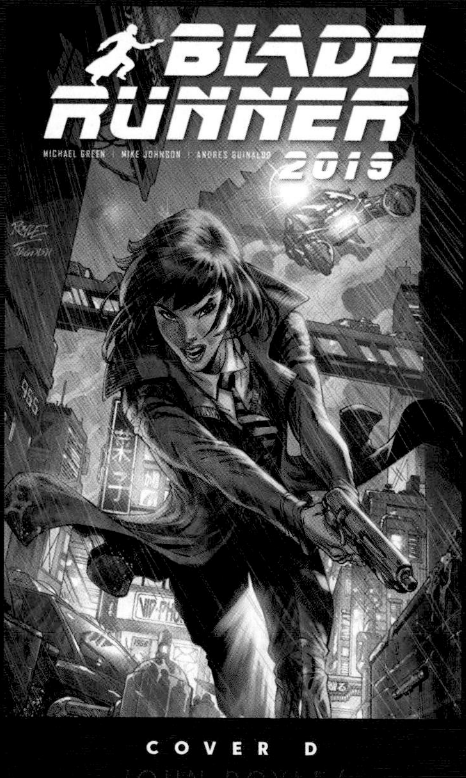
BLADE RUNNER
MICHAEL GREEN | MIKE JOHNSON | ANDRES GUINALDO
2019

COVER D
JOHN ROYLE/
JAGDISH KUMAR

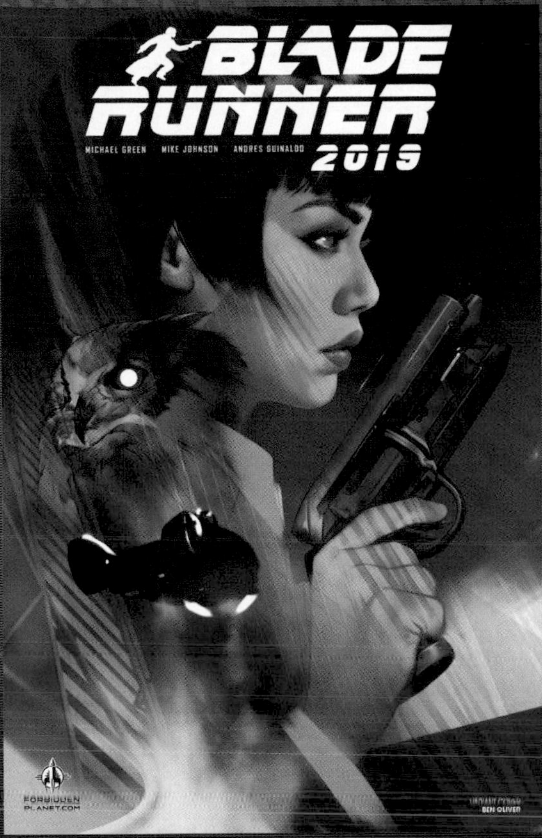
BLADE RUNNER
2019
MICHAEL GREEN
MIKE JOHNSON
ANDRES GUINALDO
FORBIDDEN
PLANET.COM
BEN OLIVER

FORBIDDEN PLANET
VARIANT
BEN OLIVER

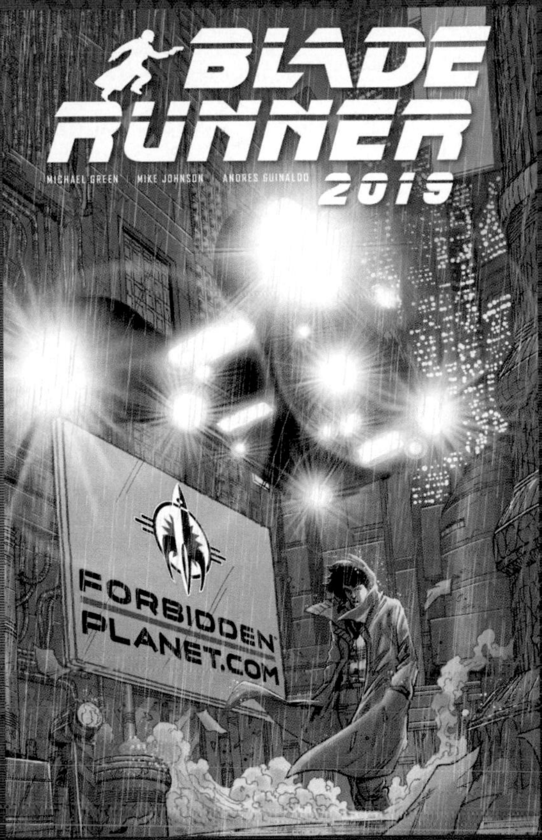
BLADE RUNNER
2019
MICHAEL GREEN
MIKE JOHNSON
ANDRES GUINALDO
FORBIDDEN
PLANET.COM

FORBIDDEN PLANET
EXCLUSIVE
ANDRES GUINALDO / MARCO LESKO

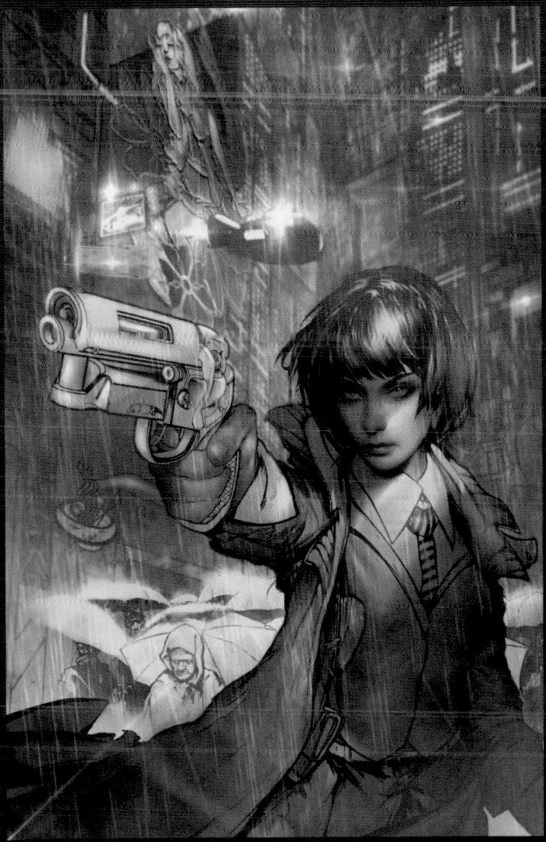

COMIX EXCLUSIVE
DAN QUINTANA

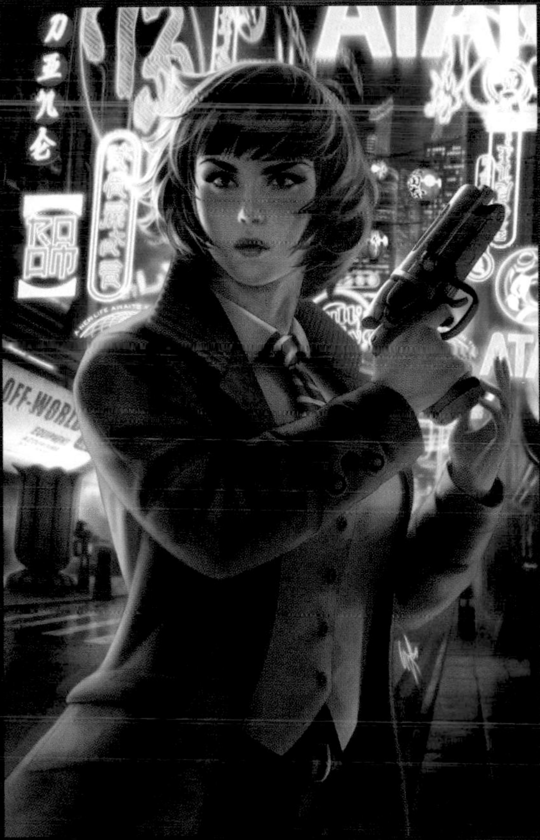
OFF-WORLD

KRS EXCLUSIVE
WARREN LOUW

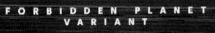

BLADE RUNNER 2019
ISSUE TWO

"10 out of 10. A must-read title."
- Bleeding Cool
BLADE RUNNER
2019
MICHAEL GREEN | MIKE JOHNSON | ANDRES GUINALDO

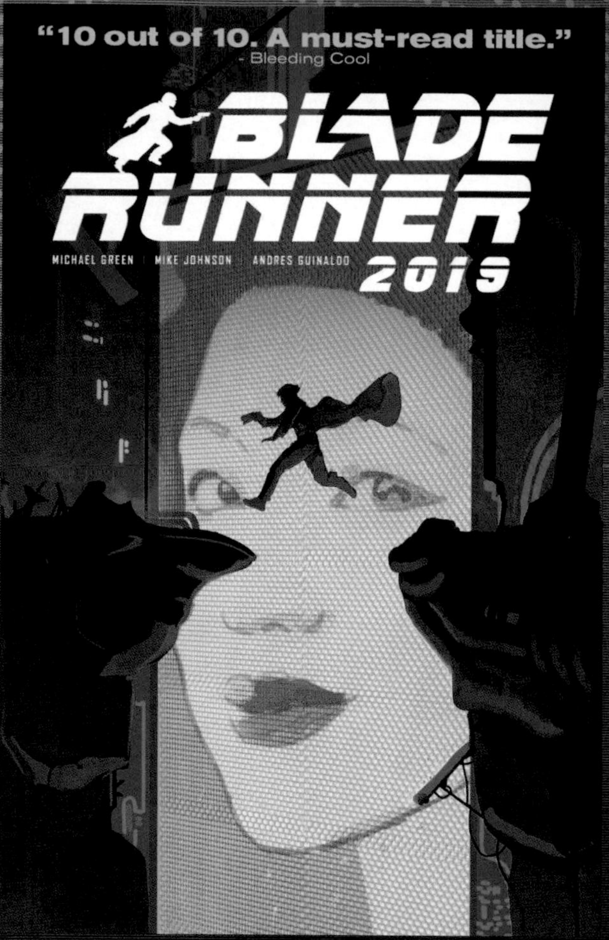

COVER A
CHRISTIAN WARD

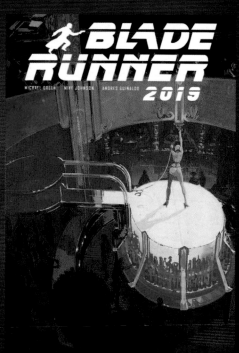

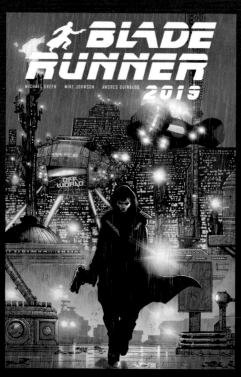

BLADE RUNNER
2019
MICHAEL GREEN | MIKE JOHNSON | ANDRES GUINALDO

COVER B
SYD MEAD

BLADE RUNNER
2019
MICHAEL GREEN | MIKE JOHNSON | ANDRES GUINALDO
OFF WORLD

COVER C
ANDRES GUINALDO/
MARCO LESKO

**BLADE RUNNER 2019**
ISSUE THREE

BLADE RUNNER
2019

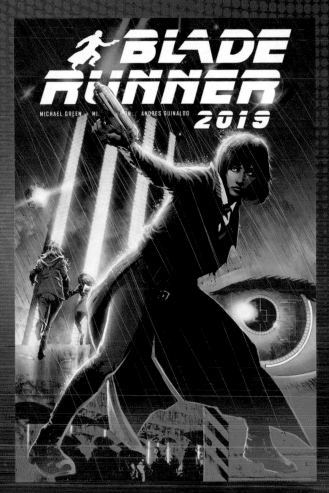

COVER A
BUTCH GUICE

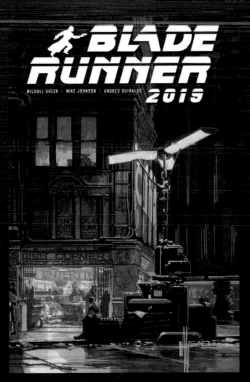

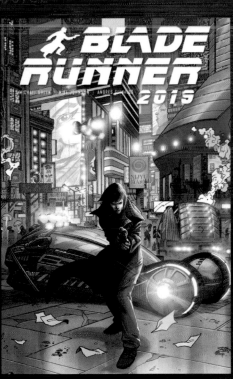

BLADE RUNNER
MICHAEL GREEN | MIKE JOHNSON | ANDRES GUINALDO
2019

COVER B
SYD MEAD

BLADE RUNNER
2019

COVER C
ANDRES GUINALDO/
MARCO LESKO

BLADE RUNNER 2019
ISSUE FOUR

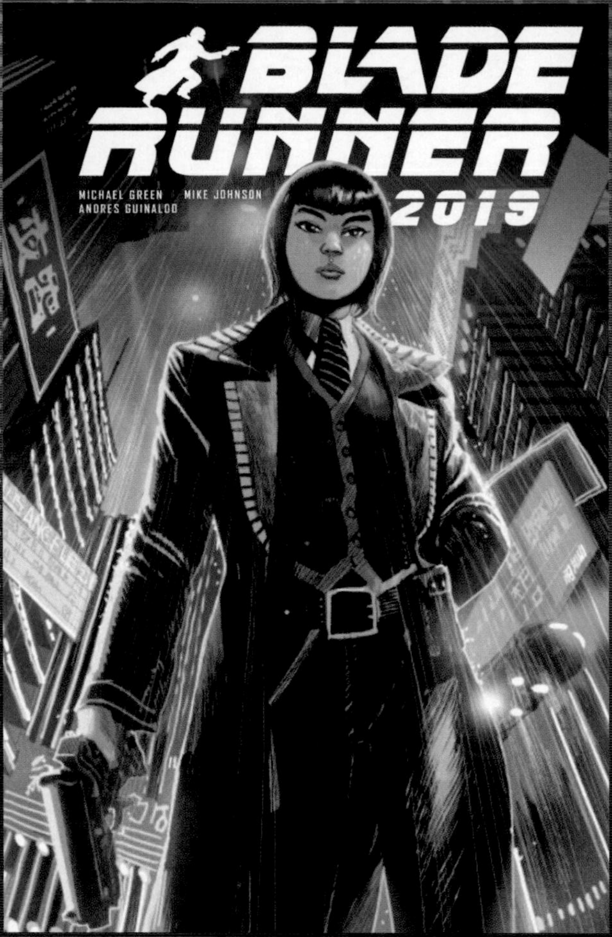
BLADE RUNNER 2019
MICHAEL GREEN | MIKE JOHNSON
ANDRES GUINALDO

COVER A
RAFAEL ALBUQUERQUE

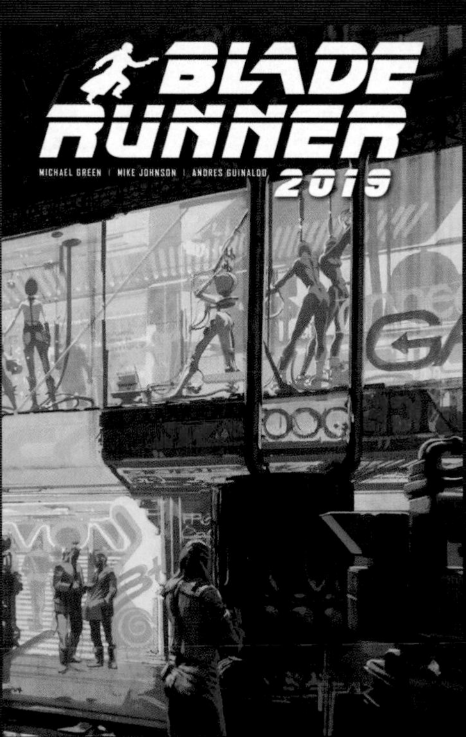
BLADE RUNNER 2019
MICHAEL GREEN | MIKE JOHNSON | ANDRES GUINALDO

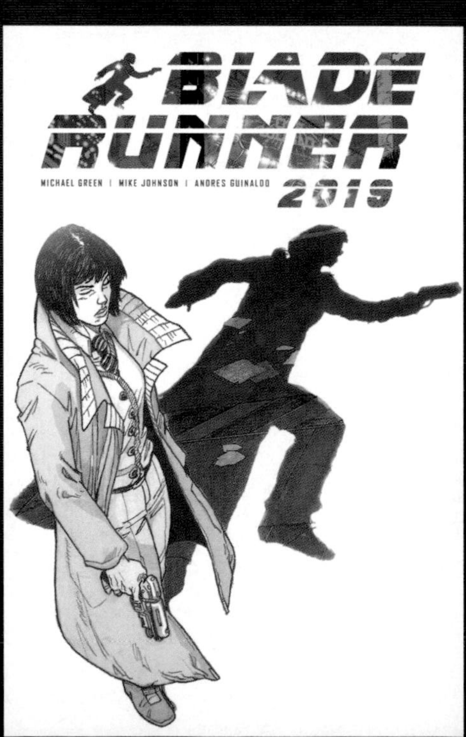
BLADE RUNNER 2019
MICHAEL GREEN | MIKE JOHNSON | ANDRES GUINALDO

# COVER DEVELOPMENT

Each cover artist supplied cover roughs (called 'scamps') for the editorial team to choose from. Presented here are a selection of scamps, from artists Andres Guinaldo, John Royle, Christian Ward, Butch Guice and Paul Pope.

**ISSUE #1-4**
ANDRES GUINALDO

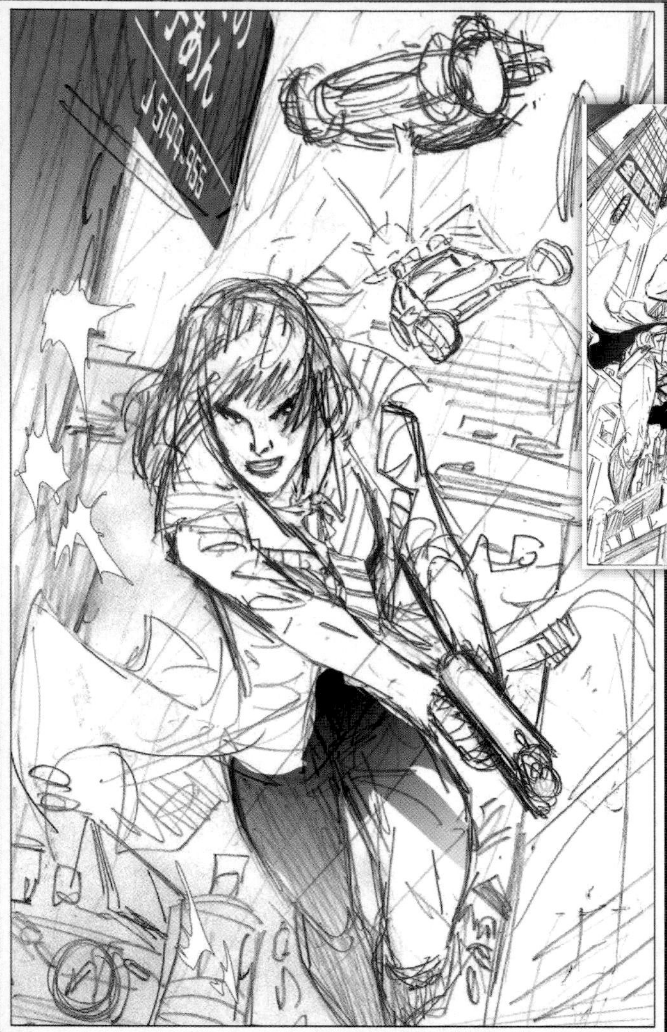

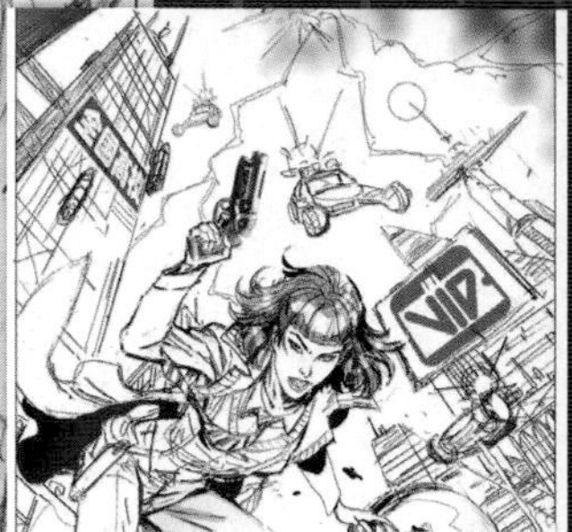

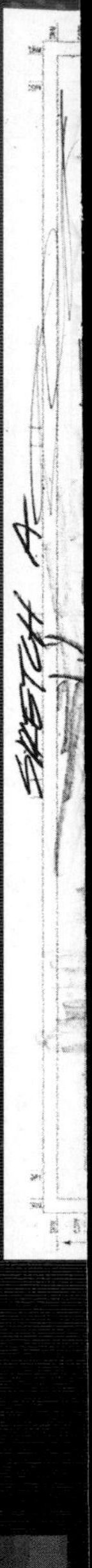
SKETCH A

**ISSUE #1**

JOHN ROYLE

Two of John Royle's cover scamps.

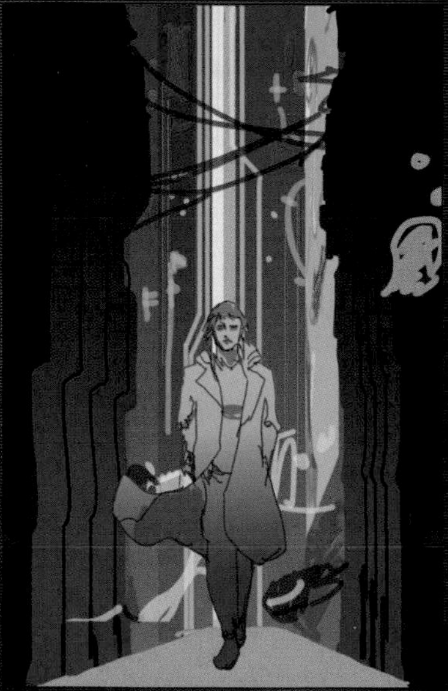

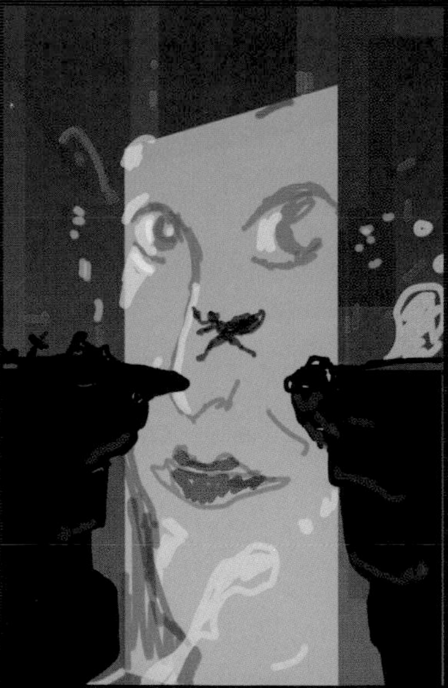

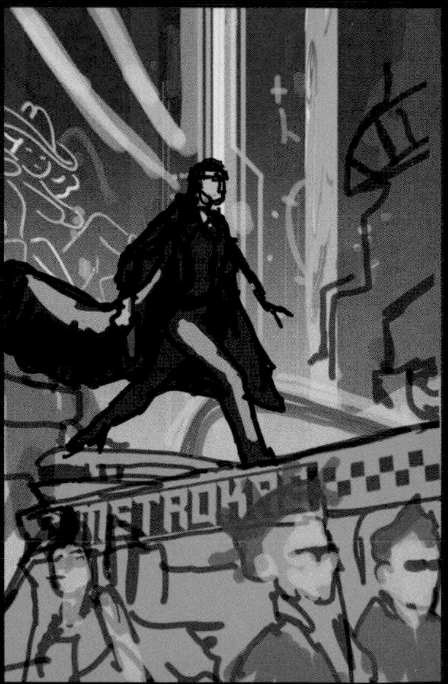

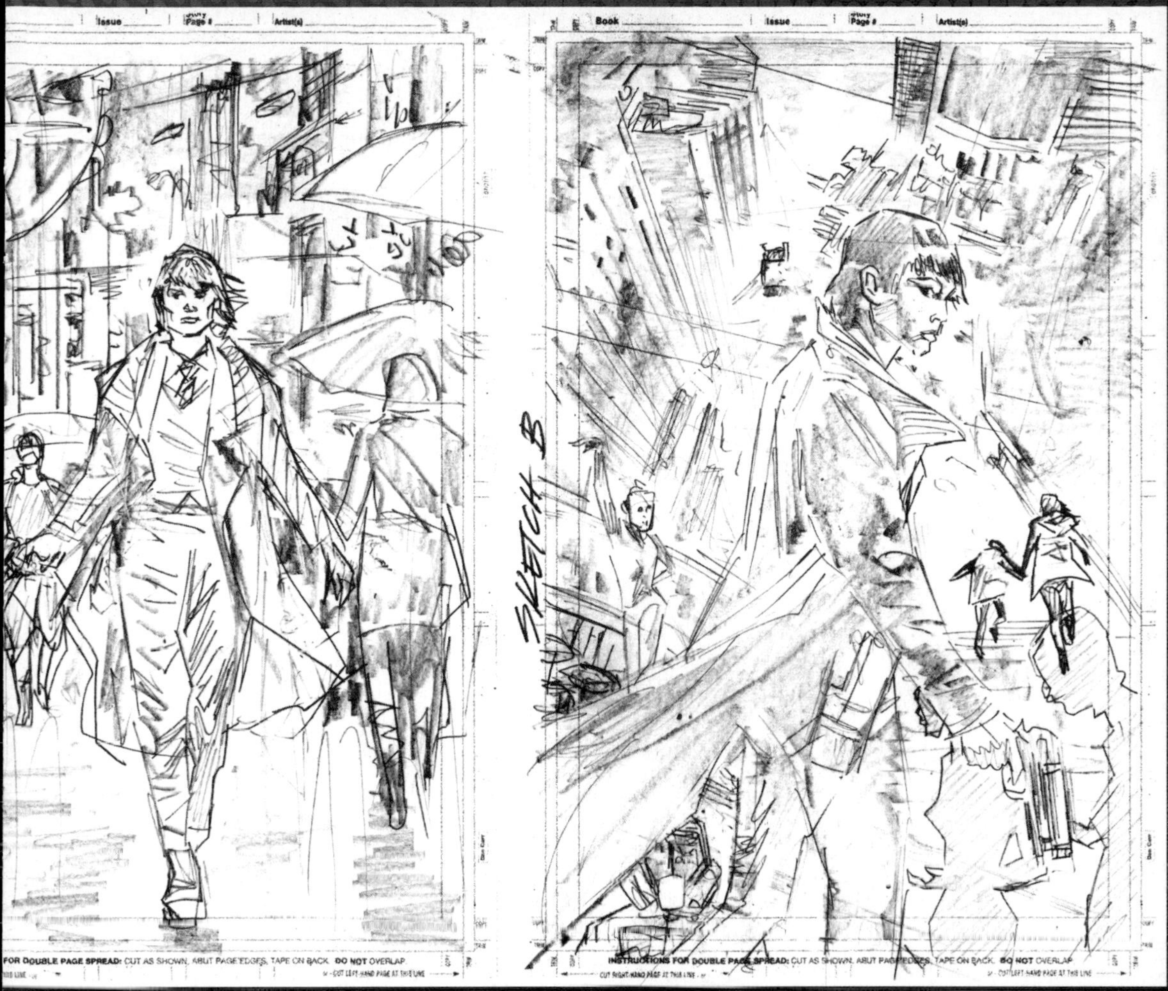
Book
Issue
Artist(s)
SKETCH B
INSTRUCTIONS FOR DOUBLE PAGE SPREAD: CUT AS SHOWN, ABUT PAGE EDGES, TAPE ON BACK. DO NOT OVERLAP

## ISSUE #3

BUTCH GUICE

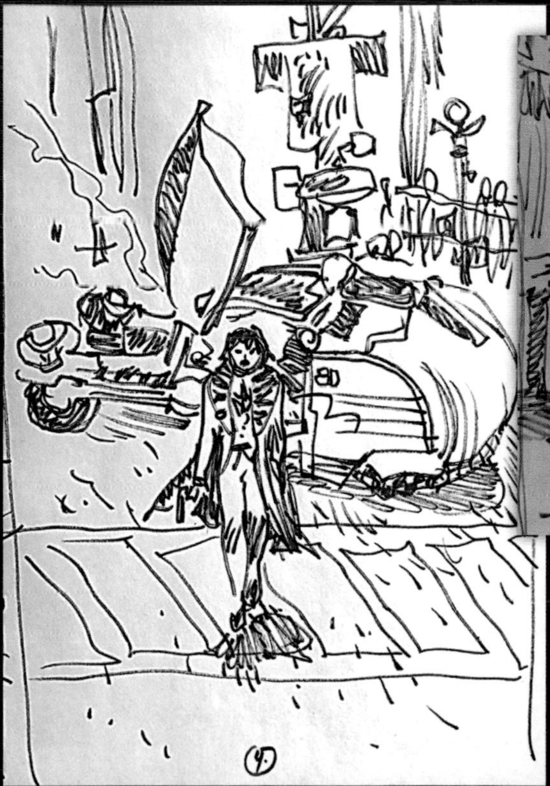

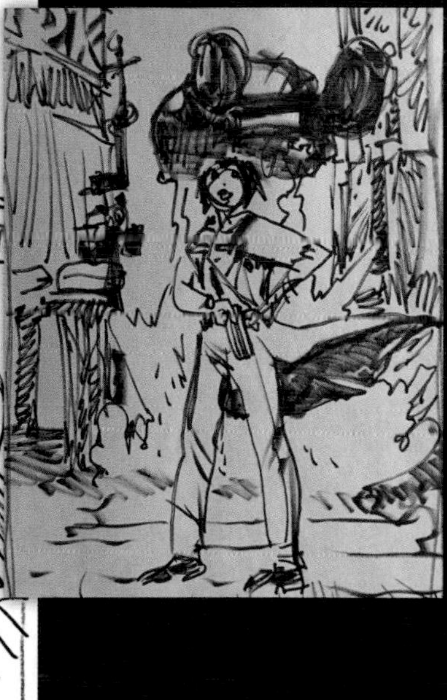

## ISSUE #4

PAUL POPE

Two of Paul Pope's cover scamps. Originally commissioned for issue #4 but would eventually become the cover for issue #5.

# CHARACTER DESIGN

Presented here is a selection Andres Guinaldo's character designs for *Blade Runner 2019*. The design of Ash was based on the following brief description by Michael Green and Mike Johnson. Guinaldo nailed the design almost straight away.

"...Blade Runner, ASH (short for ASHINA; Angeleno born, Indian by blood), wears a trenchcoat to hide something we'll see soon enough. Her hair is short, but styled in a pixie bob. Age approximately late 20s."

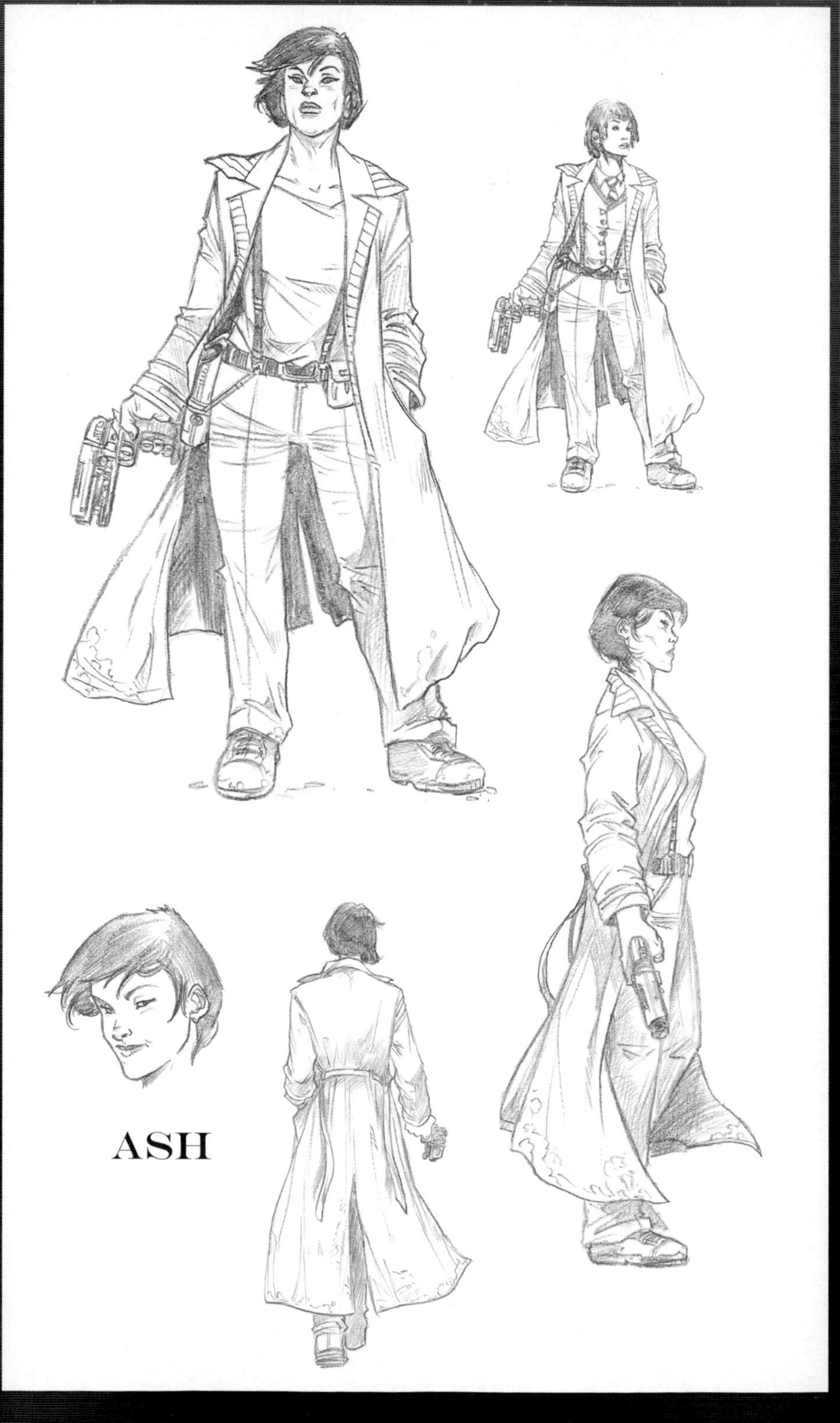
ASH

RIGHT: Andres Guinaldo's initial character sketches. (The waistcoat and braces were a later addition.)

OPPOSITE RIGHT: Secondary character designs, by Andres.

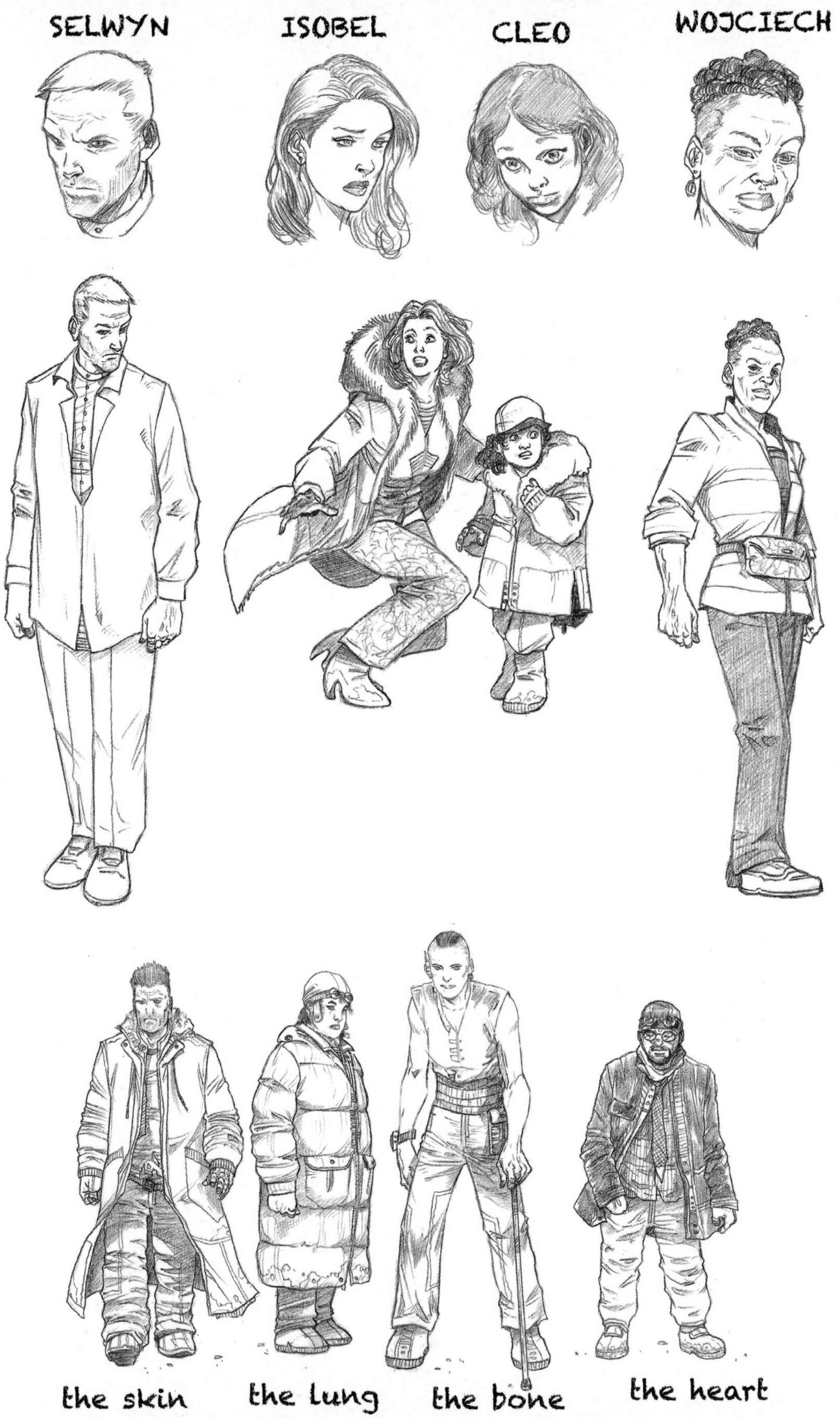
SELWYN
ISOBEL
CLEO
WOJCIECH
the skin
the lung
the bone
the heart

# ANDRES GUINALDO TRYOUT SAMPLE

The final shortlist for a suitable Blade Runner artist came down to three. Each artist was sent a sample two-page script written by the Editor. Presented here and published for the first time ever is Andres Guinaldo's two page tryout. Also presented are Marco Lesko's color tryout pages.

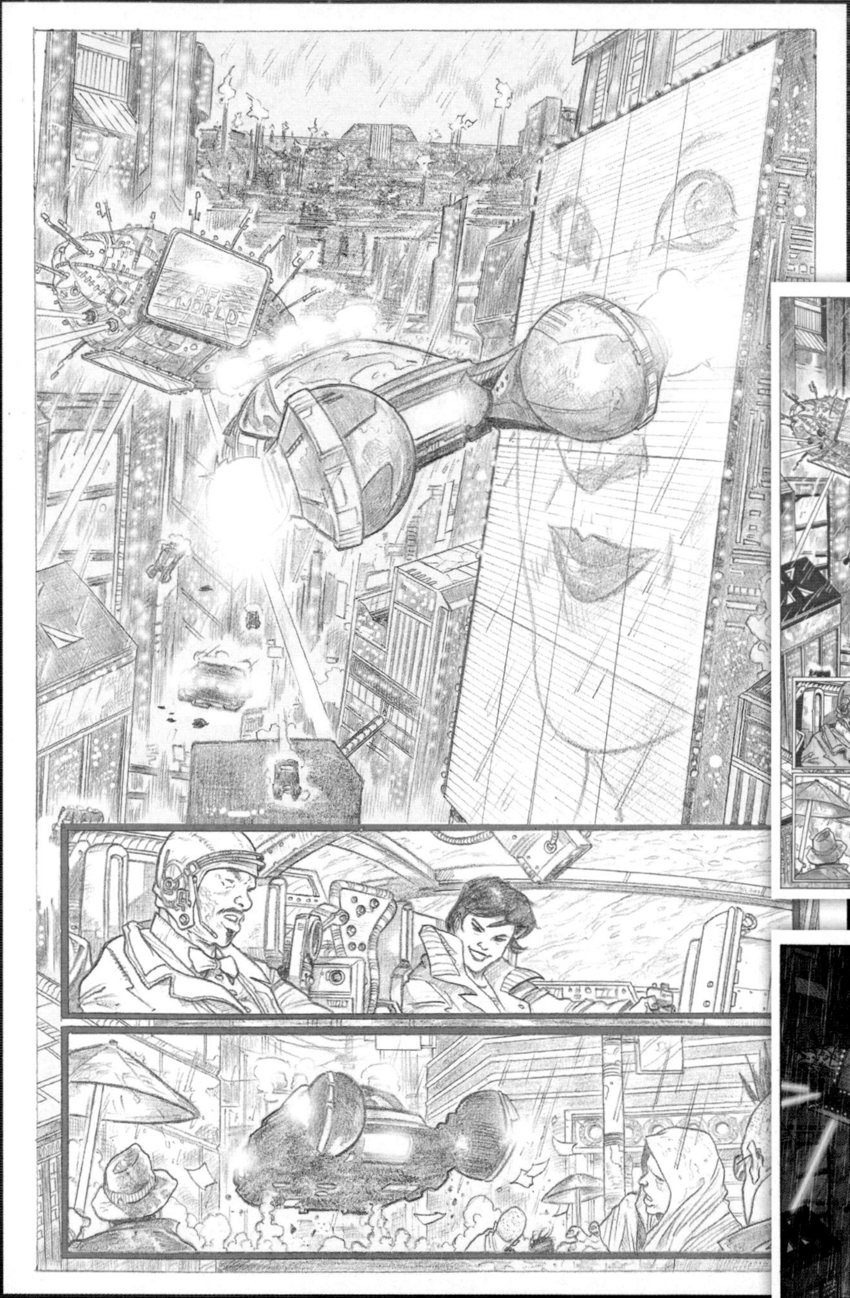
OFF WORLD

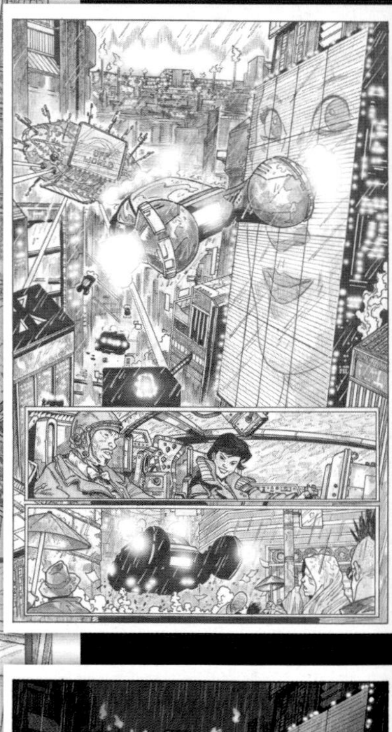

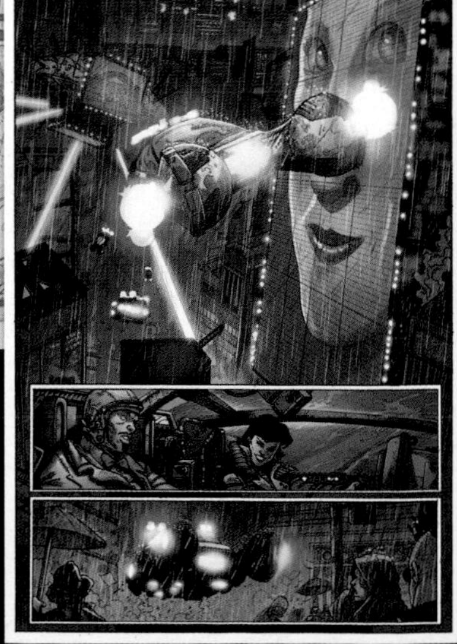

TOP MAIN: Pencils for page one. The script was written to showcase how the artist would handle both cityscapes and action sequences. RIGHT TOP. Andres' inks for page one. BOTTOM RIGHT: Marco Lesko's color tryout.

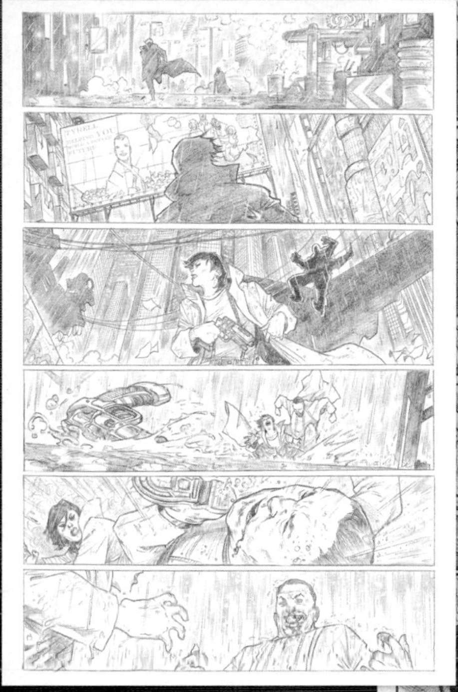

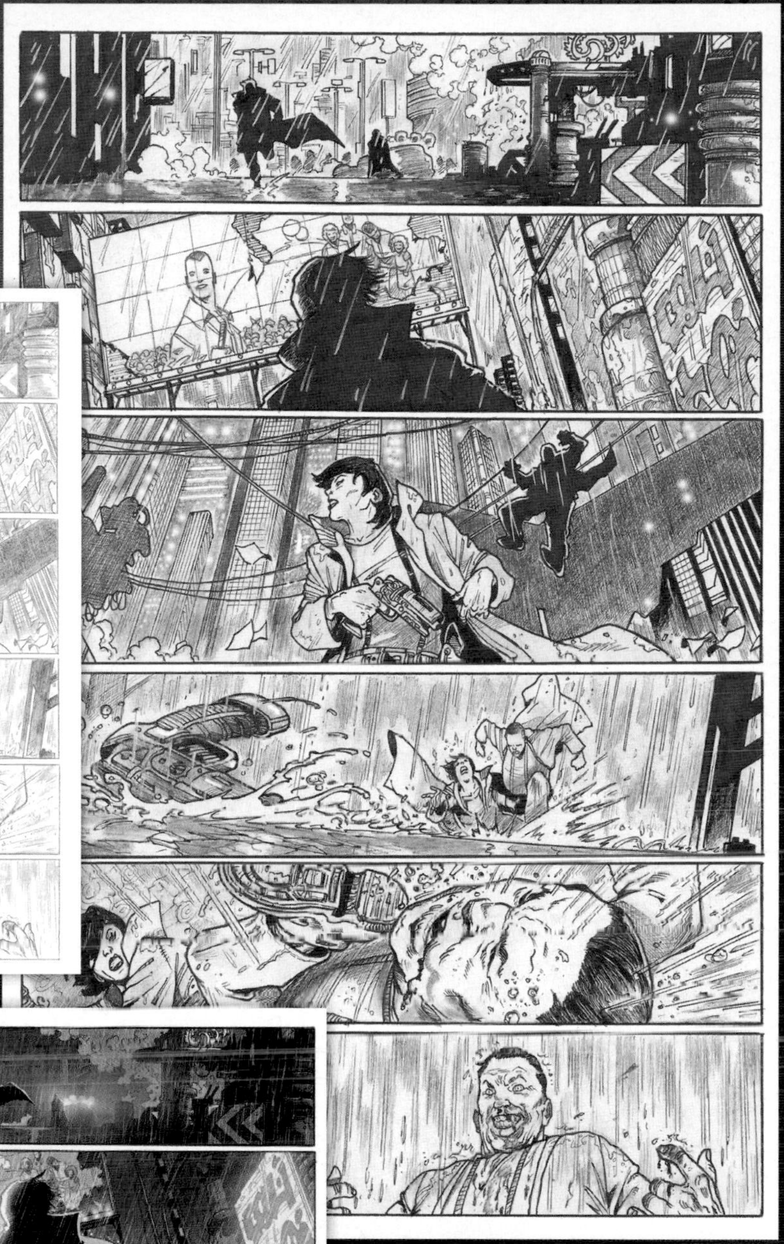

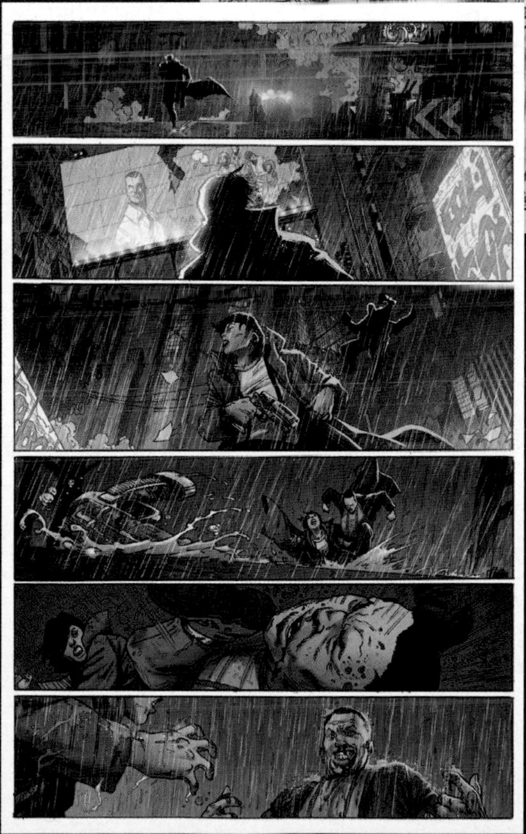

TOP LEFT AND RIGHT: Andres' pencils and inks for page two of the tryout strip.
BOTTOM LEFT: Second page of Marco Lesko's color tryout.

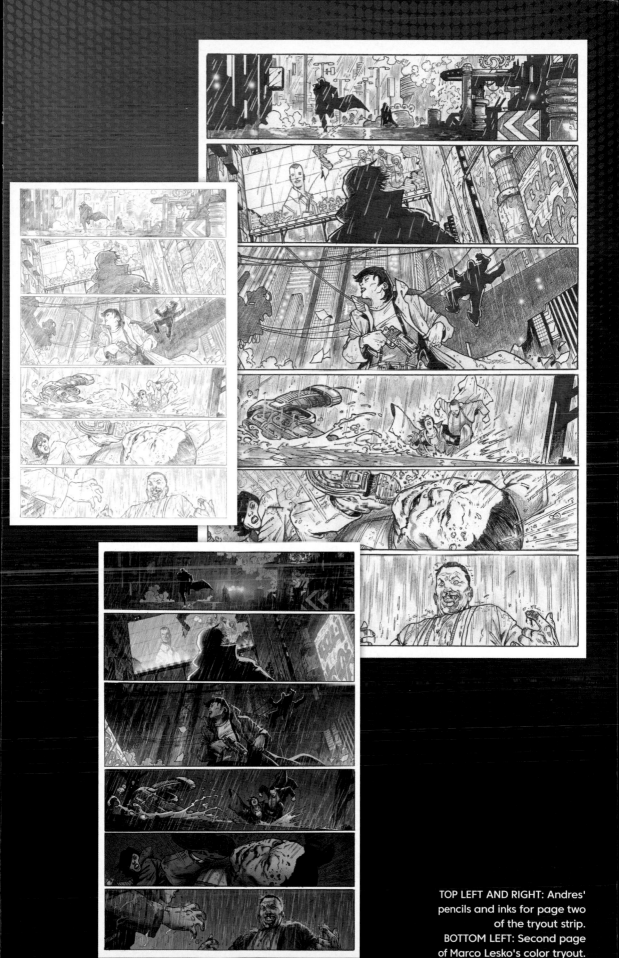

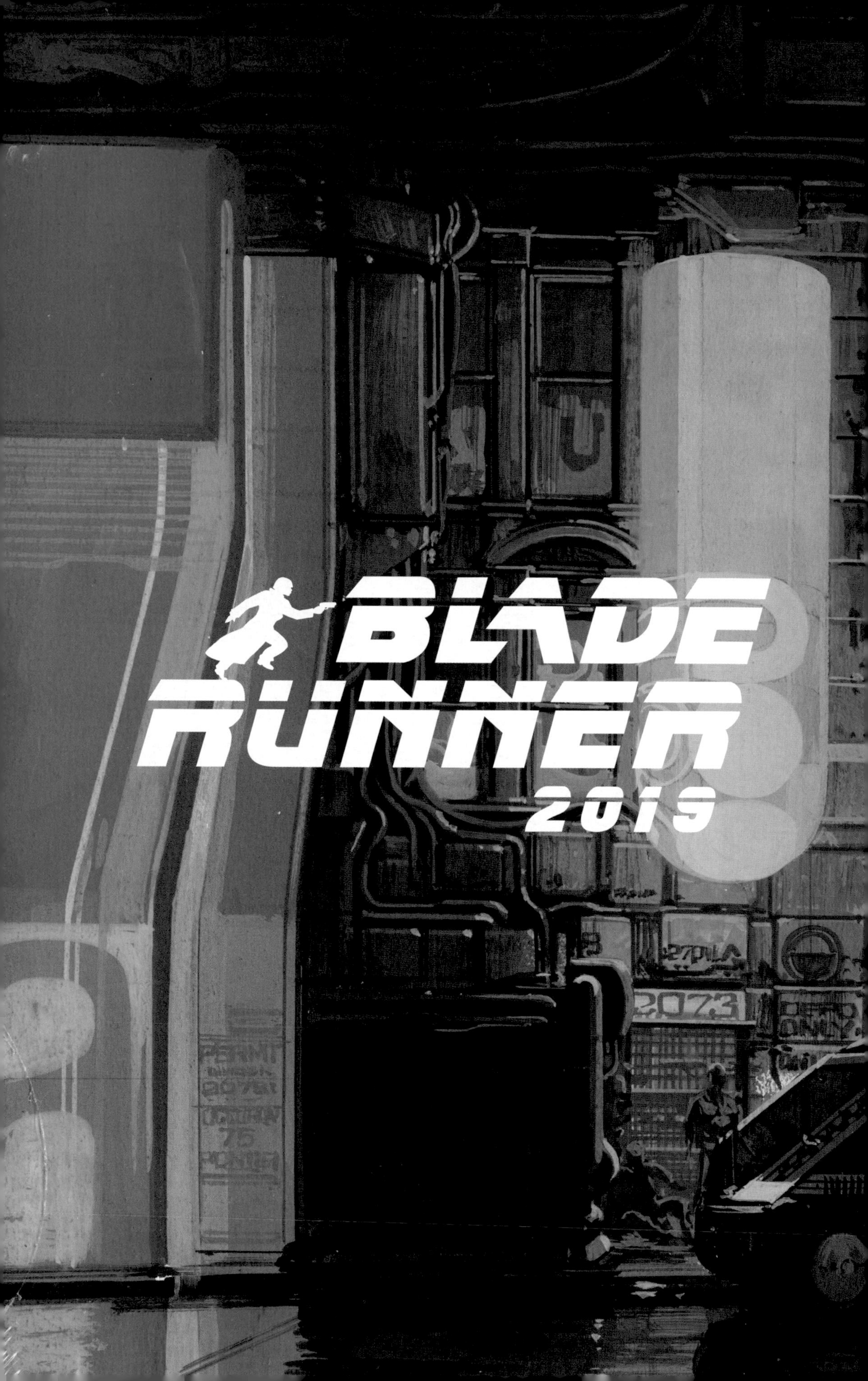
BLADE
RUNNER
2019
PERMIT
2073

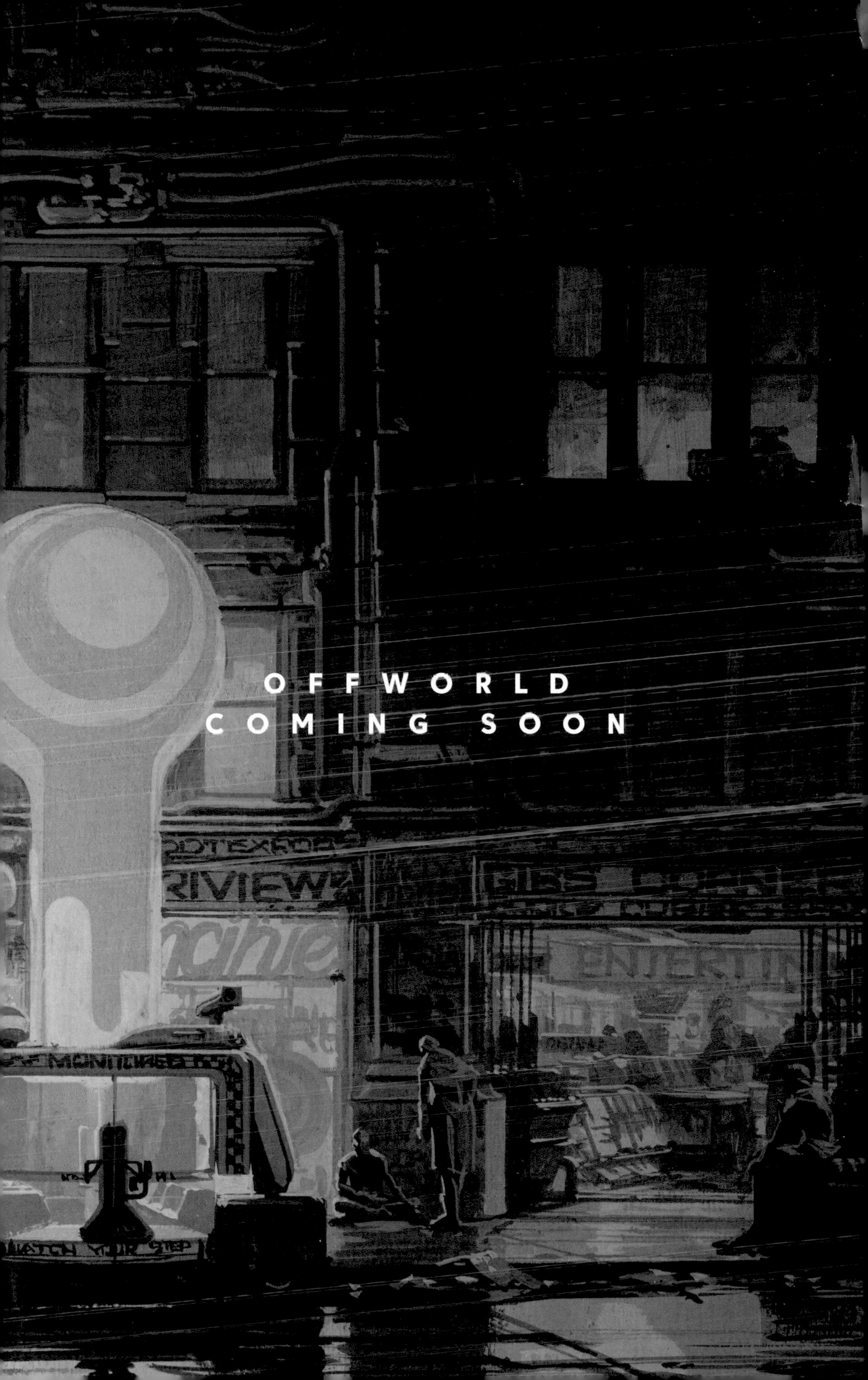
WATCH YOUR STEP

OFFWORLD
COMING SOON

# CREATOR
# BIOS

## MICHAEL GREEN

Michael Green is a film and television writer and producer. His work
includes *Blade Runner 2049*, *Logan*, *Murder on the Orient Express*,
*American Gods*, and *Kings*.

## MIKE JOHNSON

Mike Johnson is a New York Times-bestselling writer of comics, animation
and games whose credits include *Star Trek*, *Transformers*,
*Superman/Batman*, *Supergirl*, *Fringe*, and *Ei8ht*.

## ANDRES GUINALDO

Born in Segovia, Spain in 1975. Andres originally studied movie making
(direction) at Madrid University before making the move into comics. His
first professional work was drawing Joe R. Landsdale's *The Drive-in* and
*By Bizarre Hands*. He followed those with *Pistolfist: Revolutionary Warrior*,
*Helios: Under The Gun*, *Purity*, and *Cartoonapalozza*. In 2010, Guinaldo
started regularly penciling *Son of Hulk* and drew issue #5 of *Dark Reign:
Hawkeye*. He followed this with *Gotham City Sirens* #14-17, *Joker's Asylum:
The Riddler*, *Namor: The First Mutant #4*, *Red Lanterns #8*, *Resurrection
Man #9*, *Nightwing #11-14*, *Hypernaturals*, and *Justice League Dark*.
In recent years he's worked on titles as diverse as *Ninjak* and *Captain
America: Steve Rogers*. He currently resides in Segovia,
the city where he was born.

## MARCO LESKO

Hailing from Brazil, Marco Lesko has been a professional comic book
colorist since 2014. His credits include *Rat Queens*, *Assassin's Creed
Uprising*, *Doctor Who*, *Robotech*, *The Shadow* and many more. When he's
not coloring comics he spends endless hours studying color theory from
many different areas, including: cinema, conceptual art design, Japanese
anime, videogame design, and classic Disney animations.

## JIM CAMPBELL

Jim Campbell is an Eisner Award nominated letterer whose work can be
seen on everything from Titan's *Robotech* books to *Roy of the Rovers*
graphic novels to the *Firefly* series. He lives, works, and very occasionally
sleeps, in darkest Nottinghamshire in the UK in a house he shares with his
wife and an unfeasibly large collection of black clothes.